WHEN CAN I COME HOME?
A DEBATE ON AMNESTY FOR EXILES,
ANTIWAR PRISONERS, AND OTHERS

MURRAY POLNER has taught history at various colleges and universities. He wrote *No Victory Parades: The Return of the Vietnam Veteran* and has written articles for *Trans-action, Commonweal, Annals, The Christian Century, The Nation,* and others. He is editor of *The Conquest of the United States by Spain and Other Essays by William Graham Sumner.* He is currently Executive Assistant to the Chancellor of the New York City public schools.

Grateful acknowledgment is made to the New York *Times* for permission to reprint Tom Cornell's "A Draft Resister's Story"; *The Christian Century*, for permission to reprint Barry Johnson's "Seminarian in 'The Resistance'"; *Commonweal*, for permission to reprint Murray Polner's "18-Minute Verdict: Military Justice & Constitutional Rights"; and the *National Catholic Reporter* for permission to reprint portions of John M. Swomley, Jr.'s "Amnesty: The Record and the Need."

When Can I Come Home?

A DEBATE ON AMNESTY FOR EXILES,
ANTIWAR PRISONERS, AND OTHERS

EDITED BY MURRAY POLNER

ANCHOR BOOKS

DOUBLEDAY AND COMPANY, INC.

GARDEN CITY, NEW YORK

1972

The Anchor Books edition is the first publication of *When Can I Come Home? A Debate on Amnesty for Exiles, Antiwar Prisoners, and Others*

Anchor Books edition: 1972

Library of Congress Catalog Card
Number 75-175414
Copyright © 1972 by Murray Polner
All Rights Reserved
Printed in the United States of America

Contents

WHEN CAN I COME HOME?
A DEBATE ON AMNESTY FOR EXILES,
ANTIWAR PRISONERS, AND OTHERS

". . . as for these deserters, malcontents, radicals, incendiaries, the civil and the uncivil disobedients among our youth, SDS, PLP, Weathermen I and Weathermen II, the revolutionary action movement, the Black United Front, Yippies, Hippies, Yahoos, Black Panthers, Lions and Tigers alike—I would swap the whole damn zoo for a single platoon of the kind of young Americans I saw in Vietnam."

Vice President Spiro Agnew, February 10, 1970

"Would it be too much to suggest this Easter that we empty out our jails of all the protestors—the guilty and the innocent —without judging them; call back from over the border and around the world the young men who are called "deserters," drop the cases that are still awaiting judgment on our college youth? Could we not do all of this in the name of life, and with life hope, both of which we celebrate at Easter? Whereever our young people, even for reasons we do not know, stand in need of mercy let us reach out to them. The fruit of Easter is reconciliation and so much of our world remains unreconciled; the hope of Easter is our salvation and so many are waiting to be saved."

His Eminence, Richard Cardinal Cushing,
March 29, 1970

"Is nobody to be beheaded, nobody to be hanged? Where would be the warning to future ambitious and unscrupulous demagogues? I answer, that if the awful deluge of ruin and desolation that has come upon the country from this civil war should be no warning to the people not again to follow such leaders . . . would the bringing to the block of a few guilty heads, or the exile of their owners, have that effect?"

Edwin Hickman Ewing,
accepting President Lincoln's offer of amnesty
to southern rebels, December 17, 1863

Introduction

Between 1967 and 1970, while engaged in research for a book on Vietnam veterans, I naturally spent a good deal of time with large numbers of ex-G.I.s. I was quickly struck by their profound sense of grievance, their instinctive feeling that somehow, in some way, they had been manipulated and then abandoned by men and institutions they had once accepted. For the moment at least I thought that for many of them the delicate bond between rulers and the ruled had been ruptured. And I concluded:

> Never before in American history have as many loyal and brave young men been as shabbily treated by the government that sent them to war; never before have so many of them questioned as much, as these veterans have, the essential rightness of what they were forced to do.[1]

But it was hard for me to think in rigid categories. What of the other "loyal and brave young men," those who came to regard the war as "illegal" or "immoral" and who refused to serve or to continue to serve in the military services? Staggering numbers have broken the law, fled, or been flung into prison. The impact of all this is as yet

[1] Murray Polner, *No Victory Parades: The Return of the Vietnam Veteran* (New York: Holt, Rinehart & Winston, Inc., 1971), p. 165.

incalculable, but the loss is increasingly intolerable. Hundreds of thousands of the best young men of this country have been sacrificed—on and off the battlefield—for a war that remains impossible to justify or to explain.

Thus, for a variety of reasons that should become clear throughout this book, I reached a parallel conclusion about those men who had to choose a painful alternative to military service: They too had been victimized by their own government. The central issue became for me what is defined in these pages by Peter Steinfels as "the plight of young people in prison for three, four, and five years, or treading water in exile because of the moral demands of our time." Or put yet another way by Willard Gaylin: "Is eternal exile a punishment warranted for any crime? Remember about whom we are talking: eighteen-to-twenty-five-year-olds. I am not sure what purpose would be served by refusal to declare an amnesty, except further to exhibit a sense of vindictiveness and a desire to punish."

This, then, is a book dealing with the possibility of amnesty. I have here drawn together people whose work has interested me. I have attempted to include as many points of view as possible: those arguing in favor of amnesty and those opposed and those who defy simple categorization. The result, however, is hardly an "objective" book, since I have made no attempt to give "equal time" to each point of view. I have moreover tried to anticipate most of the arguments that may eventually be aired if and when there is a sustained public effort to allow these men to return home. For that above all is my major aim: to help serve as a catalyst, to initiate a national debate that would ultimately declare a general amnesty and forgive both the "victims and the executioners."

By amnesty I mean simply "an act of oblivion for political offenses; in effect it wipes out all legal recollections of them." I also intended here to embrace more than those who went into prison or exile. Drawing upon Amnesty International's classification of political prisoners,

I believe that anyone who has in effect said, "with the gift of our liberty, if necessary our lives and our reputations, the violence stops here, the suppression of the truth stops here, the war stops here" ought to receive amnesty as soon as the war ends, and in many instances, even sooner.

The following people should be included in any amnesty:

1. "Men within the military who have made unsuccessful applications for C.O. status and have refused military duty.

2. "Men who have refused to go to Vietnam or to train for Vietnam; often charged, as in Dr. Howard Levy's case, with disobedience.

3. "Men charged with desertion or AWOL who have acted on the grounds of their objection to the war or the military.

4. "Soldiers who have publicly been critical of the war policy; the charges may be sedition, encouraging sedition, insubordination, or sometimes drug charges, some of which have been found spurious on investigation; editors of antiwar G.I. newspapers are included in this category.

5. "Men who protest against general or specific conditions within the military, and not always directly related to the war in Vietnam: in some of these cases the men have been charged with mutiny.

6. ". . . civilian sympathizers with resisters and deserters. Some have been indicted for their part in organizing antiwar demonstrations, others for destroying or defiling draft files."[2]

The United States is no stranger to amnesty. For while there has never been a general amnesty, there have been partial ones, arising in part from the presidential right "to grant reprieves and pardons for offenses against the United States."

[2] Amnesty International, "Categories of Prisoners and Deserters," November 1970.

George Washington, John Adams, and James Madison all granted amnesties, as John Swomley, Jr. points out, despite the fact that in each instance they arose from actual rebellions. Lincoln was known as a pardoning President. In 1862 and again in 1863 he ordered a "full pardon and restoration of all property rights except those in slavery." The order included draft evaders too. So generous was Lincoln (and in the midst of war) that his Secretary of the Navy worried that "the authors of the enormous evils [of rebellion] will go unpunished, or will be but slightly punished."[3] But to Grant, Lincoln's rationale was clear. The President "thought enough blood had been spilled to atone for our wickedness as a nation."[4] After Lincoln's murder, Andrew Johnson proclaimed three amnesties, emphasizing repeatedly, as Swomley reminds us, that vindictiveness "now as always could only tend to hinder reconciliation among the people."

In this century, both world wars presented differing approaches toward amnesty. The post-1918 years in this country were especially embittered. The Bolshevik Revolution, the spread of Communist and socialist governments into European states, the continued pressures from revolutionary Mexico, the growth of trade unionism here, and the tensions engendered by an undigested industrialism and mass immigration all helped bring to the surface that endemic American malaise, anticommunism, together with its twins, superpatriotism and xenophobia.

Shortly after the Armistice, Allied governments began freeing their political prisoners. Between October and December 1919, Italy, France, and Belgium opened their prisons. The British issued no formal decree, but by the close of 1919 they too had let loose virtually all

---

[3] Gideon Welles. *Diary* (Boston: Houghton Mifflin Co., 1925), Vol. II, p. 43.

[4] U. S. Grant, *Personal Memoirs* (New York: Century House, Inc., 1909), Vol. II, p. 522.

their political prisoners. Said the Canadian amnesty proclamation, "an amnesty should be graciously extended
. . . [for] . . . the restoration of peace. . . ."

There was no such graciousness in this country. Here
a frightened great power, creditor of the world, un-
touched by war but anxious with buried conflicts, turned
in nightmarish hallucinations on imaginary plotters. In
so mad a setting, amnesty was impossible.

During the war thousands had been sent off to prison,
most notably Eugene Victor Debs. Others had been
jailed for draft dodging, been refused C.O. status, or
suffered because of their motley backgrounds of radical-
ism, liberalism, and/or pacifism. Others were simply swept
up in the prowar panic.

William Powell, a resident of Lansing, Michigan, received a twenty-year sentence (later commuted to two
years) for expressing doubts in the home of a relative
about German atrocities in Belgium.

Robert Goldstein of Los Angeles served three years
for producing a film, "The Spirit of '76," critical of
Great Britain, "our ally."

Equally unknown was Benjamin J. Salmon, who went
to jail because his draft board would not consider him
a conscientious objector. "I have been illegally imprisoned
because I refused to kill or help to kill," he wrote from
his prison cell. "The 'war to crush militarism' was won,"
he wrote again after the Armistice. "But this monster is
enthroned more securely than ever."

Salmon had been shanghaied into prison on a charge of
"desertion and propaganda"—an impossibility, since he
had never been in the Army. What happened was that
he refused to return his questionnaire to the draft board,
writing them later, "Ultimately, individuals and nations
must awaken and rally to Christ's standards or perish."
For his refusal, he was sentenced to nine months' imprisonment by a United States District Court. Salmon
then appealed and was freed on bail. At that moment

the draft board ordered Salmon, a father and sole support of his mother, to report for induction within three
days. He tried instead to surrender to a U.S. marshal,
was turned down, and, was immediately arrested as a
deserter on complaint of his draft board. It took a year-
long hunger strike, many more months of incarceration,
and an official attempt to have him certified insane
before the government that wanted to "make the world
safe for democracy" would free Salmon.[5]

The battle for amnesty after World War I was associated with the National Civil Liberties Bureau (forerunner of the American Civil Liberties Union) and the
Socialist party, whose main concern was getting Debs
released. While the NCLB tried to have Salmon's case
re-examined, the "patriots" hooted. The Tacoma (Washington) *News Tribune* called him Denver's "yellowest
slacker." Woodrow Wilson, an absolute moralist, would
not consider amnesty for anyone. In 1920 he told his
Secretary of Labor that he would never free Debs. "This
man was a traitor to his country and he will never be
pardoned during my administration."[6]

The Lafayette (Indiana) *Courier*, in November 1921,
summed up much of the argument against amnesty: those
who would benefit from amnesty "are in reality a greater
menace to this country than are the petty thieves and
burglars." That the test of their imprisonment was in
many instances grounded on expressions of opinion on
public matters had little or no impact on those who were
dead set against amnesty. Nor did the fact that few, if

[5] *Papers*, American Civil Liberties Union, #23, p. 40,557.
The State Historical Society of Wisconsin. See also the Hunt
case, another example of the wartime hysteria. Hunt was a
Seventh-Day Adventist whose entire family was sent to the
Colorado State Insane Asylum at Pueblo because one son's request for a C.O. deferment was equated with collective madness.

[6] Donald Johnson, *The Challenge to American Freedoms*
(Lexington, Ky.: University Press of Kentucky, 1963), p. 207.

any, of the prisoners had committed an act of violence against persons or property.

Still, by 1921 a "Joint Amnesty Committee" was formed. To their demands the federal government replied that there were no political prisoners; all inmates had been convicted after being accorded due process. Undeterred, the committee called for restoration of citizenship and dismissal of untried cases, organized Medal of Honor veterans to picket the Washington Disarmament Conference, and even set up a "Children's Crusade," comprised of wives and children of prisoners, who tried daily to visit the White House to make a personal plea to the President.

The new President, Warren Harding refused to see them but, unlike the dogmatic Wilson, he released twenty-one prisoners, including Debs. That seemed to satisfy the Socialists, but it did not satisfy the NCLB nor the small but active number of liberals and conservatives—bishops, governors, Supreme Court justices, and an expanding network of local committees—who also believed in amnesty. Senator George Wharton of Pennsylvania said that "an individual pardon meant nothing except that the Government was exercising its right to be generous." And Senator Borah of Idaho sponsored a resolution to free all political prisoners. An unemotional Calvin Coolidge finally heard their pleas and opened the prison doors on December 15, 1924, more than six years after the end of the war.

The aftermath of the Second World War was somewhat different. The war was perhaps the most popular in history and the enemy, certainly in the eyes of many Americans, among the most despicable. Yet with the surrender of Japan there were 15,805 prisoners, and A. J. Muste organized a group proposing amnesty, which included Henry Luce, Henry Seidel Canby, and Thornton Wilder.

Finally, in late 1946, Harry Truman named a three-

man Amnesty Board comprised of a former Supreme
Court justice, a past president of the American Bar Asso-
ciation, and the vice chairman of the American Legion's
Americanism Commission.

The results were disappointing. Only 1523 pardons
were grudgingly recommended, very often with little
logic or compassion. Japanese-Americans who had been
dragooned into concentration camps and who subse-
quently refused to serve in the military were freed. So
too were some religious C.O.s. But the overwhelming
majority were not. The "Three Wise Men" refused amnesty (they said) for "those who have set themselves up
as wiser and more competent than society to determine
their duty to come to the defense of the nation." Muste
answered that even in its application of religious belief
the Board was hardly consistent.

> One was granted pardon though never classified . . .
> [as a C.O.] . . . the other, who had been so classified,
> is refused pardon. Two boys grew up together and
> went to prison together; one is listed and the other is
> not. . . . A Brethren minister who refused to serve
> in Civilian Public Service is granted pardon, but not
> Methodists, Presbyterians, and others who took the
> same position.[7]

Omitted were black men who had refused to serve in
a segregated Army and Navy, Puerto Rican nationalists
who went to jail insisting they owed no allegiance to
this country, and Hopi Indians whose beliefs prohibited
participation in war. Forgotten too were the forty-three
hundred Jehovah's Witnesses who languished behind
bars—as they still do today—because the Government
decides which members of which religious groups shall or
shall not be considered "clergy."

There was, therefore, neither amnesty nor justice after

---

[7] "Amnesty Denied to Most Objectors," *The Christian Century*, Vol. LXV, No. 1 (January 7, 1948), pp. 3-4.

1945. And yet, as after 1918, other nations that had suffered far more than the United States found the humanity to free their political prisoners: Greece, Yugoslavia, Bulgaria, India, Japan, Spain. On Christmas Day 1945 President Truman did declare an amnesty, notes Swomley, for men with criminal records who had served honorably in the armed forces for at least twelve months— but not for men of principle and conscience.

Harold Ickes, once Franklin Roosevelt's Secretary of the Interior and a perennial iconoclast, could hardly contain himself in his New York *Post* column:

> Like Shylock, insisting upon the last shred of his pound of flesh, certain people seem intent on inflicting on these unfortunates the last measure of the law.
>
> I, for one, protest against such harsh inflexibility. President Truman found it easy to pardon members of the Pendergast gang who had been convicted of vote frauds in a Missouri election. And after all, the theft of votes is a deadlier assault upon American institutions than an aversion to war.
>
> Can we no longer forgive? Has the gentle quality of mercy dried up in our hearts?[8]

In spite of my obvious bias I do not think the questions raised in this book are easily answered. Can a man pick and choose his war? Would this kind of option give to an individual far too much responsibility? Which rights are inviolable, those of the nation state or those of the individual? Should not the minority in a democratic society go along with the will of the majority? Should not the opposition to a legally elected government act out their roles only on a lawful basis? Would selective conscientious objection allow men to lie their way out of the service and thereby place the burden on the less articulate, the less sophisticated? How can we reconcile the process of examination of the Vietnam war's origins and the esca-

[8] New York *Post*, November 13, 1945.

lations with continuing punishment of those who were among the earliest to act against it? And what of the thoughts of the Cuban Jose Martí, himself a prisoner of conscience, who once wrote that "to witness a crime in silence is to commit it"?

I remember reading about a short but sharp debate in Washington, D.C. at a meeting of the House Armed Services Committee, superhawks, none of whose sons or grandsons had ever served in Vietnam.

A congressman was questioning a Florida man, a former student at Berkeley, a member of a draft resisters group. The onetime student had infuriated the members because he openly admitted he was a "no-show," an inductee who had refused to be drafted.

> *Rep. Charles S. Gubser* (Republican, California):
> "What about the poor square who goes to Vietnam and gets killed? Isn't he a blot on your moral conscience?"
> *Fred W. Ingraham:* "I should think he would be a blot on your moral conscience."[9]

But amnesty *now?*, someone will ask. What advocates of amnesty are really saying is that the President ought to use his legal authority in a manner he clearly cannot while the war is still on. No government, so the argument goes, in the middle of a war and delicate negotiations, without the machinery to create a mercenary force, can effectively demobilize its conscripted army by putting service on a voluntary basis.

A friend put it to me this way: "It makes no sense to call upon a person, in this instance the President, to act in a way we would not ourselves if in his position. All amnesty now would do is to promote desertions by removing the penalties, and any President who acted in such a way would deserve impeachment."

A lawyer: "They broke the law and should take the

[9] Washington *Post*, March 4, 1971, p. A5.

punishment. Their heroes, Gandhi and King did, and so should they."

An automobile mechanic: "They're criminals. They broke the law, didn't they? Let them rot in jail or in Canada."

Thus, the partial case against amnesty made—with considerable nuances and with significant differences—by William Rusher, Ernest van den Haag, and Ronald Docksai of Young Americans for Freedom.

"No law," writes Professor van den Haag, "can ever condone civil disobedience. Civil disobedience means basically not that a person claims an exemption for himself which the law can, and in America does grant, but that the person says he's better than the government and the majority that supports it."

Since little will be done until the war ends, the case for peace is now even greater, and the appeal for eventual amnesty much more valid, especially when one remembers what these new "criminals" did *not* do. They did not rebel against their country, they did not commit treason or openly take up arms. Their sole offense, if it is an offense, was in cherishing freedom so highly that they refused to submit to a draft or military service in a war their morality and their ethics would not let them accept.

Who shall bear the responsibility for their plight? Walter Collins, a black civil rights activist now in prison, or the all-white southern jury that found him guilty of draft evasion? Dan Kelly, who in 1966 turned in his draft card to Selective Service as a protest against the war? Or his draft board, which had him reclassified 1-A, ordered him to report for immediate induction, and when Kelly balked, turned him over to the courts? He was given two years in prison, only part of which he served. Kelly was nineteen years old when this happened.

Who acted illegally? Collins? Kelly? Or a former President, who now basks in the admiration of his Texas neighbors? Or our former Secretary of State, who reminds

us in his soft Georgia tone that we are in danger of moving
ever so swiftly away from internationalism? Or a former
presidential aide, now in exile at the University of Texas,
who told a New York *Times* reporter that John F. Kennedy too would have been a hawk? And what of those
mindless aides in the world of officialdom who encouraged
and instigated this indefensible war? Who broke what
laws and committed what crimes?

Vietnam will haunt this country in a hundred ways
for decades to come. We need peace. We need unity.
We need our young men. Let's welcome them home.

The Debaters

Ronald Docksai

Ronald Docksai is National Chairman of Young Americans for Freedom. He founded Young American Conservatives, a five hundred-member YAF chapter, which won the "Outstanding Service Award" for 1966 and 1967.

I am twenty-one years old and a senior in political science at St. John's University. Eventually I want to go into law or governmental service. I am also National Chairman of Young Americans for Freedom, a young conservative organization of intellectual and political activists, with some fifty-five thousand members in over eight hundred chapters in high schools and colleges and over two hundred community chapters for young professionals. My remarks should be interpreted primarily as the personal remarks of an individual, as one who describes himself as a young conservative. However, I can say that most YAF members I have talked with in different parts of the country have views that coincide with mine.

YAF supports the Goldwater-Hatfield bill. This bill was defeated when it was first proposed in August 1970. We lobbied for it then and we will lobby for it again, in hopes of replacing the Selective Service System with a voluntary military program that we believe would serve

not only the best interests of individual liberty but our
national interests as well.

My personal view on amnesty is not too alien from
Roscoe Pound's writings dealing with sociological jurisprudence. Roscoe Pound had a profound effect in freeing
American law from the myth that legal concepts and
rules can be viewed in isolation from their social context. Many people today, particularly those on the left,
try to isolate laws from their societal contexts and are as
guilty as the old-fashioned type of reactionaries who try
to isolate laws from their historical continuum. In his
discussion of American law in *Talks on American Law*
(N.Y.: Vintage, 1961), Harold J. Berman wrote:

> . . . it is of the greatest significance that the judge can
> at times say: a statute . . . which conflicts with justice
> is not law. He can do this when the constitution is in-
> fringed; but the power of judicial review of the con-
> stitutionality of legislation has had a pervasive influ-
> ence on the entire legal system, for lurking in the
> background of every case, civil or criminal or adminis-
> trative, is the constitutional requirement of "due process
> of law." A gross injustice always suggests, at least, a
> constitutional issue. (P. 225)

My point here is that the law must have an equal effect
upon the American community, on all Americans regardless of race, creed, or distinguishing class or biological
distinctions. I think we would make a very big mistake
in trying to be so selective that individuals may decide
what laws they will and will not obey. YAF, for example,
has stated that the Selective Service Act is unconstitutional; however, we also believe compulsory Social Security and its compulsory provisions to be unconstitutional.
Further, we believe the Kennedy Medicare rider to be
unconstitutional. Similarly the Civil Rights bill of 1964
is viewed in part as unconstitutional. However, we also
realize that within the American community pluralism

is not merely a hypothetical "ought to be," but that there are other views of constitutionality and of which laws are right.

I believe that those who call for amnesty for individuals who have resisted the draft in this war are at the very best short-sighted, insofar as they are also allowing precedent for the Ku Kluxers to knock over buses or do very harmful things to the civil community. The point here is that while one may or may not empathize and/or sympathize with the draft dodger or one who flees the country, one has to realize that breaking a law in this country, whether or not that law is believed to be constitutional, is wrong. The law itself should be challenged in the courts, and we should follow the necessary jurisprudential means to amend, suspend, or change that law. However, when one does break that law, he should face the consequences, and for the peace and stability of the community, he must.

Recently in New York City the police went on strike. I believe that this would not have been the case if a precedent had been set whereby other municipal employees, forbidden by law to strike, had been disciplined in the way the police should also have been disciplined. Here one sees that when the precedent, in this instance the civil law, breaks down, a kind of domino theory of American civil jurisprudence goes into operation.

What do we do with the person who believes, for example, that the Vietnam war or any war is immoral? If he believes so *religiously,* he can of course apply for conscientious objection classification. If he is not able to and in all sincerity does believe the Vietnam war to be immoral, I believe he should do one of two things: either voluntarily leave the country, insofar as he is not repaying society for the privilege he gained as an American citizen, and flee to whatever country he particularly desires; or, if he does wish to remain in the United States,

I believe he has to face the legal consequences of his refusal to serve.

The issue here is amnesty and I cannot, in good conscience and in good intellectual regard for the stability of
the American community, favor amnesty. I know that
most members of Young Americans for Freedom, as conservatives, would not favor it either from an ideological
standpoint or from the standpoint that laws, so long as
they are on the statutes, should be obeyed. This involves
laws whether they concern marijuana or traffic on the
highway or anything else.

I happen to believe the Vietnam cause is moral. I happen to believe as well that the war as conducted by the
Johnson Administration included many immoral aspects.
By that I mean that a war that is not fought to be won
has a very shaky moral foundation.

Do I want to go to Vietnam to fight in this particular
cause? Quite honestly I would rather not, insofar as I
do not believe the war is being fought to be won. But
if I were drafted, I would go, for I believe it is my duty
as an American to serve.

To conclude, then, I do believe that those seeking
amnesty should not be granted it. If the exiles wish to
return, they should be judged in a court of law where
the circumstances of each case can be weighed individu-
ally. This is the American process within the American
system. The argument for amnesty should be considered
not merely from a political or ideological stance, but
rather from a broader stance concerning obedience to all
laws in society.

WILLARD GAYLIN

Willard Gaylin is a training and supervising psychoana-
lyst at the Columbia Psychoanalytic Clinic. He is also an
associate professor of psychiatry at Columbia University
School of Medicine and adjunct professor at Union
Theological Seminary. He is the author of In the Service
of Their Country: War Resisters in Prison.

Before I discuss the question of amnesty in specific
terms let me confess to a general bias in its favor. Not
just because of the meaning of amnesty to those receiving
it, but also for what amnesty implies about the nature of
the society that grants it.

It is one of the ironies of a liberal democracy that we
justify violation of our moral code only in defense of it.
We make a basic assumption that if a society is good, and
if its survival is threatened, we may do bad things to
preserve it. For a war to be defensible it must be because
it is in the service of essential values. In defense of our
society and its values we have a long tradition of abandoning or limiting basic rights and tradition. Today, we are
seeing a constriction of civil liberties justified for particularly those reasons. We pass no-knock and stop-and-frisk
legislation, limit certain rights to assembly, interpret conspiracy laws in a loose way—all with the implicit as-

sumption that the good society has a right to defend itself.

But it is not just today and it is not just in these limited
ways that we have abandoned fundamental rights to "preserve" them. It was under such traditionally humanist and
democratic Presidents as Abraham Lincoln and Franklin
D. Roosevelt that we saw the suspension of the writ of
habeas corpus, thereby effectively suspending the Bill of
Rights. These acts today will still be defended by certain
constitutional lawyers. The internment of over one hundred thousand American citizens in concentration camps
during World War II seems incredible today, but was at
the time also justified in terms of the necessary acts, indeed, the necessary obligations of the good society to
preserve itself. The ultimate question, of course, is how
many violations of its own values the good society can
commit before these very acts redefine the nature of
the society so that it is no longer good.

To me, the concept of forgiveness is so fundamental
that no society that does not cherish it would be worthy
of saving. I have always been irrevocably opposed to this
war, so amnesty comes naturally to me. But those who
felt this war was in the ultimate defense of our country
or its extended principles must demonstrate that those
principles justify the horrors perpetrated in their name.
Only that which is worth dying for is worth killing
for—and maybe not even then. A vengeful, unforgiving
state is worth neither.

Now, in terms of this particular crime and these particular criminals—the war resisters—I think a special case
can be made. My personal experience is limited to the
imprisoned COs, but I feel that what can be said for
them has relevance to the larger group of war resisters.

In 1967 I began to get inquiries about what one could
do when faced with the draft. These were from people
who opposed the war in Vietnam, would not serve in it,
and yet refused to lie or evade. They were asking whether

they should choose to leave the country or to go to prison, seemingly the only alternatives available to them. I was being asked to give a professional estimation as to the potential harmful effects of these two alternatives. It was a reasonable question, logically directed to precisely the person who should be expected to know the answer. I was a psychoanalyst; therefore my field was human behavior and environmental influence. In addition, my special interest was the application of psychoanalytic concepts to social problems. I had been working in the area of psychiatry and the law. With all this, I was totally unequipped to present any intelligent answer. I had never spent one hour within the walls of any penal institution. My subjective impression of prison was formed by too much exposure at too early an age to too many Saturday afternoons in the movies. Balancing this was a limited intellectual conception based on the few articles on prison reform, rehabilitation, and so forth, that I had chanced upon. While I knew prisons were unlikely to be as pictured by Warner Brothers (they had let me down badly on college life), my knowledge of the conditions in institutions in general indicated that prisons were likely to be a long way from the ideal. I began to read the available literature on prison life—the meaning and purpose of imprisonment, the intended and actual impact of imprisonment, and more important, I began to wonder on what facts the war resisters themselves who had elected to go to prison based their decisions. For them it was no theoretical decision but two to five years of their lives.

I inquired at the Bureau of Prisons as to who was currently doing research in this area. To my amazement I found that no one was—at least not officially. Even the barest statistics as to numbers of imprisoned objectors, racial and religious background, had not been tabulated. But with the growing resistance to the war by the end of 1967, and the prospect of an increasing number of men choosing imprisonment over service in the Armed Forces,

it seemed crucial for the future as well as for the present
crisis to know more than just the statistics. Who were
these people? What factors influenced their decisions?
What were their motives? What were the determinants
within and without each individual that shaped his
course of action? I therefore requested permission to do
the research myself, and after six months of correspondence and a trip to Washington to prove that I was "respectable," I was given permission to study these
prisoners.

The question has arisen in my mind as to why I was
given this permission, particularly since before the research was over—despite a contractual agreement—the
Bureau of Prisons, unhappy about the conclusions I was
drawing, interrupted the research and revoked my privileges of visiting the prisons. I think the reason for the
original permission was a genuine concern over the spector
of a vast new class of prison inmate, one which the prisons
were ill-equipped to handle. Middle-class men traditionally do not go to prison. In a sense there was an analogy
between the war and the prisons. Both situations were
tolerated far beyond the time they might have been because they did not affect the people who count. The injustice, inhumanity, and sheer inefficiency of prisons
have been perpetuated because the people who go to
prison, being the poor, are also the dispossessed and have
little impact on the decision-making process of our government. They are, in a sense, a constituency without rep-
resentation. Similarly, the war has lasted as long as it has
because the middle class—while in general defending the
principles of the war—had protected its children from
service. The influx of the middle class into penitentiaries
because of the marijuana laws and the antiwar movement has already caused more establishment concern over
the prisons than has been seen for many a year. Similarly,
when the middle-class boy began to get drafted the war
began to lose its popular support. I am convinced that

at the time of the Berrigans' original conviction the government would gladly have sent them to an island retreat to luxuriate in the sun if it could possibly have justified it. It is also quite likely that many people inside the prison system breathed a sigh of relief when Benjamin Spock was freed. These men are not wanted in prison. They are conduits to the public mind and conscience. The last place in the world the prison managers want such illuminative and illuminating men are inside the dark corridors of prisons.

What type of man is the imprisoned war resister? Who are the criminals about whom we are contemplating amnesty? When I first raised the question it was with a certain bias. It seemed natural to presume that the CO in prison was analogous to the college radical. I had been on the college campuses; I had heard many times many men threatening to go to jail rather than serving in the Army. I had seen them burning their draft cards. In actuality the prison population was quite different from the college radical. Close to 80 percent of them were Jehovah's Witnesses. These were men who under the principle of the law would have been exempt as conscientious objectors just as the Quakers were, except that it is of the very nature of their religion that they are not allowed to serve a secular authority. Their objection to the draft is not simply that they are pacifists but that it would violate this basic principle against serving the state. So, unlike the Quakers, they are not prepared to do alternate service, for that too would be a violation of their principles. The actual number of political or moral war resisters independent of this group of Jehovah's Witnesses fluctuates between seventy-five and one hundred at any given time. It therefore represents a select and very special group. The original statistical breakdown alone indicated that it could not have been a group congruent with the college radical, for that group traditionally has a disproportionate number of Jews and a low number of Catho-

lics. In the original sampling of the war resisters there
was not one Jew (although one day after I started the
study a Jewish war resister was admitted) and a high
percentage of Catholics—ten out of the twenty-one white
members being Catholic.

They are a markedly heterogeneous group, and to fully
appreciate that they would have to be described individ-
ually. Yet some generalizations can be cautiously offered
about the original group I studied. Most of them had a
personal sense of moral outrage with the war and a strong
conscience, which would permit them neither to participate in it nor avoid the confrontation. While they
were political, they were still not politicians. They were
not for the most part organizers, and when they attempted
such activity they often failed. They were activists, but
activists who believed in action by example and witness,
rather than exhortation.

Politically they subscribed to no clear-cut dogma. Only
two of them were professed Marxists, and even that in
the modern sense of the word. Two of them were conservative, Goldwater Republicans. Many did not even
think in political terms. There was a high percentage
of sympathy with the anarchist-pacifist writings, and many
of them described their political philosophy as essentially
"Christian pacifist." There were only two who by any
stretch of the imagination would have been called "hippie"
types, unless one wanted to include the Catholic Worker
group (four members) who in dress and manner of living
might have been misinterpreted as such, but who in intention and action were entirely different.

Two would not have been in prison at all if they had
had the money to go to Canada. But this would have represented a hardship on their families, in one case because
of the bond that the family had put up, and in the other
case because job opportunities would have been limited
for him, as he was black.

Some should not have been there at all. One was an

Amish boy who was raised in that religion but who in his late teens stopped attending the church, although he continued to subscribe to its principles. His draft board refused him CO status.

Another fulfilled totally the new ruling as to CO status but came from a small southern town where his draft board shared his ignorance of his rights. There was no lawyer to consult or guide his appeal.

Three came in specifically to test the legal validity of certain aspects of the war and the draft—two felt that the peacetime draft was illegal, and one proposed the right of individual conscience on the basis of the Nuremberg trials.

Over half were true pacifists (or were at the time of admission) who had subscribed to total nonviolence.

At least a third had clear-cut advance indications that they would not have been eligible for the draft if they had chosen to exercise their rights to deferment.

In personality they tended toward the quiet, contemplative, and introspective. There was a relatively low level of aggressiveness and hostility, particularly when allowing for the elevation from the norm that one would have expected to see in a prison environment. In sociological terms they were service-oriented individuals who believed that a man must be judged by his actions, not his statements, and that ideals and behavior were not separable phenomena. And assuredly they were not the population at which the Selective Service Act was directed, for under the intention of the act most of these boys were indeed conscientious objectors.

Why, then, did they enter prison? As an act of witness; as an obligation to pay the price if one breaks the law; as a political gesture, feeling that if enough of those who opposed the war would refuse to serve, it would ultimately destroy the system by overloading the already shaky prisons; as a propagandistic purpose to dramatize the opposition to the war. And for others, simply because they had no choice; they could not kill and they would not avail themselves of a conscientious objector law that they saw as too selective and therefore prejudicial to those excluded.

It should be remembered, however, that the Army never needs more than a small percentage of the eligible male population. Because of this, there are many outs. Besides the preferential treatment of the educated—which may be defended on the basis of maintenance of the country's institutions—there are other loopholes less readily defended which, whatever their intention, ultimately serve the purposes of the knowledgeable and well-to-do. These escape mechanisms are built in. All that is necessary is sufficient education, sophistication, money, or influence to exploit them. To catalogue some: expensive medical help to legitimize borderline conditions for deferment; membership in the reserves (I have never been quite sure for what they are being reserved); the privilege of commission, which seriously diminishs the possibility of risk, damage, or even inconvenience; appointment to a relatively safe service like the Navy or Coast Guard, and in particular that institution called the National Guard, which seems to be available for any and all purposes except guarding the nation.

All these alternatives were available and, at the time of my original study, there was the simplest of all—the capacity to maintain yourself as a student. Yet the men who went to jail chose not to avail themselves of these. In this sense they were imprisoned by their own conscience.

Not all war resisters went to prison. Some chose to flee the country, and this may be seen by some as a less courageous or less noble way. I am not so sure. But then, what is the nature of even this criminal? I suppose we would have to say that he is a frightened young man who is unwilling to die with no conviction of the purpose that his death might serve; or he is an angry man who resents being put in the position of having to kill or be

killed; or at worst, he is an irresponsible man who in refusing to undertake one burden, has other burdens, not
inconsiderable, imposed upon him. Really to pass judgment on a question of amnesty you ought to consider not
only the nature of the criminal but the nature of crime
and, beyond that, the purpose of punishment.

The nature of this crime is peculiar. Anything may be
said to be a crime that violates a statute. In this case we
are dealing specifically with the Selective Service Act. The
nature of the crime here is unique because of the special
circumstances of the law. The draft is a sometime thing—
only periodically required, skipping generations, appearing and disappearing with war and peace. It is not a
part of ongoing tradition. It is not a conventional and
assumed aspect of the American Way of Life—although
it may be becoming so. Since we do not see it as a stage
of normal citizenship—it comes as an interruption, an
unusual demand rather than a usual duty—it seems arbitrary and quixotic, hitting one, bypassing another, and
because of that it will be greeted as unfair. And what is
asked of this very small minority of our population is
that they be prepared to do no less than kill or be killed.
Most citizens are never required to face the decision, let
alone the act. Again we turn to a chosen few and demand
an exorbitant price. The privilege of a government in
asking this must be reserved for the most critical times,
for the most compelling purposes. These young men have
refused to be placed in a position where they will be
asked to kill or be killed. Presumably the purposes did
not have the sense of moral urgency to them. Whether
it would have had to the majority of us if it was a decision involving "us" rather than "them" can never be
answered theoretically. It is one of the dangers that arise
when the legislators and legislated are different popula-
tions. Their crime may have been in being premature
prophets. At any rate, they raised a question and came to
a conclusion that was at one time unpopular and now is

the accepted view of the majority. Who is there left who
believes that Vietnam is worth the loss of any more lives?

But if you require a draft system that is to work, it must
punish violators severely enough to guarantee a sufficient
enough number of men to conduct the business of war. It
is almost a certainty that most of the men in the armed
services today, if given a free choice, would not be there.
Faced, however, with the limited choice of Army or
jail, the majority chose the Army. To that extent the
Selective Service Act is successful. But the threat of
punishment is effective only if the threat is carried out in
the face of defiance. We therefore manage to keep in the
Army that large population that it is assumed will go only
under duress by imprisoning a small sample group for
which the law was not intended in the first place. They
are the innocent minority who must be sacrified to insure
the efficiency of the punishment system. It would seem
to me, however, that with the end of the war we can
now recognize that they have served their purposes and
we do not need them in prison any more.

My own feeling is that if a war is of such a nature that
you cannot convince the population of its worth, it may
not be worth waging. I remember enlisting at the age of
seventeen to go to World War II and I remember very
well the anguish, and, yes, tears of a good friend because he was physically unfit. Few of us had to be
drafted. I suspect World War II could have been won
without a draft, or at least the purpose of the draft would
have been merely to insure administrative order and fair-
ness. I suspect that it is when a government does not
trust itself, its purposes, or its population that it will require a draft—when it cannot assume either the responsibility of its citizenry or the worthiness of the cause.

But when a person has broken a law, even an arbitrary
one, ought he not be punished? That is a significant question and one well worth asking. It is "ought" questions
that usually define the real ethical issues. Ought they

be punished? What is the purpose of punishment? I am not as ready as some liberals to state that there is no place for punishment in learning or in rehabilitation. I can conceive its serving the purposes of discouraging some crime. The loss of freedom is not something a person takes lightly. The degradation of arrest and arraignment are traumatic experiences. We know punishment can be effective in individual cases of child raising, but here we make the crucial assumption that punishment serves the purposes of the offender rather than the punisher. It may be worthwhile for a mother occasionally to punish her child for her own satisfaction, provided the punishment is not too severe, since her child's well-being is dependent on her peace of mind. But we are not talking about a gentle pat across the rump; we are talking about the deprivation of two to five years of life—no, more important, two to five years of youth—and about a government not expected to have pique or petulance.

Does punishment serve to rehabilitate *these particular criminals?* What is there to rehabilitate? They are not for the most part violators of law in general. Only this law. For the most part, they had been well habilitated in the society.

Will the threat of punishment discourage these men from repeating their crime? What repetition of the criminal act can there be? When the war is over and there may not be any more draft they cannot possibly violate that law. Indeed, were there to be another war, this particular individual would probably be over age and exempt. Recidivism has no meaning in terms of a draft evader.

Or are we still insisting that prisons be penitentiaries— places of penance? These particular prisoners will never be penitent—not with the judgment of history already on their side.

What about the concept of example? If they are let off, in future wars will it not make it easier for others to avoid service? Does memory really last that long? Do

the young people today really know what happened in
1942 or 1917 or 1863 or if they did know, could they
possibly relate to it?

Is there some absolute moral principle that demands
punishment independent of its purposes? I do not know,
but if so we should not take lightly the price that these
men have already paid. The nature of punishment must
bear some quantitative relationship to the nature of the
crime to avoid being monstrous. Is eternal exile a punishment warranted for any crime? The men I met in prison
have paid a price in loss of youth, in loss of self-confidence, in loss of ideals. All could have been classified as
being committed to the principles of nonviolence and
passive resistance when they entered. By the time they
were discharged, none of them accepted these principles.
Perhaps the most touching example was a dialogue I
had with a former seminarian. I asked him how he would
have described his political position. He said, "When
I came in I would have called myself a Christian pacifist,
but all of that has changed." I attempted to make light
banter with him and said, "What has changed, the Christian or the pacifist?" He smiled wryly and said, "Both, I'm
afraid. The pacifist by conviction. The Christian out of
despair."

I said at the outset that in general I was in favor of
amnesty and that I felt it would serve the society that
grants it as well as the individual to whom it was granted.
For its own sake our society will progressively require
a general amnesty. Without amnesty this war will never
end in our own minds. The country will bear the burden
of guilt for its thousands of estranged sons. Guilt is an
unbearable emotion. We will go to great lengths to avoid
it. If a set of facts produces too much guilt we may deny
the facts rather than suffer the emotion. Men of good
will supported this war in its early stages, presumably
for purposes of high ideals. As time went on and their
investment became greater, more and more people were

killed, and the doubts began to set in. The frozen position of responsibility finds doubts such as these unbearable, for it produces a burden of guilt. With each killing, their stake in the war became greater, and consequently the need to justify it and rationalize it became greater. If it is too painful to admit a mistake, one solution is to deny that there was a mistake. This can be done by selectively recognizing only that evidence that justifies the war and its perpetuation. This may supply an alternative explanation (beyond "playing the game") for the individuals in high places who were for years emotionally committed to the war when they were part of the government and who underwent a conversion within months of leaving. Then they no longer had a personal need to maintain the rightness of the war.

If too much is invested, too much time elapsed, the truth can never be faced. We saw something similar with the radicals of the 1930s who sacrificed greatly for their dedication to the Communist Party. They simply could not face the evidence. Even as late as the Slansky trial in Czechoslovakia in 1951, and ultimately the Khrushchev revelations, some of them simply could not believe. So great was their sacrifice—giving up home, status, family, jobs—that they had to deny their senses rather than surrender overinvested illusions.

If you were a man of good will who had made Vietnam policy on the decision that it had been a just war in the national interests you would be the last to be objective when contrary evidence began to emerge. As long as personal guilt is present, there will be the tendency to discount and discredit the evidence to preserve oneself from having to believe things too painful to be believed. If we are to be done with this war we must alleviate the suffering even of its proponents. We must free all of the victims. Certainly among those victims are our political refugees. We must forgive these young men for being prematurely right.

There is a distinct possibility that the prisoners and exiles would not accept amnesty. But, judging from the men I spent time with, I think they would—particularly if it was expressed in terms that the previous decrees under which these men were prosecuted and jailed were considered null and void, and particularly if their freedom and the full civil status, which they value dearly, were restored. Very few of them refused parole if it was offered. (It is to the disgrace of the processes of justice that very seldom was it offered, as is generally the custom with most first offenders. There was a distinct discrimination against the political prisoner.) I think the resisters would be comfortable with amnesty. It fits into a tradition they understand—a tradition they embrace—of decency, love, and kindness. Let me repeat that these men have paid an enormous price. Do we really want to have them paying it all of their lives? Remember about whom we are talking: eighteen-to-twenty-five-year-olds. I am not sure what purpose would be served by refusal to declare an amnesty, except further to exhibit a sense of vindictiveness and a desire to punish. There is a joy in forgiveness, and a relief. It offers a pride and a pleasure that America could use today. America needs amnesty now. America is ready for it now.

A television panel show some time back interviewed a group of parents of imprisoned war resisters. After the interview of that panel a group of parents of children who were killed in Vietnam were interviewed, in a rather cruel and cynical contrast. Perhaps the producer expected some dramatic accusatory confrontation by the bereaved parents. If he did, he underestimated the human mind and the human spirit. The parents of those who were killed were most sympathetic and compassionate to those mothers with boys in jail. "I'd rather have a live boy in jail," one said, "than a son dead forever." America doesn't need either. Let us be thankful for those who are alive. Let us welcome back those of our youth who are still capable and wanting to come back. We need them.

WALTER GOODMAN

Walter Goodman's last book was A Percentage of the Take. *He has also written* The Committee: The Extraordinary History of the House Committee on Un-American Activities, All Honorable Men *and* The Clowns of Commerce *plus numerous articles in* Commentary, The New Leader, *the New York* Times Magazine, Life, *and others.*

There are times to deal with certain problems and times not to deal with them. If you raise the issue of amnesty while the war is still on, you run into the reasonable objection: Doesn't that encourage young men to avoid the draft?

I would hope, however, that when the war is over and things quiet down and there is no longer any need to worry about some men running from the draft, then the nation might be able to say, "All right, the time has come; let's bring these men back and accept them and finish with punishment and revenge."

A question often raised about those who refused to serve, and which I have examined in magazine articles, is whether these men were merely frightened of going into the Army and were simply using the principle of conscientious objection as a pretext. There is, of course, no way of generalizing, but in the case of the men I have met, I was left in no doubt of their sincerity. Was there an element of cowardice in their desire to avoid a certain kind of duty to their country? Perhaps; but the men with whom I spoke at some length convinced me that they were not consciously using the C.O. argument as a means of covering up something else. They were sincerely conscientious, by any definition.

So, if the issue of amnesty hinges in part on their honesty, then amnesty should be given.

A question is raised as to the potential for common ground that would allow an act of forgiveness such as amnesty. I have not found much bitterness against the C.O. or would-be C.O., although I am certain it exists. I found suspicion, though, and an incapacity to understand why some men refused to go. For example, I spoke with a group of Catholic lawyers. The immediate response of several of them was, "Aren't these kids who don't like the war simply saying that 'this is a war that we personally didn't choose and therefore we are not going to fight?' What kind of position is that?" It is not a philosophy; it is not an antiwar position; it has nothing to do with our traditional ideas of service to our country; and so to these lawyers it seemed illegal as well as immoral.

I suppose that underlying their suspicion was some degree of bitterness over the resisters getting away with something that others—boys they knew—were not. I think to an extent they were justified because the whole selective service scheme has actually worked out that way. The children of the well-to-do, the educated and more sophisticated classes, generally have escaped the draft. The children of "middle America" have had to serve, fight, and return to be ignored. The bitterness of those lawyers, if I sensed it correctly, was not directed just at resisters—although they were a fine focus for it—but at the college students who were able to escape their obligation while other kids had to fight and possibly die. Their anger is understandable.

My own feeling is that the resisters have in some fashion made a contribution to the country. For all their political and logical deficiencies and their pretensions to superior virtue, they have served to remind us that our republic finds strength in the tensions between the exigencies of government and the imperatives of belief, between the demands of authority and the refusals of exasperating individuals.

Those of us who like the idea of an eventual amnesty are somewhat hypocritical; I would be loathe to make a campaign for amnesty now, simply on tactical grounds. You would be doing harm to those you want to help, because you would only be arousing resistance—particularly, I believe, from Congress. Representative Edward I. Koch, who introduced the first such bill, has excellent motives. I know that he has traveled to Canada and talked with the young men there and has been moved by them. But it is nevertheless an unpropitious moment to advance so emotional an issue. It can only create unnecessary opposition.

I do not accept the argument that amnesty is immoral because it excuses those who have broken the law, because it rests on the premise that all wars are equally sacred, equally valuable, equally accepted by the nation. We know, after all, that some laws are only nominal laws, and some, while not nominal, reach into specially sensitive areas, and have to be so employed in a sensitive way.

Still, those of us who favor amnesty have to face up to this "argument." If a law is passed in this country and if it becomes a man's duty to go into the Army, then how can one say, "Well, we will forgive those who choose not to go."? That is, we are forgiving you for the crime you are now committing or have recently committed or are yet to commit. Can we have a law and an amnesty at the same time? I do not think so.

It is partly for that reason that I would advocate waiting until the moment when the draft laws have lost their effect, when the war is finished, when, possibly, the bitterness of the moment has somewhat abated. At that point, it would be possible to raise the issue of amnesty. Then we can say to the resister and to the exile, "You may have done wrong as far as the law was concerned, but our society does not consider it a great moral wrong and is now willing to forgive you, or at least punish you no more than you've already been punished."

After the war and after the draft, we are going to be faced with an extinct law—but a dead law that is still punishing large numbers of men. We will not be able to do anything at that moment for those men who had to go, and we will have to address ourselves to the question of whether there is any longer a good reason to continue punishing men who were sincere in not wanting to go and who certainly had no wish for anybody else to go either.

Another troubling aspect to this matter, which goes beyond the question of amnesty, is the manner in which we get out of Vietnam. We probably will not get out gracefully; we certainly will not get out victoriously. What effect will that have on American life in the coming years? After Korea there was a backlash. When and if we ever free ourselves from Vietnam, it will take someone in the White House who can command the kind of trust and faith necessary to keep the inevitable recriminations within bounds. I do not believe Richard Nixon is the man for this job. On the other hand, if the Democrats are in power, particularly if the President should have a reputation as a dove, then he will be a natural target of the impulse toward vengeance, toward placing guilt and building up conspiracy theories. He may have trouble keeping the animals at bay.

Much of the agony over this whole issue might have been avoided if we had allowed a man the legal option of being a conscientious objector to a specific war. Why should the officially approved C.O. only have the right to say conscientiously, "I am against all wars."? Why isn't it equally a matter of conscience to be against this one war? If this country is able and ready to recognize that conscientious objection is valid under certain circumstances—and we have for many years been able to do that—where is the logic in restricting it in this manner? The restriction may be practical, reflecting a desire to hold down the number of proclaimed C.O.s, but it isn't logical. There are historical reasons connected with the existence of "peace churches" like the Quakers and Mennonites, which fall under the freedom of religion clause in the Bill of Rights. But even that does not make the principle logical or indeed moral.

The government does itself no service when it tells an opponent of our adventure in Southeast Asia that America can offer him nothing between the fields of Vietnam and a prison cell. To allow the selective C.O. alternative service in hospitals, schools and ghettos would be a show of regard for the individual, a gift to the nation, and a sign of grace in the state. And because we failed to do this, we are having to pass through a good deal of needless pain here at home.

INTERVIEW WITH
CONGRESSMAN EDWARD I. KOCH

Edward I. Koch is the Democratic congressman for the Seventeenth District, in Manhattan, New York City.

MURRAY POLNER: *Congressman Koch, in general terms first, why did you, the only one of the New York delegation, possibly the only one in the U. S. Congress for that matter, go out on a limb and introduce the whole issue of amnesty?*

EDWARD I. KOCH: Well, I think you have to set the climate for the discussion that I believe will take place after the war; my position is that amnesty is only one of a number of options. I have not taken the position that amnesty should necessarily be provided to those who have left the country and gone to Canada to evade the draft.

I believe that we have to find an acceptable solution that will permit the men to return without going to jail. Now there are some who have not violated U.S. law; they have emigrated and have received their Canadian citizenship and, as I understand it, could come back freely to the United States. There are some, perhaps most, who have in fact violated the law, if they got their draft notice and then left, or if they have deserted from the Armed Forces. So we are talking about different groups of people in terms of the law. What I have said is that we have to consider the options that should be made available to permit their return to the United States.

It is interesting to note what happens every time I get on a program with a right-winger such as Jeffrey St. John, who might not like to be classified as a right-winger but surely he is a conservative and a very likable and very intelligent guy. He invited me to debate the subject with him and when I made my opening statement, which was that we have got to find options that will permit their return, he said, "I'll give them an option—send them to *jail*." So I said, "Well, that's one option; how about instead of jail for five years, which is presently the law, how about two years?" And he said, "Yes, well, that's all right." I said, "How about instead of jail we find some constructive work to do; you and I know what jail does. How about some service in the ghettos, the Indian reservations, doing something constructive for two years?" He said, "Well that is something that I would consider." And it became very clear—and I have found it is this way every time I have this conversation with an intelligent and sincere individual—that all he wanted to be sure of is that a guy does not get off scot free. That's really the heart of it. They are not so much interested in his going to jail; it is just that there be some kind of note taken that you can't with impunity evade the law. I understand that. And so what I say to those who ask is that amnesty is only one of the options. I say that probably we will find it easier to deal with this if we find some other option such as an alternative civilian service to be rendered for a period of time by these men.

M.P.: *Why have you emphasized this issue?*

E.I.K.: I'm also the proponent of two bills relating to selective C.O. status, one prospective and the other retroactive. Let me start at the beginning. The bills provide that selective C.O. status be recognized; that means granting C.O. status to those opposed to participation in a particular war, instead of requiring that they be opposed

to participation in all wars. Selective C.O. status would
be granted if you were able to establish your opposition
to participation in a particular war because of moral,
philosophical, religious reasons—comparable to those
that have to be established by a traditional C.O. It would
not be for reasons based on political opposition. It would
obviously be difficult for someone to establish that he is
a selective C.O., but the fact is that if he does not establish
it, and it is his burden of proof, he is going into the
Armed Forces. Those who can establish that they are
bona fide objectors ought to be given selective C.O.
status. So, I introduced two bills in the spring of 1969.
One, prospective in coverage, simply clarifies the definition of conscientious objector. The other, which is called
my "second chance" bill, covers those men already affected
by the Selective Service Act—whether they be in exile, in
prison, or in combat against their consciences.

My "second chance" bill would permit those who have
left the country to come back. It has eight co-sponsors.
If the exiles were able to establish that they were qualified
as selective C.O.s at the time they left the country and
are presently selective C.O.s to the satisfaction of their
local draft boards, they would be given the opportunity
of performing alternative noncombatant or civilian
service for the two-year period that one would have to
serve in the military forces. Pending criminal prosecutions would be wiped out. Those who went to jail, again
providing they qualified, would be given selective C.O.
status and freed. They then would perform alternative
noncombatant or civilian service. The same alternatives
given to a C.O. would be given to the selective C.O.

I have read a number of newspaper stories on this subject; one in particular in the New York *Times* had a very
vivid impact on me. Among other things it said that there
were five thousand draft evaders in Canada. Then I received some calls from parents in my own district—not
very many, but some. I decided I would go to Canada to

see for myself. I called the World Council of Churches because I knew that they had representatives working with the young people in Canada. They had also been in touch with my office concerning my selective C.O. bill. A young man, Rev. Richard Kilmer, agreed to be my guide. It was a very short trip, I think it was December 29 and 30, 1969, and we—Kilmer, David Brown, my administrative assistant, and I—went to three cities: Toronto, Montreal, and then Ottawa.

In Toronto we met with a group of Members of Parliament, who were very concerned about the problem and had fought with their own government to make certain that immigration officials, who were turning back Americans coming over the border to evade the draft, be directed not to do so. And as I understand it there was a change in regulations that they got through the immigration service at the direction of Prime Minister Trudeau, stipulating that the fact that someone was a deserter or an evader of the draft was not to be a bar to his being granted landed immigrant status.

M.P.: *When you met some of those young evaders or deserters, were they interested in the possibility of amnesty?*

E.I.K.: In the one major meeting that took place in Ottawa, I met with about twenty-five people in the home of a Canadian, who was very much involved in assisting the draft evaders. He provided a kind of underground railroad. The exiles were there, some with their infant children. Most of them told me that it was not just the war in Vietnam that caused them to leave the United States, although that was the major cause, but that it was American society, which they pictured as crass and commercial and did not conform to what they wanted. Very few of them in that room were deserters, but those who were spoke of the brutalities they had witnessed in the military. One was a Marine, another had been in the Navy, and some of them had been to Vietnam and had come home and deserted. Some of them said that even if they were not punished and were given amnesty—and that was the word they used—they could not be induced to return to America unless other conditions changed in our society.

One couple from the Midwest, both teachers, said after the meeting broke up, "Congressman, we want you to know that we don't feel that way, that if we could come back without going to jail, we would like to." My own feeling was that a good number of these people, knowingly or unknowingly, who said they would never come back unless the other conditions in society changed, were simply rationalizing. I am sure it is true that a few would not come back, but I do not accept it as applying to very many. There was great emotion expressed about their not being able to come back to the United States on passes, so to speak, to see their families, and they asked, "Could it not be arranged that we might come in on a weekend to see our families?" I could sense the great impact this loss of the family relationship had had on them. A number of them talked about the fact that their parents could not understand what they had done and were ashamed of them. Some of the parents, particularly the fathers, would not accept telephone calls from their children and in effect said, "For me you are dead." It was really heartbreaking. Others, however, said that their parents visited with them and maintained the family relationship, and that too was very moving to me.

M.P.: *Would you extend amnesty to those who deserted the military? If so, how can you reconcile your position as a Congressman sworn to uphold the laws of the United States with that of forgiving desertion from the armed services?*

E.I.K.: There is no conflict in my having to uphold the laws of the United States. I would never intentionally violate the law. I served in World War II; now I'm opposed to the war in Vietnam. I think it is immoral and unconstitutional. I can list all of the reasons why we ought never to have been involved in that war, and why our involvement should be terminated now. But I would go, if called. This is not reflecting on the courage of the men who have not gone; it takes a certain kind of courage to do what many of them have done, too. With many of them it is a matter of principle. All I am saying is that I believe that our Congress should provide the mechanism and options whereby they can return. This is not in conflict with my having sworn to uphold the laws of the United States.

The two bills that I mentioned earlier and the discussions that I have initiated are predicated on the fact that the war in Vietnam, because it is the kind of war it is, is a cancer that is destroying us. It would be far better for the country, were there, to use the President's hackneyed phrasing, a way of bringing us together. Good, bring us together, Mr. Nixon. You do that by introducing some justice into this area where the war has caused much injustice, where our laws have made it necessary for principled young men to choose between violating their consciences or violating the law. That is the reason I have introduced my two bills to provide for selective conscientious objector status.

I am opposed to any option that would say to all these young people, "Let them spend some time in jail." That would not be any one of my options because I also happen to know what jail does to people. You do not change a man's character in jail, and I just do not think that this country is going to be made better or the individual involved in this moral dilemma is going to be rehabilitated by putting him in jail.

The other options are those that would create an opportunity to do constructive service, whether VISTA or the Peace Corps or some new humane endeavor. Those are the kind of options I mean.

M.P.: *Some have claimed that amnesty might lead to*

reconciliation. Others have said that it would cause a tre-mendous amount of bitterness, particularly by those who invested a great deal of their emotional resources sup-porting this war. What have you found to be the case?

E.I.K.: There is no question that both of those are valid points of view. Let me tell you what happened when I came back from Canada. I was walking near my home, down Eighth Street in New York City, and I met a woman whom I know quite well. I did what I generally do when I meet a constituent. I said, "How am I doing?" And she said, "Oh, I think you are doing fine, Mr. Koch, except for that trip to Canada." I said, "Well, why?" And then she began to weep. "Why should we let those boys come back from Canada, those yellow bellies, when my grandson is in Vietnam and may be shot and lose his life?" I said, "Look—what I want to do is to save all the lives, the life of your grandson, and the lives of these young men who have gone to Canada. What I want to do is to bring all of them home." The explanation didn't mean too much to her. She couldn't accept it but she did say, when we parted, "Well, all right, I like everything else you do."

My mail reflects the division on these points. One letter I received was from a mother, well written and very bitter. How, she wrote, could anyone think that the evaders could be let off. Her son had died in Vietnam. Another letter was from a parent who said that his son had gone to Canada and that he had cut him off as though he were dead. It was heartbreaking to read. So, setting the issue of exile aside, I sent a little note to him just saying, "It is so sad that you should find yourself in that situation and I hope you are able to work it out with your son."

You asked me why I started to concentrate on amnesty. I think the best answer is that while we cannot offer an amnesty or other options until the war is over, we can start the dialogue now.

M.P.: *How do you perceive this issue of amnesty developing?*

E.I.K.: Its time will come. When an idea reaches its time, nothing can stop it. I think that is what will happen here. There are enough people involved that the pressures will build up in the Congress, and there is a fundamental American desire to do the right thing and to attempt a national reconciliation. At least I hope that is what is going to happen. How many of us come from families where our grandfathers and even fathers left European countries in the very same way, to escape service in their conscript armies.

M.P.: *What kind of an amnesty would you favor?*

E.I.K.: I do not favor amnesty as such. I do favor alternatives that would permit young men to return to this country and perform some kind of national service without having to go to jail. I suppose some might call that a conditional amnesty. We and other democratic societies have passed through this before. Great Britain has had a selective C.O. classification for its citizens who could not in good conscience take up arms since 1941, a year when they were under nearly overwhelming attack by the Nazis. In our own Civil War, Abraham Lincoln sought to bring the country together and offered amnesty during the war to southern rebels if they swore allegiance to the Union.

I am always amazed that we were more merciful to those who killed their northern fellow citizens than we are willing to be to those, who for whatever reason, have refused to kill any human beings.

INTERVIEW WITH ROBERT JAY LIFTON

Robert Jay Lifton holds the Foundations Fund for Research in Psychiatry professorship at Yale University. His books include Revolutionary Immortality: Mao Tse-tung and the Chinese Cultural Revolution; Thought Reform and the Psychology of Totalism: A Study of "Brainwashing" in China *and the recipient of the National Book Award,* Death in Life: Survivors of Hiroshima.

MURRAY POLNER: *You have had a good deal of experience with Vietnam veterans, particularly those who have been opposed to the war. You have also had extensive experience with the victims of the Hiroshima nuclear attack. In general, what might be some of the psychological experiences of a young man exiled in Canada or a resister in prison?*

ROBERT JAY LIFTON: I think there is a sense of being a victim and a sense of being cast out. Gradually, even in brave men, that becomes internalized to some degree. For instance, a draft resister who goes to Canada is likely to have a sense of pride over not having succumbed to military induction for a cause he feels to be evil. But at the same time, he may have another image, some inner question. It might be a question about himself, whether, for example, he did it out of fear. He might internalize society's over-all judgment of him as betraying his country.

These images can exist side by side. Anybody who goes into exile to evade the draft is likely to experience such ambivalence.

The sense of being disloyal, even though it is irrational by his own standards, can become connected with a sense of guilt, together with a sense of isolation, of being cut off from the mainstream of one's own country. In fact, the increasing psychological separation from society, here in their own country, must be a real burden for many young people. Still, there is a great difference when that experience occurs in the center of their culture. It is an inner exile. Being in exile in Canada or Sweden could result in a profound sense of estrangement.

M.P.: *Would this be true for those who went to prison?*

R.J.L.: Much of it would hold true and a lot more as well. I have no expert knowledge of this because I have never worked with people in prison. But from reading about it you get a very strong sense of its dehumanizing experience. Prison tends to break down one's humanity even in people who are dedicated to higher moral purposes. It is so total an experience that people often collapse under it. Incidentally, I did work with people who had been in prison in a political context when I studied Chinese thought reform or so-called "brainwashing."[1]

There tends to be an internalization of the prison experience too. In American prisons I have read about, prisoners have to cope with a strange series of manipulations and rituals involving the guards as well as other prisoners, and which include a considerable amount of sadism and advanced psychopathy. Prisoners lose their capacity to react spontaneously. They begin to set up techniques of self-protection. In important ways they really become divested of their humanity. Even among conscientious ob-

[1] *Thought Reform and the Psychology of Totalism: A Study of "Brainwashing" in China*, New York, W. W. Norton & Co., 1961. (Paperback reprint, Norton Library Edition, 1963.)

jectors, it has been shown that many of them tend to take
out their inner rage on one another, or, for example,
against those who were given shorter prison sentences,
who were made to suffer less than they for the same
cause. All sorts of patterns manifest themselves, patterns
they would consider unworthy of their moral stand. Their
potential for psychological conflict is strongly evoked, as
is the potential in everyone for dehumanization. Prison
does that.

M.P.: *To what extent would an act of amnesty help or
harm the outcast in prison or in exile?*

R.J.L.: I think the psychology of amnesty would not
be simple. This is, first of all, conjecture, because it would
have to happen and then be observed to really know ac-
curately. Nevertheless, I would suspect that to some
extent, the amnesty perceived by those who suffered in
prison or in exile may be seen as counterfeit. They might
not accept it as a meaningful, or appropriate, or even an
adequate gesture on the part of the government.

You might also find a paradoxical reaction here of resentment—resentment of the effort of a government to assume the moral authority of granting amnesty, to make a
gesture that is in any case too little and too late. I think
this has to do with a whole psychology that I call counterfeit nurturance, in this case an ostensibly noble gesture on
the part of the offending force, the American government.

But having said all this, I believe that, from the standpoint of the resisters and from the standpoint of society, amnesty would be a very positive psychological
experience. From the standpoint of the resisters who
have been in prison or those in exile, it would be a form
of recognition, rather than being simply condemned by
their society. In some way there would be a gesture made
toward the value of their act, and therefore, their own
worth. It would recognize as well the direction they took,
and could in that way contribute to their own self-esteem.

I think it would do a great deal toward diminishing their alienation from their own country. This would be very important since many of them are estranged on many levels, often in disturbing and complicated ways. It does not mean that they would suddenly embrace their government. Far from it. But they would at least be in a position of recognition by their society and feel themselves more comfortable about finding their way and taking various actions, including actions that were critical of their society.

M.P.: *You suggested earlier that there would be psychological advantages to the country at large if there were an amnesty. Could you elaborate on that?*

R.J.L.: I see the Vietnam war as a culmination in a very extreme way of a major historical crisis for this country. I think the crisis began long before the war and is more basic than the war itself. But still, the war is its culmination, and has in turn contributed to something close to the breakdown of the American national polity and social structure. The descent into random violence, with major groups in society turning against—and being turned against—each other is ominous indeed. The fabric of American society, which perhaps has always been more tenuous than we would like to believe, is being threatened in a very real psychological way.

The whole process—what I think of as a malignant spiral—follows upon our specific actions in Indochina—not just the face of the war, but the way we are fighting it, what we are doing there on a day-to-day basis. I refer, of course, to the atrocity-producing situation we have created there—to the over-all atrocity of extraordinary scope that we are perpetrating—with the result that the entire country has, in an important sense, been "living in atrocity." Whatever the psychological defenses call forth, and they are considerable, Americans can no longer avoid the sense of having fallen into evil. The country is deeply confused, but there is a feeling, vague but disturbing and widespread, that not only the GIs sent to Vietnam but the whole society is in serious moral peril.

Vietnam has torn us apart, but I think that amnesty would be a very significant step in the direction of recovery. It would hardly be enough and it would be a very small step. But amnesty could be a way of turning legal processes away from justification of what is actually an immoral and illegal war, and turning them instead toward a recognition of and sympathetic expression toward those who resisted the war. An amnesty law would be a very significant act, since our society is one of laws, and the law is so essential to our tradition. It would also be a very significant psychological act, a humane act for all of us.

I would add that amnesty could also aggravate certain tensions. The American government has an enormous impact upon the rank and file of Americans, including those we call middle Americans as well as the various ethnic groups in the country, many of whom remain antagonistic toward the peace movement. Many who have supported the war and expected victory feel as betrayed by Vietnam as those of us who have been in the peace movement, perhaps even more so. For them, amnesty could seem a further act of betrayal on the part of the government. Among veterans—dove and hawk—there could be mixed feelings. But an official decision for amnesty could bring these contending groups together in some form of constructive dialogue around the principle of welcoming *all* of America's young men back into the society and recognizing their struggle for integrity under the difficult conditions everyone has faced.

Yet so much of the rage around the war has been stimulated by the government and by certain chauvinistic positions taken by the President, Vice President, and others in positions of power. If these same leaders—or, more likely, their successors, or perhaps the Congress—were to take the very humane position of amnesty, these tensions and resentments against those who did not fight could be

ameliorated. Some people, of course, would remain en-
raged and nothing would reconcile that. But I do think
there are many Americans who move in and out of chauvinism and who are ready for a more decent and humane
policy. I think amnesty could reawaken in many Americans traditional sentiments associated with individual conscience, whether on a religious or secular basis. It could
bring out the best side of people whose worst side too
often has been evoked for political reasons. I have mentioned a number of tensions, because I think these are
important for proponents of amnesty to face, but if the
policy could be built around a far-reaching alliance between respected leaders and ordinary people, these tensions could be outweighed, and in part resolved, by a uni-
fying principle that, for a change, will be life-enhancing
rather than life-destroying.

M.P.: *You have been working for some time with
antiwar Vietnam veterans in group therapy sessions. How
might they cope with a possible amnesty?*

R.J.L.: They have begun to think and talk about
amnesty, and they favor it. I think the matter is complicated for them, though. Even dovish veterans are probably ambivalent to an extent. One side of them may feel,
"We really suffered, we went through it, it was an extraordinarily painful experience for us"—causing them to resent
those who avoided the war and were "getting off easy."
But once they have had that reaction, having now come
to an antiwar position—which for veterans takes a lot of
soul searching and is really a very genuine and, in my
experience, a very moving transformation—they bring the
power of their transformation to this judgment and call
forth their reasoning powers.

I have heard them refer to those who avoided the war
as their brothers. Coping with this question becomes another step in their spiritual journey. They will, for the
most part, cope with it very positively. Having taken the
antiwar position, many of them have made gestures to

draft resisters in one way or another. They talk with sympathy about conscientious objectors, admire their stand, and see it as the one that they too might or should have taken, if only they knew earlier what they had to learn so painfully about the war.

Clearly, other veterans not specifically identified with an antiwar position could have a greater degree of resentment. They too would have their ambivalence with the element of resentment stronger and the capacity to accept amnesty weaker when compared to the antiwar veterans. They are psychologically defending against a deep sense of absurdity and rage. There is sometimes a desperate effort to preserve significance and justification for all they suffered and experienced. How could the war have been worthless? How could it have had no meaning? The most terrifying idea of all to some is the simple truth that, as John Kerry put it, the war has been fought for "the greatest nothing in history." In order to defend themselves against this realization, prowar people must come out with wildly chauvinistic images, as if to preserve the most extreme dehumanization and numbing that they have known in Vietnam or read about from a distance. Even now there is an article in _Harper's_[2] in which some wounded veterans do just this and say every Vietnamese ought to be shot. It is a kind of psychological defense against feeling, and against the inner recognition of what the war really was. And, in that sense, they would have much the same rage toward amnesty and toward those granted amnesty. Still, some small voice in them, the same small voice that knows the war is dirty and absurd, that voice that you encountered in all two hundred of the veterans you interviewed, that same voice might have a little bit of sympathy or even respect for those granted amnesty and for the justice of their position. Now that voice might not always be able to be recognized within them but it would be there.

[2] March 1971.

M.P.: *Would the same be true with the parents or the wives of those who were either wounded or killed in the war? In other words, how might a parent whose son may never get up off his back or a wife who will never see her husband again react when they find the guy who went off to Canada is allowed once again to return home, absolved of his guilt?*

R.J.L.: A very difficult, touchy, and painful situation. They have the psychology of the survivor. Once a woman's husband or son comes home wounded or maimed, she is a survivor. These wives and mothers can go in either direction. A number of them have this terrible poignant need to find meaning in the sacrifice that their sons and husbands have made. They come out endorsing war as a form of significance. It is the traditional way of survivors of any war.

Still, a small minority of this group have come out against the war and have found that significance they need in a peace-minded survival. To my mind this is a more humane and healthier pattern, but much more difficult to develop. And of course, as in the case of veterans themselves, there are many family survivors, perhaps most, who fall in between these two positions and have great difficulty articulating their feelings.

I think these themes would be the issue around which the problem of amnesty would be viewed. Insofar as they feel the need to defend and endorse, sometimes desperately, the war, they would be resentful of amnesty. Insofar as they could accept the peace-minded survivor's resolution, they would be sympathetic to amnesty.

M.P.: *Much of your writing has dealt with the question of psychic numbing, which perhaps you can briefly explain here. But as this war drags on endlessly, to what degree is there a relationship between raising up yet another controversial question and the fact that the American public might very well not want to deal with more difficult issues such as amnesty?*

R.J.L.: First of all, by psychic numbing, I mean simply desensitization. People undergo psychic numbing in a variety of ways. They simply cease to feel. There is a gap between event and inner experience. And of course the American people, like people during all wars, have undergone profound psychic numbing. They do not allow their imaginations to dwell on what happens at the other end of their weapons. In general, people focus on the more romantic side of war and on the idea of patriotism. This war, however, is hard to romanticize, even on the part of its defenders. Certainly the American public has not wanted to see or deal psychologically with the nature of this war, as a large over-all atrocity. Psychic numbing has been necessary to the state to keep the war going and prevent earlier and more effective resistance to the war. Yet some of the truth of the war has broken through the numbing. The My Lai story and other evidence of atrocities have gotten through in partial degree. All sorts of psychological measures or defenses are called forth against full recognition. But still, numbing is imperfect.

How does this attitude of numbing deal with the question of amnesty? Again, it is not easy to say. Some people will simply not want to think about the whole thing. They are tired of the war and once it is over they will not want to be called upon to have opinions or emotions about it any more. They will resent the issue on that basis or else ignore it. Others will find the numbing, insofar as they have retained it, again threatened by the issue of amnesty because the implicit assumption with amnesty would be that the war was indeed dirty and that there was something admirable or at least acceptable about opposing or refusing it, even if that meant breaking the law.

M.P.: *Are there any other important psychological issues to consider?*

R.J.L.: I think there is another area we must look into, one that is indirectly related to amnesty and its implications, namely, the drastically altered male role.

I have seen some very interesting and moving things happen to veterans concerning the male role. To oversimplify, some of them begin with a vision, or ideal vision, of the tight-lipped, supermasculine, cruel but courageous hero, ready to shoot and kill for his cause. But they move toward a very different sense of maleness, one with greater emphasis upon sensitivity, introspection, thoughtfulness, "softness," aesthetic sensibility, and the capacity for tenderness.

It is a very different kind of male role, moving, say, from John Wayne to Country Joe and the Fish. The John Wayne hero battles and dies gladly for his cause in an unquestioning way. To Country Joe and the Fish, in their "I'm Fixing to Die Rag," the satirized notion is, "I'm going to die for nothing, absurdly and meaninglessly."

The new expression of the male role has to do with a judgment about such matters, a rejection of what might be called blind courage for reason, for thoughtful examination, for humane purposes. I think that this kind of shift would be very much reasserted by amnesty. Those who went abroad or who chose prison certainly embraced this second, more sensitive, less unquestioning, less chauvinistic male role. Their form of maleness, their form of courage, and their form of integrity in relation to a view of the male role would be encouraged and supported by amnesty. That would be a very positive step for the country because America has suffered from its supermasculine ethos and from the accompanying terror of homosexuality. It has led many Americans to jingoistic decisions and has fit in with corresponding political and social positions. It has also blunted the capacity for tenderness and for aesthetic sensibility.

I am not saying that amnesty by itself could convert Americans from the first to the second model of the male role, but it would be a positive element in that shift. Now that shift is already occurring in important ways in the youth movement. Amnesty would have the additional virtue of reinforcing some of the best that is in the youth movement; that is, a capacity for empathy, sensitivity, stress upon each person's right to his own idiosyncrasies and inclinations, rather than a very sharp definition of maleness and femaleness with the narrow restrictions often contained within that definition.

M.P.: *We were talking before about amnesty as a kind of recognition. What did you mean by that?*

R.J.L.: Whether or not it was so stated in the amnesty decision there would be a recognition of the moral choice made by those who went to prison and those who went into exile. In other words, it would be treated as a serious moral decision with elements of value of purpose and one that connects with other moral traditions that are respected. This would be a way of society's seeing the moral vision that it now seems to be blotting out in simply sending these young people to jail or exile. That is a form of recognition. Now I am using recognition on several levels —legal recognition, of course, meaning restoration of full rights and ending of fugitive or prisoner status; psychological recognition, in the sense of affirming to some degree the value of the act of resistance, and therefore of the individual granted amnesty; and personal recognition, in the everyday sense of being remembered, welcomed, granted respect. As yet America has not been able to afford or to hold forth such recognition because it has had to maintain the twin deceptions that it is fighting a just war and that to refuse to fight that war is an immoral act. One has the impression that much of the energies of our leaders are spent in blocking out the kinds of recognition we are talking about. But now, with a wider appreciation of the war as something close to an over-all atrocity, the possibility of granting recognition to draft resisters for their superior courage is much closer to people's consciousness. The whole issue of amnesty becomes quite discussible.

M.P.: *Nonetheless, in many societies, the warlike cul-*

*ture often makes amnesty seem very difficult to achieve,
despite the good intentions of a great number of people.*

R.J.L.: Yes it does. And that is another reason why it
would be such an important step. That supermasculine
ethos fits in with warmaking and the warlike ethos. One
reinforces the other. Amnesty, in interrupting that super-
male stereotype, would also be a break in the general
warlike ethos of the culture, together with the inclination
to romanticize war and to lend it dignity. Amnesty would
cause a fundamental questioning of the place of war in
society simply by its recognizing and re-embracing those
who had so sternly and iconoclastically rejected the war.

In the same spirit, the warlike ethos that has passed
from generation to generation would also be questioned,
if it were not in fact interrupted. Maybe it is worth saying
a word about this, too. One veteran I interviewed told me
how his father had been a pilot in World War II, but was
otherwise a man quite troubled and weak. He regaled his
son with stories about heroic deeds during World War
II, stories that fascinated the boy and created in him admiration and a kind of curiosity and yearning for similar
experiences. Now, I think this is a very fundamental
process and it has been described by a friend and colleague
of mine, a psychoanalyst named Martin Wangh. He wrote
a paper in which he talks about this ethos being passed
from father to son. I have seen evidence of it in my own
work. It is very real and it perpetuates the kind of male
ethos of the sort I have been talking about, as well as the
values of war and the psychological affirmation for fighting
in a war.

Not only that, but it creates within each generation a
sense that each man, if he is indeed to be a man, has to
fight in the war of his generation. It is very strange when
you come to think of it. World War I, World War II,
the Korean war, and the Vietnam war. Almost from
grandfather to grandchild. One vet I spent time with went
back as far as the Alamo, which he said his grandfather

used to talk to him about, as he himself described the sense he had about the responsibility of each generation to fight bravely—and above all to be counted among the fighters. This is a disastrous ethos. It might have made a little more sense when men were defending their own territories or fighting with their hands or very limited weapons. But we have moved into ultimate weapons and advanced technology and we have seen enough of the latter in Vietnam being employed against an underdeveloped society.

In any case this ethos becomes absolutely grotesque and profoundly dangerous to the survival of the species within the framework of our technology.

What does amnesty do? Well, amnesty helps to interrupt the generation-to-generation warmaking ethos. Amnesty says that at least a small group of young men within a generation can be judged as worthwhile and even brave for rejecting that ethos, for breaking the deadly chain—for saying "no" to fighting the war that one's generation was "expected" to fight. Amnesty would recognize, dignify, and institutionalize that interruption of the glorification of war over the generations and indeed, the ethos of the "necessary war" for each generation. That would be a very important goal to which amnesty can contribute.

I see amnesty as one part of a number of social transformations within our country and in the world in general. I mentioned the earlier general crisis I see our society in the midst of. To get out of this crisis, even to survive, we are going to need a number of such transformations. Again, many of the protest movements are trying to say this, at some times more effectively than at others. Nonetheless, that is the inner message of protest. In general psychological terms, there has to be a transformation away from psychic numbing, much of it associated with sophisticated technology or with large organizations or so-called technobureaucracies, which dominate so much of our society.

There are struggles now on many levels, people trying to move to a more viable pattern with more capacity to feel and to empathize, while at the same time dealing with high technology and with large organizations, creating new forms of community, and engaging in a large number of social experiments. Amnesty would be very much in that spirit. But the fundamental change to which amnesty might contribute would be the crucial one for our time: from war to peace, from imagery of war to imagery of peace, from warmaking to more humane pursuits.

MARTIN E. MARTY

Martin E. Marty is Professor of Modern Church History at the University of Chicago and Associate Editor of The Christian Century. *His most recent books are* Righteous Empire: The Protestant Experience in America, The Search for a Usable Future, *and* The Modern Schism. *He is also co-editor of the Macmillan annual* New Theology No. 1–8 *and* Ecumenical Studies in Church History.

My concern here is whether Christians, theologians, and reflective thinkers have any special point of view on the question of amnesty. I believe it important not to confuse amnesty in the political sense with any traditional categories of Christian witness, e.g., forgiveness. Forgiveness is a word that usually relates to the way Christians view God-man relations. It also deals with man-to-man relations and is seen to have been made possible, in the Christian tradition, because of a special act of God, usually seen as an act that He took in Jesus Christ. Now, there may be parallels or analogies between that kind of divine-human or man-to-man transaction and between amnesty and forgiveness, but there are also many differences, and I believe it only introduces confusion to bring the two together.

The Oxford English Dictionary defines amnesty as

"forgetfulness, oblivion and intentional overlooking." While some biblical language calls forgiveness a forgetting or a divine willingness not to remember one's offenses, the transaction involving forgiveness usually recognizes a God who remembers and who may even punish and then create something new, a forgiven person.

In the civil realm amnesty is an act of oblivion, or a general overlooking of past offenses by the ruling authority. We have to remember in this case that the past offenses, from the viewpoint of a ruling authority, are not necessarily offenses against what a Christian perceives to be a divine law. Thus, to take an obvious example, if a German was told he should execute an innocent Jew and then found some way not to, the ruling authority might have condemned the negligent executioner; but from the viewpoint of anything transnational this was not an offense. It was an offense only in light of one ruling authority.

Now, to bring that home to the United States: If the Vietnamese involvement is as immoral as many of us have felt it to be, and given the perspective our nation will acquire in a few years, should the young men who went to Canada or anywhere else in the world as exiles to avoid getting involved in committing an offense, be given amnesty? From the viewpoint of the ruling authority it is a past offense. From the viewpoint of a divine law it may not have been a past offense. It may have been a better following of divine law. We can perceive from this that there are great differences between Christian concepts of forgiveness in the light of breaking the divine law and political concepts of amnesty in the matter of breaking human law.

My point of view from one angle is radical: Everybody gets amnesty. From another it is conservative: One does preserve some sense of order and principle. There is no reason why anyone who was in exile during these years should have to serve in any kind of penal situation. It would only serve to add further to the burden of his life.

But I believe that some analogues to alternative service could be developed for many kinds of people.

The very fact that we have to *talk* about amnesty in America suggests that we are in a new stage of our national development. Maybe it is good that we have to. Maybe this is a sign that we are past national innocence, past the days of simplicity, of "my country right or wrong," of involvement on any terms that we might like, in any kind of war. We are learning complexity and we are joining the human race. This can be a creative moment for ethical reflection. This will not be the last time that our nation is going to be thrown into such ambiguous and complex social-ethical issues; we can begin to learn from this. Until we have believable policies that almost all of our people can share and until we come again to some national consensus, we will find that this kind of issue will be coming up and we will have to discuss it.

Just as the Vietnamese war greatly enlarged the numbers of people who could accept the concept of selective conscientious objection, so perhaps Americans can make a great leap forward and show the maturation of their society by indicating their willingness to live with the concept of amnesty at the end of the Indochina conflict. Needless to say, we do not have to wait until the end of that protracted war to begin to invite back the young men who left, but I am realistic enough to assume that not much will happen until then.

What specifically can past events within the Western and American Christian traditions add to this topic? It is almost impossible to speak about *the* Christian tradition on a topic of this kind. To begin with a cosmic generalization, we ought to say that from the fourth century down to the recent past, almost wherever Christians happened to be, they were running the show. Eastern Christians in their regimes, Western Catholics and then Protestants and Catholics running their regimes, did not only provide support for the powers that be. In occasional modern revolutions they helped upset power and, when a new regime took over, they began to endorse it. There are some biblical passages in the New Testament that suggest that Christians should always be working with the powers that be, but of course there are ten passages to one asking them also to seek a kingdom that goes beyond the kingdoms of this world. The tendency in Christian history has been to be supportive of the established situation. Very rarely have Christians placed themselves in the circumstance of making contributions to subjects like pacifism or conscientious objection or amnesty. The people who have made the major contributions have been the outsiders, the statistically small groups, the minority groups such as the Quakers and the Mennonites. These people are willing to say that the individual conscience takes priority over whatever the state demands. It is true that during the Constantinian period (after the fourth century) there were moments when Christians made specific contributions toward the humanization of war. It is true too that Christians have in some ages provided sanctuary, particularly in feudal times, for victims of injustice.

Individual Christian humanists have often pleaded the causes of people who have sought amnesty. The Christian tradition has not necessarily always been inhumane. But the main burden of the Christian tradition in the Western world has been to support the kind of people who have forced others into exile, and not vice versa.

What does it do to our system of law if we grant amnesty, if we are oblivious of past offenses from the viewpoint of civil authority? Here the Christian lives in a certain kind of tension. He will tend to agree with Romans 13, where St. Paul took the position that over the long haul in history we are better off with order than with disorder, with law than with lawlessness, with sociality than with autonomous competitive individualism. If one wants to agree with that, he must be prepared to give certain kinds of sanctions to order and to the principle of

law. Nothing that I am saying on the matter of amnesty
violates that concept. Take the system of law very seriously; but then appraise it in a larger context and ask,
what was the purpose of the law, what was its intention?
Was it just to induce conformities to any kind of leader-
ship, to anything it wants? Or was it for the normal circumstances of life? Then there may be countless occasions
wherein there may have to be suspensions of that law,
when the state winks at violation, when it finds the law
unenforceable. This does not necessarily imply that all law
is bad, but that it is in a process of constantly evolving.
Law in relation to a matter like the Vietnam war could
not evolve, change, and develop fast enough to help people face the issues of conscience related to it.

If amnesty were not a moral act I would not for a moment support it. It may not be a *normal* moral act; it may
not be the kind of moral act on which the whole society
can be built. It is the exception. Søren Kierkegaard speaks
of "the teleological suspension of the ethical." There are
many moments in biblical history where somebody is
asked to do something against the normal act. Not only in
the Hebrew Scriptures, where there are many instances,
but also in the root of the Christian tradition, the New
Testament writings, there are many instances where
Jesus came into contact with people who represented a
system of law, the normal order. They would test him. Is
it right to heal a man on the Sabbath, when one was not
supposed to be working? Jesus replied to them: "You pull
an ox or an ass out of a ditch; would not you also help a
man on that day?" There *are* exceptions. "There are times
when even the ceremonial bread was eaten by your sacred
forefathers," he would say. "The Sabbath is made for man,
and not man for the Sabbath." So it is with our laws, or in
Paul Ricouer's terms, it is possible to assert an ethic of
distress, in a time when one has to suspend the normal, for
the sake of the day when one can resume the normal.

What can we say to the tens of thousands of people who

sacrificed sons for Vietnam? We have to take very seriously their sacrifice, their grief, their loss, but essentially
moral acts should not be viewed as public relations problems. These people have worse problems than seeing
other people come back alive from exile. Most of these
refugees from our system were already terribly inconvenienced people. Were I in a family where someone
had been lost in Vietnam, I would be much more resentful of the affluent sons of senators and representatives
and university professors who were able, certainly before
any draft laws changed, to get exemptions and to get
by without any kind of inconvenience. Remember that
most young people were not in any way inconvenienced
by Vietnam. The exile was. He was often thrown into
situations in which he was ill-equipped to thrive. He was
the subject of suspicion overseas; he left behind a girl-
friend, brothers, sisters, parents, friends, etc. He faced
the unknown.

The parents and the widows of those killed in Vietnam
who supported that venture will not be enthusiastic about
these people. Many of those people, however, never did
support the cause. Or they supported it minimally and
through the years became increasingly disaffected. There
is no reason why *they* would feel resentful about exiles.
They will concentrate their sense of disappointment and
even rage on the executive and legislative leaders who
were slow to take other kinds of action and contributed
to the prolongation of a war that had become morally,
politically, and militarily senseless.

Using the concept of an ethic of distress, "doing what
one must do and then saying one's prayers," there are
many ways in which amnesty can be seen as moral, or at
least not as a violation of morality. Therefore it can be
supported. Guilt enters into this discussion—not necessarily theologically if one's conscience is at ease—but politically, if one is guilty of offending the existing laws or
avoiding the expectations and demands of legitimate exist-

ing authority. The question of guilt enters in here mainly psychologically; that is, if someone comes back as a result of the amnesty it is possible that he again resumes life with peer groups. It is possible that he does meet people who sacrificed in other ways during this nightmare, and in their presence he develops a pattern of guilt. Just to be born in the twentieth century we know that we are involved in guilt. Here we have to be very sure that those who can work off any sense of ambiguity or guilt will be given opportunities in contexts like VISTA, the Job Corps, and the Peace Corps to serve society; every kind of structure possible should be made available to them.

To what extent will amnesty or alternative solutions for those who refused to serve hasten reconciliation in this country; will they further infuriate Middle America? Here again we have what is essentially a question of public relations. We should not worry too much about "what everyone will think" of an act if it is the right act. At the same time, polarized and torn and immobilized as we became because of the Vietnam war and similar circumstances, many of us do hunger for reconciliation. Amnesty might be an important part of what we have to learn to live with if we want a better future, and reconciliation should incorporate it. We should not take a cheap way out of Vietnam. We should never say, "Well, we blew it; we goofed; we made minor misjudgments." We did some *terrible* things. We may have been well-intentioned in others, but we remained blind and wilfully ignorant along the way when we should have been awakened. In the middle of it all the only way we could come to ourselves was to deal with people among us who could create at least some minor sense of abrasion. Statistically we are talking about a group so small that most of the nation is not going to be aware of or even troubled by it.

Can Christian theologians play any role in furthering the view I take on this subject when the question is publicly raised after the war? I don't have *any* imperial views of theologians. Most of them deal with small numbers of people; they write books bought by hundreds or a few thousands of people. Most of them aren't in the public eye. In our society of religious pluralism people do not turn to these theologians with bated breath, waiting for their answers on pressing matters. Yet they do have a secondary impact of considerable importance. That importance is not one that should lead the theological communities to any sense of isolation, independence, or a quest for monopoly. We are all in this together. I would be more interested in having the theologians speak *to* the Church than *for* the Church. It is to be hoped that they can bring to bear the biblical, traditional, and philosophical moral insights of tradition to a new kind of social problem or question.

ARYEH NEIER

Aryeh Neier is Executive Director of the American Civil Liberties Union.

The American Civil Liberties Union supports amnesty as an outgrowth of its position both on the draft and on the war. The American Civil Liberties Union considers the present draft to be unconstitutional because the Congress has not borne the burden of demonstrating that national security is threatened in such a way that only a draft can meet the threat. In addition, the American Civil Liberties Union believes the waging of the war to be unconstitutional because there has not been explicit congressional authorization of the war. In consequence we are for amnesty because we consider the people who have fled the country or served in jails within the country to have been resisting an illegal draft and an illegal war. We seek a method for them to re-establish themselves as citizens.

If you look at the history of the courts in dealing with questions of this sort, you will find that the courts seem incapable of confronting questions as momentous as these during actual times of war. A court that attempted to reverse the policy of the President would simply find that it would be disregarded, its jurisdiction curbed by the Congress.

During the Civil War Chief Justice Roger Taney him-

self signed a habeas corpus order for a man named Merry-
man, barring his imprisonment by the military authorities. Lincoln simply refused to obey Taney's order, and
the court action was nullified. After the war similar kinds
of orders were entered by the courts. But since the war
had ended, the jurisdiction of the courts was again
respected.

During World War II the Supreme Court was unwilling to uphold the claims of any of the Japanese-Americans
whose liberties were being infringed upon by the detention
camp policy. Only after the war ended did the Supreme
Court act favorably in any of these cases. The passions
had subsided and the courts were able to reassert their
authority as protectors of constitutional liberties. I am inclined to think something of the same sort may happen
with respect to the war in Vietnam.

We are not going to win cases challenging either the
draft or the conduct of the war during the course of the
war, but those cases may not be mooted when the war
actually ends. After the war, a court will be much more
likely to act favorably on the cases that we have brought.
One case challenging the constitutionality of the war in
Vietnam is especially interesting. The Second Circuit
Court of Appeals ruled in the case of *Berk* v. *Laird* that
the constitutionality of the war was something that could
be decided by the court, that it is justiciable. The court
then sent the *Berk* case and a companion case, the
Orlando case, back down for trial to District Court judges.
In those trials, the young men involved, through their
counsel provided by the New York Civil Liberties Union,
were asked to bear the burden of showing what standards
were necessary for a war to be constitutionally authorized
and why those standards have not been met in the conduct
of the war in Vietnam. That burden was borne by the
briefs that were submitted in those cases. However, the
federal judges who ruled in those cases, Judge Dooling in
the *Orlando* case and Judge Judd in the *Berk* case, went

off on what I think are wholly untenable grounds. They decided that the congressional appropriations for the war over a period of time amounted to implicit congressional authorization of the war. On appeal the argument is being made that something as momentous as war cannot be entered into by the United States through the back door. There has to be explicit congressional authorization. Backhanded approval through authorization of military expenditures is not the explicit approval that is required by the Constitution. There are rules in both houses of the Congress that purport to prevent members of Congress from using authorization measures as the means for deciding substantive questions.

I think that any court able to consider this question outside of the power context that exists during an actual time of war would have to overrule the decisions by Judge Judd and Judge Dooling. I do not expect those decisions to be overruled during a time of war. Courts will find any way possible of ducking the issue. Even if they were to confront it squarely and rule the war unconstitutional, I cannot see how the courts could change the course of history. It is just beyond their power to play that significant a role in American life. One would have the kind of situation in which Andrew Jackson said of a ruling by Chief Justice Marshall, "Judge Marshall has made his decision; now let him enforce it."

Since the resisters and exiles broke the law, some have said they should pay the penalty as did their heroes— Gandhi and Martin Luther King and Thoreau. I would turn this comment back to the society that has the opportunity to be gracious, to be humane, to be forgiving, even when it regards people as having broken the law. There are a great many people who think that it is somehow inevitable that if a person has broken the law he should be prosecuted in some way. It is seen as a breakdown of law if a person is not prosecuted. In fact, however, that runs counter to the entire tradition of law in the United States. One of the ways in which the law's ability to be flexible is reflected in American law is that a prosecutor's decision not to prosecute is absolutely unreviewable. Nobody can ever compel a prosecutor to prosecute someone whom he does not want to prosecute. That enormous area of discretion that the prosecutor has available to him is an incorporation of the concept of civil disobedience into our law. It says that when the prosecutor recognizes morality or harmlessness in action, even if there is an infraction of the law that has taken place, he doesn't have to go ahead and prosecute. One sees this exercise of discretion at all times. We have laws on the books in New York State and most other states that make adultery a crime. The State Legislature reinforced its commitment to penalizing adultery as recently as 1967 when it had before it a penal code that eliminated the crime of adultery. The legislature explicitly restored it, yet there hasn't been a prosecution for adultery in New York State since the nineteenth century. This despite the fact that there are adulterous acts that are affirmed to have existed by courts in divorce cases and the information is very readily available. The prosecutor recognizes that public opinion will simply not allow that kind of a prosecution.

At a different level, if someone has been badly injured by another person, and a relative in turn attacks the person who has inflicted the injury, if the attack is not out of proportion to the original crime, the chances are that a prosecutor will not prosecute. The prosecutor recognizes the passions that are involved in the crime that has been committed. That kind of civil disobedience is encouraged by our laws, which provide such an enormous area of discretion to prosecutors. If there is general public rejection of a law, prosecutors simply will not prosecute.

It is my belief that the law does not crumble if that kind of discretion is exercised by prosecutors. It's that kind of discretion which, even failing any formal kind of amnesty, can and should be exercised by prosecutors. They should simply refuse to prosecute people who return to this country following the end of the war. After Congress enacted its draft card burning law there were a handful of prosecutions, symbolic prosecutions, but then nobody took the draft card burning law seriously. Even though thousands more draft cards were burned and returned, federal prosecutors simply stopped prosecutions of draft card burners and draft card returners. The law doesn't crumble under such circumstances. There is that much flexibility in any humane approach to the law.

Another way in which this flexibility is built into our law is in the concept of the jury trial. One of the most famous cases in American history is that of John Peter Zenger. In the Zenger case, the jury was instructed by the judge that all it had to decide was whether Zenger had published the little book about the British judge. That much was acknowledged by Zenger. Zenger's attorney, Andrew Hamilton, appealed the judge's ruling on the law and said to the jury that if they did not think this law just, they ought to nullify it by acquitting John Peter Zenger. The jury did that. Juries engage in that kind of nullification of the law under certain extreme circumstances when they believe that there are extenuating circumstances that merit their exercise of their discretion not to convict somebody of a crime. That discretion in the hands of the jury, taken together with the discretion in the hands of the prosecutor, should be seen as a method of accommodating protests that are deeply motivated by principles of conscience, protests that do not pose any continuing threat to public welfare and public safety, and that the society can be large enough to digest and accommodate.

Even if one believes that the war is legal and proper and constitutional and that the exiles and resisters disobeyed a valid law, there is a time for healing to take place after a bitter struggle of the sort that the United States has been through. That process of healing can be speeded by amnesty. We have mechanisms in the law, without ever tackling the constitutionality of the war or the draft, for putting amnesty into effect.

I'm not sure that I agree that advocates of civil disobedience have always felt that punishment was a necessary part of civil disobedience. Martin Luther King was advocating disobedience of laws that were themselves unconstitutional and therefore invalid as laws. He was willing to suffer punishment not because he believed that there was some redemption in punishment but because punishment was the inevitable consequence of the actions he engaged in. I think the same thing can be said for Gandhi. There was a willingness to suffer punishment, but it didn't mean that punishment was a necessary consequence—that the morality of civil disobedience would be diminished if punishment didn't follow surely and swiftly upon the act of civil disobedience. One could also argue that to many of those to whom amnesty would apply, there has been punishment, through exile. Certainly if amnesty comes about it can't be as a consequence of anything that they would have expected. It would be a fairly remarkable kind of event. They would have to have lived for a period of years assuming that amnesty would not come about, with all the painful personal consequences that flow from an anticipation of being a permanent exile.

It is possible to say that for each person who escaped the war, somebody else had to serve in his place. I think one ought to balance that idea with an understanding that if it were not for the people who engaged in the kinds of protests against the war that led them to be possible beneficiaries of amnesty, the war would have been much more extensive. It would have been drawn out much longer, and many, many more people would have had to suffer the consequences of the war. In a sense some others had to serve in their place, although they made it possible for many others not to serve at all. They were willing to risk their own futures in a rather dramatic manner as a means of narrowing the scope of the war and even bringing it to an end. I don't know if it is ever possible to make a perfect equation between those people whom they saved and those whom they harmed. But I don't think that they can be held as having perpetrated any great harm upon others.

I have a difficult time drawing distinctions between the deserters and those who simply escaped the draft by going to Canada, often after having gone through lengthy periods in which they claimed rights of conscientious objection. I think that a lot of our procedures for determining whether a person is a conscientious objector are entirely too rigid and mechanical. I think it's quite possible for a person to arrive at his sense of outrage against a war right in the middle of a battle. It doesn't have to be something that is bred over a long period of time, and I would not differentiate deserters from any others.

A few years after the end of World War II, the United States was engaged in friendly relations with Japan, with Italy, and with Germany. They were the people who had been fighting against us, and it was possible for us to engage in friendly dealings with those countries soon after the war. I don't think it should be any more difficult for the people who have suffered losses during the Vietnamese war to engage in friendly dealings with people who were enough opposed to the war to flee participation in it.

James Reston, Jr.

James Reston, Jr., is a novelist and journalist who was a staff writer for the Chicago Daily News *and is now an instructor in creative writing at the University of North Carolina. His first novel,* To Defend, To Destroy, *examined the conscience of an American intelligence officer caught in the moral dilemma of Vietnam and is based on the three years (1965–68) that Reston spent in the Army.*

A chief aim of this country in the next few years must be to restore the idealistic impulse of its young people. The withdrawal of the creative and intellectual elements of an entire generation from the political process has been the greatest price America has paid for the Vietnam war. Morally and practically, this country cannot afford the cynicism and despair that take different forms in the hippie and radical cults. Morally, it is wrong for a country, having admitted an historical mistake, to continue to persecute those who have been saying the war was a mistake for years. And practically, no country, particularly this one, with its immaturity at this moral juncture in its history, can afford to lose its intellectual and moral resources to this degree.

The figures on what the war in Vietnam has done to a generation of Americans are staggering. Beyond the 345,000 killed and wounded, there are over 50,000

American exiles in Canada. Members of the Canadian Parliament expect this figure to reach 150,000 before the war is over. The FBI received 146,554 draft violation complaints between 1966–70, and needless to say, the Bureau does not receive the name of every draft evader. Over 89,000 American soldiers deserted the military in 1970 alone. And in 1968 the number of men in federal prisons for draft-related cases was 723 out of a federal prison population of 20,000.

These are the cold facts, but there is no way to compute the psychological casualties or the damage to the values of a generation. Beyond the rampant despair all around us, we now have a sad new element: the bitterness of those who offered themselves up as soldiers in 1965–66 for patriotic reasons, and now find out that they were lied to by their President.

Thus, for the Vietnam generation, the country must prove itself worthy of respect again, not, as some would have it, the other way around. That will not be easy after the depravity of Vietnam. The issue has broadened in the tortuous years since 1965. Ending the war may not settle the question for many. There will have to be substantial movement toward a just society at home and a humanitarian approach abroad for the best elements of the young to respond once again. This will involve a major shift in priorities: a merciless slashing of the military budget to around forty billion dollars a year, which such experts as Adam Yarmolinsky, an aide to Secretary McNamara, have said can meet our true national security interests, and an attendant push on the social front of the cities, the rural poor, and the environment.

The more immediate issue, however, is restitution to a generation that has both fought the war abroad and been the vanguard of protest at home. This must come, in my opinion, in the form of major concessions to the dissident young, concessions that should in no way demean the sacrifices of those who fought in Vietnam.

The most important of these is amnesty to all political exiles abroad. This step is the logical result of a domestic application of Vietnamization, which is simply the national recognition of a mistake, couched in bureaucratic language. An amnesty proclamation should come automatically after the presidential election in 1972, or upon the achievement of a minimal draft, or upon the achievement of a troop level in Vietnam that can be supported by volunteers—whichever comes first. This does not mean that Congress can wait until 1972 to act. This measure should be passed at the earliest possible date, so that it would be an early sign to a generation fast abandoning its country, that the nation intends to make amends.

The way in which amnesty is declared is nearly as important as the proclamation itself. A sanctimonious tone of forgiveness of a country to its errant young will miss the point. The country has erred; the instincts of the exiles have been right. Amnesty must come as an honest and courageous attempt at national expiation. We will get our exiles back only in this way. The majority are not waiting for their country to forgive them. Rather, as I have been told by one who has counseled hundreds of Americans in Toronto, it is a question of whether they can ever forgive their country.

The terms "treason," "draft dodging," and "desertion" have lost their old flavor in this war, especially as the intrigue, duplicity, and secretiveness of the U.S. involvement becomes known. The American public will quickly forget these concepts when the war ends. I suspect that draft refusal, and even draft evasion and desertion, will be overlooked, and even widely admired after the war, just as today a jail sentence during the southern civil rights campaigns of the early sixties is admired. Historically, the shortness of the country's memory is borne out. Dr. Evan Thomas, brother of Norman Thomas (who has perhaps the best pacifist credentials of any American alive today, for having refused service in 1917 and for having chaired

the War Resisters League in World War II), told me a
story that shows this. After Evan Thomas was released
from military custody in 1919, nearly a year after he had
been sentenced in a military court to ninety-nine years for
"refusing to eat," the outcome of a hunger strike,
Thomas tried to get into a number of medical schools.
None would have him, including New York University.
Ten years later, N.Y.U. sought him out and begged him
to attend their medical school. This he did, and some
years later he was a resident physician at the N.Y.U. Medical Center.

So moods will change, and this country's mood toward
its exiles will change naturally. But the number of
psychological victims is so large today that Congress cannot leave the matter to natural process. It must act
dramatically and early. Its motivating drive must be a
healthy sense of national guilt, and a desire for rehabilitation.

Amnesty for political exiles abroad should, however, be
only one aspect of a general program of restitution. It
would be irresponsible to grant amnesty to the exiles without attending to the whole pattern of harassment that the
war has brought.

The campaign might start with the investigative
machinery that has been created during the Vietnam years
to track down the subversives and to report on the dis-
sidents. This system is a hangover from the Johnson era,
when victory in Vietnam was a national goal, and when
the refusal to participate in the war was treason. But the
FBI and the military investigating agencies still work by
directive today, and the bureaucratic ball is rolling more
smoothly than ever. Department of Defense Directive
1325.2, entitled Unauthorized Desertion and Absence,
directs the services to turn over to the FBI the names of all
AWOL soldiers after sixty days' absence. In fiscal year
1969 the FBI received 51,000 such names and appre-

hended 14,000 of them. An FBI spokesman proudly told me that this constituted a higher apprehension rate than in fiscal year 1968, when 38,885 soldiers deserted. The FBI has also received from the Selective Service System an average of 28,000 draft evasion complaints every year since 1966, but in 1970, the second year of Vietnamization abroad, the Bureau could point to 923 convictions, the highest figure yet.

The combination of a well-oiled investigative machine; the talk of an end to the war, of an all-volunteer army, and of an elimination of the draft; and the court decisions strengthening the pleas of conscientious objectors create tremendous uncertainties. Should an objector go to Canada before the FBI picks him up? Should he stay and try to win in court? But what if he loses? What device will stall the induction process for two years, when the draft call may be eliminated, and there may be a different President?

So uncertainty reigns for those who have refused induction and for those who face it. I know a twenty-two-year-old who refused induction over a year ago and has waited ever since to be picked up by the FBI. He has honorably tried to face his moral obligation as he sees it, has spent over a thousand dollars in legal fees, and has stayed in the town of his refusal holding up a career he wished to pursue elsewhere. He has adjusted himself to the thought of jail, but not to the reality of waiting. I told the fellow to remove Vietnam from his life now as best he could, and continue about his business. He has paid his dues.

But the point is that now that the national goal has changed, a relaxed system of police action consistent with our withdrawal policy must follow. Clearly a public pronouncement by the Justice Department on its Vietnamization program for the United States is needed. That statement should be an amnesty from the uncertainty of possible arrest. The Congress acted to remove the uncertainty of the draft by limiting eligibility to nineteen-year-olds. So it should limit eligibility for arrest to a set period, perhaps a year, after which time the individual would be immune.

For those who have been convicted on draft refusal charges and remain in jail, an amnesty is also due. They are perhaps the most hopeful breed of all draft resisters, for they have stayed here, which may indicate that they feel the country *is* worth fighting for.

The draft refusal or draft evasion questions have largely been an issue for the college educated. This is reflected in the exile population. The impulse to flee for the evader is abstract, political, sometimes self-serving, whereas the impulse to flee for the deserter is often a gut reaction of outrage at what he sees in the military. What sort of amnesty is due the less fortunate, less educated young Americans?

The main area for concern here is the proposed all-volunteer army. In the two summers I worked in the Neighborhood Youth Corps in New York City, I saw poor youngsters time and again take the military option as the only escape from the hustle of the streets. The Pentagon with its new recruitment program is perfectly aware of this opportunity. If you travel around the country, you notice the heavy advertising for the services in the rural areas or in the poverty neighborhoods. The so-called combat skills get the biggest push, because the Army has the hardest time getting volunteers for these jobs—presumably because they have little civilian application. Thus, recruiters armed with Madison Avenue techniques appeal to the *machismo* of the eighteen- and nineteen-year-old for whom virility is something to be proved. I will never forget an eighteen-year-old I met in basic training, who had volunteered to be a helicopter gunner, one of the most dangerous jobs in Vietnam, because his recruiter said the job was like riding shotgun on a stagecoach in the old West. Such men are fighting the American war in Asia.

Thus, the poor youth of this country deserve an amnesty from the military dupe. The Army must cease to be the sole escape from the Appalachias, the inner cities, and the small towns of America. A system of humanitarian alternatives of equal stature, duration, and sacrifice to military enlistment should be devised. The streets of Brooklyn or the roads of eastern Kentucky provide infinite possibilities for regional service if youth were mobilized in social programs.

Therefore, I have proposed a Voluntary National Service, of which military service would be only one branch. It must be voluntary, because only in voluntary programs will the idealistic impulse of youth be kindled. It must be a national service, because social construction ought to be on a par with social destruction as an outlet for patriotism. As someone once said to me, allow youth to vote for life as well as for death.

In 1931 the Supreme Court of the United States heard the case of *MacKintosh* v. *United States*. MacKintosh was a Canadian and a theology professor at Yale who applied for American citizenship. When asked if he would support the Constitution and fight in wars against enemies of America, he replied that he reserved the right to judge whether the cause of America was just beforehand. He was denied citizenship. I think that we have moved to the point where American youth, the potential cannon fodder for future wars, should reserve the right to judge whether they will fight or not. Of course, they must be told the facts to make that judgment. And beyond that, they have the right to judge whether they will serve the country at all.

The goal must be to change our national emphasis: to enact the social legislation, to face the sins of the past, so that young people will freely and in good faith want again to serve a country that has proved itself humanitarian in action and in intent.

WILLIAM RUSHER

William Rusher is the publisher of National Review, *the prominent journal of conservative opinion. He has served as Associate Counsel to the U. S. Senate Internal Security Subcommittee and has written a book,* Special Counsel, *drawing on that period of his life. He is a former co-chairman of the American-African Affairs Association and is one of the two "Advocates" on the weekly national educational television program of that name.*

Amnesty is essentially an act of charity, a gesture whereby a government spares individuals the normal legal consequences of acts which, at the time they were committed, constituted crimes, but for which the government at the time of the amnesty is prepared to waive punishment. Amnesty therefore tends to take place in an atmosphere of reconciliation: after the period of conflict; after the period of necessary commitment; after the period of national danger. It is therefore, it seems to me, inconceivable that a rational government would either proclaim an amnesty *in medias res,* so to speak, or announce *in medias res* that it firmly intended to proclaim an amnesty in the future.

Take, for example, our Civil War. Abraham Lincoln, in the brief period of time that was given to him to consider such questions toward the very end of the Civil War, was (as I read history) quite eager to let off the leaders of the Confederacy lightly. He rather hoped that Jefferson Davis would get away to England. Davis did; but with regard to lesser figures, including leading military personalities and political figures of the Confederacy, Lincoln's intention quite clearly was not to engage in vindictiveness but to grant a rather general amnesty. As I recall, the ultimate political solution was to grant an amnesty to anybody who would take an oath of allegiance to the United States. I think it would have even applied to Jefferson Davis; but Davis would never take a new oath of allegiance to the United States, and died in England. Robert E. Lee, however, did take such an oath, and became president of Washington and Lee College and a very distinguished man in his later years.

That is what I would call a classical situation for amnesty. It isn't always the situation. At the end of the Second World War, the victorious Allies did not embark upon a policy of amnesty. They proceeded to round up as many of the political, civil, and military leaders of the Axis as they could find and try them—condemn them to long prison terms, or, in a number of cases, execute them. So amnesty is by no means a general impulse of human nature. It grows out of the assessment of a victorious political entity that it has, on balance, more to gain than to lose by the reconciliation of the defeated forces through the act of amnesty.

At present we are still engaged in a military operation in Vietnam. We are asking men every day to risk their lives; and it is, as I said, inconceivable to me that in that type of situation the government of the United States would either start granting amnesty now, for individuals who have disobeyed its orders, abandoned its jurisdiction, deserted its Army or otherwise traduced its laws, or proclaim now an intention to do so in some hypothetical future period in which, when we come to it, amnesty might be a desirable course of conduct. I don't think the government is going to do it; I think it would be fatally mistaken to do so. It would be bitterly unfair to the great majority of American men who, when called upon for military service, performed their service as required.

I am by no means certain that there ought to be any amnesty at all in the present situation. It depends upon what happens in the future. It depends on the price, socially, that would have to be paid. Amnesty is a commodity that can be afforded by a society that has turned the corner and is in a winning political situation. For example, take the United States at the end of the Civil War. The federal government's power was again supreme; the South was prostrate; the issue of secession had been resolved, and it was a supreme case for amnesty.

At least two things can be said about Vietnam. First, the Vietnam war does not necessarily entail a military victory, and so may not have a clear-cut termination like the Civil War. The Vietnam war may fray out into a series of semicontinuous guerrilla incidents in the Southeast Asian theater, in which we will still be asking, if not Americans, then South Vietnamese, Cambodians, Laotians, Thais, and Malaysians to risk their lives in defense of their countries, year by year. Whether or not, in that type of military and historical context, there should be amnesty for men who deserted their country and their Army and their comrades, in the midst of America's own heated commitment to the struggle is, I think, a very serious question, and one to which the answer might very well be "No." In other words, we might decide against amnesty for such men because, in that continuing situation, it would be a politically counterproductive act.

The other consideration is this. American society today is facing a largely new and extremely serious challenge. I am not attempting to minimize the challenge presented by the Civil War, which was certainly fundamental. But the present crisis is at least as fundamental as the Civil War, and in fact lacks the capacity for explicit termination that the earlier crisis possessed. Why do we have people deserting, refusing to serve, fleeing to Canada and Sweden, or showing up in Japan or Russia and pleading asylum, and so on? It isn't merely a criticism of a particular war. (It may be that in some cases, but I think it is not that in most cases.) What we are facing here is a more general disaffection with respect to American society. These people are saying, "I have looked at you, America, and I don't consider you fit to fight for, let alone fit to die for—certainly not in any cause except one that happens (for largely accidental reasons) to appeal personally to me. Certainly you, America, no longer appeal to me as something to which I want to commit myself."

Now, if that is the case, it too bears upon the ultimate question of amnesty. Because if we assume that the American society will emerge from the Vietnam war relatively on top of the situation, with the Communist thrust in Southeast Asia substantially slowed to a halt, the threat to the American society raised by these assertions remains a significant fact, a political and social challenge to the viability of the society itself. And amnesty, as we have already said, is an essentially charitable gesture performed by a society that has won the political argument. So long as the political argument continues in any serious way, amnesty is less likely, for the sound reason that it is less desirable.

Seriously to consider the possibility of postwar amnesty for those who did not serve, certain basic requirements would have to fulfilled: the Vietnamese conflict would have to be terminated on political and strategic terms acceptable to the United States and the free world; and the challenge of the resisters to the essential authority of the United States government would have to be visibly and successfully put down. If these events were to take place, there would still be those—perhaps a tiny minority—who would continue to challenge and repudiate the authority of the United States government. In a situation such as that, if you can imagine it developing, I think it would be appropriate for whoever is then our Chief Executive, or for the members of Congress, to consider the alternatives of a tacit amnesty or tracking down the unrepentant and punishing them or simply ignoring them.

Here again I think the Civil War analogy is a useful one. You will recall that I said that amnesty was available to all Confederates who would take an oath of allegiance to the United States. Not a bad idea! I'm not at all sure that we shouldn't symbolically require these gentlemen who have so cavalierly repudiated our laws and defied their obligations and deserted their country when it needed them, to take some form of oath of loyalty to the country they have betrayed.

If President Lincoln had been forced to continue, over a period of a decade or more, a guerrilla war throughout the South against hundreds of thousands of people who had taken up arms against the central government of the United States and were proposing to secede from it and overthrow its laws, I doubt very much whether he would even have considered amnesty until that argument was settled forcibly, firmly, and finally. I don't think we should consider amnesty until and unless the same situation exists in respect to Vietnam. That is the essential distinction between the two. Put another way, the possibility of amnesty is in direct proportion to the success of American arms in Southeast Asia, and every step and every development that lessens the chances of success, lessens also the chances for amnesty.

My definition of "success" is, basically speaking, the denial of political control of Southeast Asia to the Communist bloc, which would be achieved by Mr. Nixon's Vietnamization policy, successfully pursued.

There are certainly degrees of innocence or guilt among those who chose not to serve. For instance, I don't happen to be one of those who deeply admires a man who, simply because he dislikes a law, chooses to violate it and then takes the punishment for it. But nonetheless, I "disadmire" him less than I would a man who violated the same law and then ducked out to avoid the punishment. I think that a person who has violated a law of the United States and paid the penalty of jail or a fine, or whatever it was, is entitled to have his life go on—the general proposition being that he has "paid his debt to society." Amnesty is not required in the case of such a man; he has paid the price. Moreover, I don't think the President has anything he can *give* to a person who has already paid the price. You can't remit a prison sentence already served.

I think, however, that the obloquy ought to remain. I have very specifically, at *National Review,* considered hiring men who were just out of prison, or in some cases still in prison awaiting discharge. It so happens that for other reasons we have not gone ahead and hired any, but it is necessary and appropriate that a man who has paid the penalty be considered to have paid the penalty.

Punishment should be explicit. I don't see how the President of the United States can remove moral guilt. He can only remit the penalty. Assuming that there is a moral obligation, I don't think the President can remit the moral obloquy involved. All he can do is remit the sentence, and if that's been served he can't even do that.

However, in the case of the exile, we have a body of people who are largely moved by the considerations I mentioned earlier: a sense of total alienation from the American society, a deliberate intention to reject it all. Now they, I think, are in a still less enviable position than the man who has paid the penalty, because they have specifically *not* paid the penalty. They have protected their tender skins while violating the same law as the man who paid the price for the violation, and I think the American society has very little to say to them except "Goodbye and good riddance." If at some point in the future they want to return, as far as I am concerned they should be prosecuted for their crime, unless, as I said

earlier, we are at that point in some strategic situation
where amnesty is psychologically sound, America re-
soundingly having won the political point.

The case of the deserter is still worse. It depends in
part upon the circumstances in which he deserted. In the
case of men who deserted while on patrol in Vietnam,
placing in immediate peril the lives of their fellow soldiers,
I believe the penalty ought to be death. If a man deserts
at Fort Dix, it is obviously a much less heinous offense,
although there again desertion is a severe crime and
ought to be treated severely. Both kinds of deserters, then,
are in a still less meritorious category than either of the
previous two that we were discussing.

I might say, too, that I think desertion is largely overlooked or understressed. We have, as a society, embarked upon a course of military action in Southeast
Asia—one may argue its wisdom, or even if one wishes its
constitutionality, but it is nevertheless a fact. For the pur-
suance of that course of military action under our present
laws we are still relying upon a conscripted military, that
is, people drafted to serve. A certain number of men in
this country therefore have to be sent—if not against
their will, clearly against their best interests and probably
against their personal wishes—to Vietnam to risk their
lives, and perhaps to die. This number of men is a specific,
discrete number; it is not infinitely elastic. Every man who
absents or removes himself from this manpower pool as a
matter of personal volition, by deserting or by fleeing to
Canada to avoid induction, clearly mathematically increases the risk of injury or death to every other man
left in that manpower pool. Every man who crosses the
border to Canada to avoid military service is increasing
the chance of injury or death in the Armed Forces of the
United States for every man who stays here and does his
duty.

The President and the Congress should not be moved,
in their attempts to provide for the ongoing survival of

the American society and the success of its policies, by concepts of mercy and charity that would be totally appropriate from a strictly theological standpoint. I remind you that every man who goes (or went, when death penalties were more common in this country) to the electric chair or the gas chamber after committing the most heinous crimes could be accompanied by a priest or a rabbi or a minister, who would assure him (at any rate in Christian theology) of the possibility of redemption: that if one was genuinely repentant, if one sought forgiveness and appeared sincerely to want it, then it was entirely possible within God's mercy that He would forgive. Many men have gone to the gallows and the gas chamber and the electric chair believing that, and relying on it, and I think it is entirely appropriate that this should be so. This does not mean, however, that every governor who allowed the imposition of the death penalty was misbehaving or acting inappropriately. The governor's job was simply different; his job was to enforce the laws, and to impose the prescribed penalties. What happens to a man between himself and his God is not something that I think Richard Nixon can very well prescribe or make adjustments for, or seek very effectively to imitate.

We are dealing here with acts that happen to fall within the statutory description of specific crimes, but that have a much more profound symbolic significance—which is one of the reasons why we have to proceed much more carefully in this matter of amnesty. Forgiving a man for breaking into a house is one thing; forgiving him for attempting to repudiate and destroy his society, when he remains unrepentant for having done so, certainly may be quite another thing.

And this is the aspect of this whole particular series of desertions and so forth that interests me most. We seem to be dealing with a relatively new form of repudiation in this society. Again the analogy of the Civil War comes to mind, but that was a fairly political repudiation. Specific states, claiming themselves to be totally sovereign, withdrew their support from the constitutional compact and embarked upon a separate course. Certainly that was a form of secession. Here we have, not states, but, one is tempted to say, certain social categories seceding—such as one group among the younger generation. I certainly do not think it is the entire younger generation; I don't even think it is the majority. But one group among the younger generation unquestionably has made up its mind, or had it made up for it, that the American society is simply not fit to live in. And that group exists here, if at all, under protest. It leaves for Canada or Sweden, in many cases, if it can; it acts out in many cultural ways its disaffection from the society. This is the real and profound and underlying problem here—not disagreement with a particular war policy in Vietnam. These people would object to any American policy, anywhere. The Vietnam war is objected to, but not more or less than a number of other things. What they are really objecting to is America itself.

The question is raised as to whether the Soviet infantryman who refused to march with his unit into Czechoslovakia during the 1968 invasion, or perhaps a German soldier who refused to be a guard in a concentration camp, were acting out a role that was similar to the role of those who refused to serve in Vietnam. The hypothetical Soviet soldier who refused to march into Czechoslovakia was doing two things, which have quite different consequences. From the standpoint of the Soviet state, there is no question that the refusal represents a challenge to its authority, and it should not be surprising to us that the Soviet state would take offense at this and would punish him. I don't say that I would approve of the punishment, but that is because I regard the Soviet state, and the Nazi state and other states of that type as states that no moral man could legitimately support.

Now this, I suppose, may seem at first glance to leave

me open to the rebuttal, "Ah, but what about the man who doesn't regard the American society as a state that no moral man could legitimately support? Because doesn't it at last come down to a question of individual choice?" The answer is, I think, "Yes and no." It does come down to a matter of individual choice. Whether I support the United States and obey its laws, whether you do, or whether anyone does—we in this world being in some degree free—is our decision to make. But whether or not we have the moral *right* to resist its prescriptions or to escape the consequences of doing so depends on the nature of the particular state. The Soviet state, the Nazi state, simply did not provide mechanisms whereby a moral man could live out what he deemed to be the life necessary to his concept of morality. The American society, however, has always permitted conscientious objection by people with religious scruples, and we are now permitting conscientious objection by people with nonreligious scruples if they are against war in general, rather than merely against particular political decisions. This is simply unheard of in the Soviet Union, or in Nazi Germany. Furthermore, we have an elaborate mechanism whereby political change can be brought about on the basis of majority rule and representative democracy. All of these things, it seems to me, make it more difficult for an individual to make a moral decision to repudiate the American society. This society cannot be repudiated by a moral man as easily and breezily as the Nazi or Soviet society. I repudiate the proposition—I think it is an impudent proposition—that this country is in any serious way comparable, in terms of the freedom available or the moral choices that can be exercised by individual human beings, to either of those states.

EDWARD F. SHERMAN

Edward F. Sherman is Professor of Law at Indiana University School of Law and formerly a Teaching Fellow at Harvard University School of Law. He was appellate counsel in the Harvey and Daniels and Amick-Stolte cases and defense counsel in the Captain Thomas S. Culver, USAF, court-martial.

Amnesty is more than an act of grace by a government. As the Supreme Court observed in 1915, amnesty "is usually addressed to crimes against the sovereignty of the state, to political offenses, forgiveness being deemed more expedient for the public welfare than prosecution and punishment."[1] It has often been resorted to in this country after conflicts that have divided our people and driven some to oppose the laws or policies of the government.[2] It can be a way for a society to remedy injustices to individuals who, due to their conscience or the pressures of the times, have violated the law. It permits them to return to society as useful and productive citizens without the

[1] *Burdick* v. *United States,* 237 U.S. 79, 95 (1915).
[2] Presidential and congressional amnesty have frequently been granted in the United States after wars and internal conflicts, going back to the post-Revolutionary War period and as recently as the administration of President Theodore Roosevelt. See *Constitution of the United States of America, Analysis and Interpretation,* 88th Cong., 1st Sess., pp. 456–61.

risk of prosecution or the stigma of a criminal record.

Amnesty should not be advocated lightly, for improper use of the power could undercut the deterrent effect of the law. However, there are situations in which it may be the only feasible method for remedying injustices and re-uniting useful citizens to their society. This seems to be the case with certain classes of servicemen who have been court-martialed in the Vietnam war period. Many service-men have been done serious injustices in courts-martial arising out of their opposition to the war in Vietnam. Most of them have already been severely punished by incarceration in military stockades, brigs, and prisons. Those who have been discharged find themselves branded with criminal convictions and frequently less-than-honorable discharges. The number of servicemen court-martialed or discharged less than honorably for activities connected in some way with opposition to the war in Vietnam is substantial, possibly in the hundreds of thou-sands.[3] They are predominantly young and include a

[3] There have been approximately 550,000 courts-martial since the commitment of American ground troops to the Viet-nam war in 1965. More than half were for AWOL or deser-tion, and about 10 percent for various types of disobedience. See *Annual Report of the United States Court of Military Appeals*, etc., 1965–1971; Report of the Special Civilian Com-mittee for the Study of the U. S. Army Confinement System (1970), pp. 101–2. Some 100,000 servicemen have received less-than-honorable discharges during the Vietnam war period. It is difficult to estimate the exact number of courts-martial and less-than-honorable discharges which are related to anti-war activities or sympathies. The offense charged is often a vague military violation, such as AWOL or disobedience of a general order, and military records frequently do not reveal the motivating forces which led to the particular offense. Fur-thermore, military courts have held that evidence of personal beliefs is irrelevant and therefore inadmissible in prosecutions for AWOL and disobedience. See the description in Yarmolin-sky, *The Military Establishment: Its Impact on American So-ciety* (1971), pp. 356–57, of the court-martial of Pvt. Mi-chael O'Connor, one of the rare cases in which defense

disproportionate number of blacks. Their continued estrangement from our society, fostered both by their own resentment and by their competitive disadvantage in obtaining civilian jobs because of their military record, is a subject of increasing concern in our society today.

Some categories of court-martial convictions are more obviously appropriate for amnesty treatment than others.

1. *Servicemen Court-Martialed after Improper Denial of Conscientious Objector Status.* Perhaps the most compelling case for amnesty is that of servicemen who were refused conscientious objector status in the military under stricter standards than are applied by draft boards. Although military regulations governing discharge of servicemen who become conscientious objectors after induction purport to apply the same requirements as draft boards follow—that the individual be opposed to war in any form by reason of religious training or belief—the military has in fact applied much stricter standards during much of the Vietnam war. Shortly after the American troop buildup in Vietnam in 1965, the military decided to tighten up on discharges of conscientious objectors. At all levels of processing of conscientious objectors, from the immediate commander to the officers in the Pentagon who make the final decision,[4] a new and hostile attitude

---

attorneys attempted to raise the defense of "irresistible impulse" caused by antiwar beliefs in an AWOL prosecution. The number of courts-martial directly based on antiwar activity—such as making "disloyal statements" and participating in demonstrations—has been rather small, in the hundreds. A larger number of courts-martial have been based on acts of disobedience or defiance, arising out of antiwar attitudes. A very large number of AWOLs and desertions, at least in the tens of thousands, have arisen out of antiwar sentiments. Finally, a sizable number of "undesirable" administrative discharges have been related in some way to antiwar activity or expressions of antiwar sympathies.

[4] In 1962, Department of Defense Directive 1200.6 (now replaced by DOD Directive 1300.6, August 20, 1971) estab-

toward conscientious objector discharges set in. The statistics graphically reflect this change of attitude. In the
two years before 1965, almost 50 percent of the applicants for conscientious objector discharges from the Army
were found to be sincere and were discharged (twenty-
nine out of sixty-nine applicants in 1963 and 30 out of
62 applicants in 1964). In 1965, the percentage slipped
to 25 percent (twenty-six out of 101), and then, dramatically, to about 4 percent in 1966 (five out of 118) and
1967 (nine out of 185).[5] By 1968, the Central Committee for Conscientious Objectors advised in its hand-
book that "although many men were discharged on
grounds of conscience previous to the spring of 1966,
since that time almost all discharges have been denied
regardless of merit."[6]

This new military hostility toward discharges based on
conscience, apparently motivated by the belief that conscientious objection posed a threat to manpower needs
for Vietnam, meant that many servicemen who met the
legal standards for discharge were retained in the military. There were many cases in which the wrong legal
standard was applied by the military (for example, finding that an applicant was not motivated by orthodox re-

---

lished procedures for discharge of servicemen whose conscientious objector beliefs crystallized after induction. Procedures
were established in each service whereby the applicant is interviewed by his commanding officer, a chaplain, a military
psychiatrist, and, if he requests, a hearing officer of the rank
of captain (lieutenant in the Navy) or higher. The reports of
these interviews are forwarded through command channels
to the official who makes the final decision (the Army Ad-
jutant General, the Chief of Naval Personnel, or the Secretary
of the Air Force) who usually relies upon the recommenda-
tions of a board of military officers appointed by him.

[5] Statistics provided by Department of Defense, November
1968 (unpublished).

[6] Central Committee for Conscientious Objectors, *Hand-
book for Conscientious Objectors* 91 (10th ed., 1968).

ligious beliefs)[7] or in which an applicant was found not
to be sincere although there was "no basis in fact" in the
record to support that conclusion.[8] The reason that the
military could disregard the law in this way was that military determinations, unlike draft board decisions, were
virtually immune from judicial review. A long line of
federal court decisions supports the doctrine of "nonre-
viewability" of military determinations premised on the
policy, as the Supreme Court expressed it in 1953, that
"judges are not given the task of running the Army."[9]
Thus the military were able virtually to eliminate all conscientious objector discharges, in violation of the standards required by Department of Defense and service regulations, and servicemen could do nothing about it.

The unavailability of civilian court review was altered
in mid-1968 when a United States Circuit Court of Appeals, in the landmark decision of *Hammond* v. *Len-
fest*,[10] ruled that federal courts could review the military's
refusal to grant a conscientious objector discharge without making the serviceman go through a court-martial
first. Within a year, four other circuit courts (out of a

---

[7] A number of in-service conscientious objector applications have been rejected in the past on the improper ground
that the chaplain or a reviewing officer found the applicant's
views not sufficiently "religious." The Supreme Court decision
in *Welsh* v. *United States,* 398 U.S. 333 (1970) determined
that orthodox or traditional religious beliefs are not essential
for conscientious objection.

[8] See, e.g., *Crane* v. *Hedrick,* 284 F. Supp. 250 (N.D. Cal.
1968) (denial improperly based on the ground that discharge
was not "practical and equitable") *Bates* v. *Commander,* 413
F. 2d 475 (1st Cir. 1969) (denial improperly based on the
fact that applicant had written letters expressing "political"
opposition to the war); *Application of Tavlos,* 429 F. 2d 859
(5th Cir. 1960) (denial incorrectly based on the ground that
applicant's beliefs were only rooted in a "personal moral code").

[9] *Orloff* v. *Willoughby,* 345 U.S. 83, 93 (1953).

[10] 398 F. 2d 705 (2d Cir. 1968).

total of ten) took the same position.[11] The *Hammond* decision had a tremendous impact on the military's handling of conscientious objector discharges. Suddenly, the military was no longer immune from civilian court review, and the officers who administered conscientious objector discharges were faced with the unpleasant prospect of having their refusals overturned in federal courts because they had applied the wrong legal standard or had "no basis in fact" for their findings. As the number of suits seeking to overturn the military's refusal to discharge climbed into the hundreds, many of them successful, the military beat a hasty retreat. By 1970 the percentage of favorable decisions was back up to the rate of approximately 50 percent that had prevailed before 1965.

This change, however, came too late to help hundreds, possibly thousands, of servicemen who met the legal standards for a conscientious objector discharge. Some of them, after being refused a conscientious objector discharge, were court-martialed for refusing to obey an order that conflicted with their beliefs. Others, seeing no other legal recourse, went AWOL, usually only to have to return to face court-martial. Many more never applied for a conscientious objector discharge because they were not given adequate advice or assistance by their sergeants or officers,[12] or because they knew that the military was turning down virtually all applications. Faced with duties and orders that violated their conscience, they often refused to obey or went AWOL and were court-martialed as a result.

The case of Private David Brown is fairly typical of

[11] *In re Kelly,* 401 F. 2d 211 (5th Cir. 1968); United States *ex rel. Brooks* v. *Clifford,* 409 F. 2d 700, *pet. for rehearing denied,* 412 F. 2d 1137 (4th Cir. 1969); *Bates* v. *Commander, supra* note 7; United States *ex rel. Sheldon* v. *O'Malley,* 420 F. 2d 1344 (D.C. Cir. 1969).

[12] See *United States* v. *Sigmon,* CM 416,356 (2 Jan. 1968); *United States* v. *Quirk,* CM 416,445 (31 May 1968).

the conscientious objectors who were refused discharge
early in the war and who now appear to meet the legal
standards for discharge. Although Brown had decided
during his second year in college that he wanted to go
into a church vocation, he did not consider himself a
conscientious objector. Therefore, when he found himself
likely to be drafted in 1966, he enlisted in the Army
administration specialty school to serve as a chaplain's assistant. After two weeks of basic training, he reached the
decision that service in the military was incompatible with
his beliefs and applied for a conscientious objector discharge. The chaplain who interviewed him found his
beliefs sincere but based upon contacts with "pacifistic
organizations and individuals rather than on religious convictions" (an incorrect test for conscientious objection).[13]
Upon disapproval of his application, he was ordered to
draw combat equipment, which he refused to do. He was
given a special court-martial and sentenced to three
months at hard labor. While serving this sentence, he
submitted another application for discharge, and once
again the chaplain noted that his beliefs were "pacifistic"
rather than stemming from religious conviction. The second application was disapproved, and he refused to put
on his uniform and report to work in the orderly room.
He was given a general court-martial and sentenced
to eighteen months at hard labor and a bad-conduct
discharge.

After his first court-martial, Private Brown brought a
writ of habeas corpus in a federal court to require the
Army to discharge him as a conscientious objector. The
court denied the relief on the ground that it could not
review military determinations.[14] In his second court-
martial, he was not permitted to raise the improper denial
of his application for discharge or to introduce evidence

[13] See note 7.
[14] 263 F. Supp. 686 (D.N.J. 1967).

that his refusal to obey the order was based upon religious scruples. Thus, he was convicted of disobedience even though the evidence might have shown that he should have been discharged as a conscientious objector and therefore never should have been subjected to the order. (The military courts, after some uncertainty, now seem to have accepted the position that wrongful denial of a conscientious objector discharge is no defense to a court-martial for disobedience of orders.)[15] Private Brown was finally discharged dishonorably after serving most of his enlistment term in military prisons and now lives in a pacifist community in New England.

Multiple courts-martial of servicemen who claim to be conscientious objectors have been rather common during the Vietnam war, and lack of adequate legal advice often exacerbated the penalty that the individual received. For example, Private Felix Chavez, Jr., after deciding in the fall of 1965 that he was a conscientious objector, refused to comply with military orders. He was sentenced to six months by a court-martial. After serving his sentence, he applied for a conscientious objector discharge, but, while the application was pending, he was court-martialed again for refusal to obey orders and given six months more. While serving this sentence, his application was disapproved, and when he was released from the stockade, he was again given orders that he disobeyed. At this point a suit was filed in a federal court to stay the court-martial and declare him a conscientious objector, but it was dismissed on the ground that military determinations are not

[15] The Court of Military Appeals avoided this issue in *United States* v. *Noyd*, 18 U.S.C.M.A. 483, 40 C.M.R. 195 (1969), by stating that the trial judge had in fact considered the defense of improper denial of Noyd's conscientious objector application. The court has since limited the situations in which such a defense can be raised in a prosecution for disobedience of orders. *United States* v. *Stewart*, 20 U.S. C.M.A., 272, 43 C.M.R. 112 (1971).

reviewable.[16] Chavez was then court-martialed and sentenced for a third time, but, after serving the sentence, was finally discharged with a less-than-honorable discharge. His case points up the fact that a serviceman who refuses to obey orders can be subjected to an endless series of orders and court-martial sentences, which only end when a court-martial gives him a punitive discharge or his commander either tires of the game or finds the cause hopeless and decides to have him discharged administratively.

Conscientious objectors in the Vietnam war period have not only been subjected to rather severe punishments (courts-martial for disobedience or for AWOL have often resulted in several years at hard labor), but they have also experienced considerable maltreatment in military prisons. There are many reports of harassment and brutal acts against conscientious objectors by stockade and brig guards, especially in the early years of the Vietnam war when the military attitude toward conscientious objection was still extremely hostile.[17] Acts of defiance of authority by conscientious objectors have often resulted in harsh repression. For example, Pfc. James Robinson, a nineteen-year-old Marine who went on a hunger strike in the Camp Pendleton brig in 1967, was badly beaten and force-fed with tubes daily and then subjected to solitary confinement.

Amnesty for conscientious objectors who received court-martial offenses arising out of acts of conscience should not be difficult to administer. Genuine conscientious objectors should be relatively easy to identify since their military and court-martial records often provide sufficient facts to make a determination that they should

[16] *Chavez* v. *Ferguson*, 266 F. Supp. 879 (N.D. Cal. 1967).

[17] See e.g., R. Sherrill, *Military Justice is to Justice as Military Music is to Music* (1970); F. Gardner, *The Unlawful Concert: An Account of the Presidio Mutiny Case* (1970).

have been granted conscientious objector status.[18] However, amnesty should not be limited merely to those who
can now prove that a legal error was made in failing to
classify them as conscientious objectors. Although these
present the clearest case for amnesty, there are other cases
with equal claims of injustice that should be considered
even though no clear legal error can now be found. Since
the manner in which the military administered conscientious objector discharges in the Vietnam war period was
often inadequate and sometimes discriminatory, many
bona fide conscientious objectors cannot now present a
clear case of legal error. If the acts for which they were
court-martialed, such as disobedience or AWOL, can
clearly be shown to have been caused by their conscientious objector beliefs, and if there is a reasonable explanation for their failure to pursue or obtain legal relief, they
should be considered for amnesty.

2. *Servicemen Court-Martialed for Acts Arising out of
Moral Opposition to the War Who Were Not Conscientious Objectors.* A number of servicemen who have been
court-martialed in the Vietnam war for acts arising out of
their moral opposition to the war could not have qualified as conscientious objectors. They include selective objectors who are opposed to participation in the Vietnam
war but not in all wars and individuals whose beliefs are

[18] The most recent Department of Defense Directive on
Conscientious Objectors (1300.6, August 20, 1971, pp. 3–5)
states that the sincerity of conscientious objector beliefs "cannot be routinely ascertained by applying inflexible objective
standards and measurements on an 'across-the-board' basis,"
but that relevant factors to be considered from the supporting
documents include "training in the home and church; general
demeanor and pattern of conduct; participation in religious
activities; whether ethical or moral convictions were gained
through training, study, contemplation, or other activity comparable in rigor and dedication to the processes by which traditional religious convictions are formulated; credibility of the
applicant; and credibility of persons supporting the claim."

primarily political or philosophical rather than religious.

An example of a selective conscientious objector is Captain Dale Noyd, who was court-martialed in 1967 for refusing an order to train fighter pilots for Vietnam. Noyd, a career officer with an excellent military record, had attempted to get the Air Force to reassign him to duties involving minimum conflict with his beliefs or to discharge him as a conscientious objector. The Air Force refused, on the grounds that he was only opposed to the war in Vietnam. He was convicted and sentenced to a year at hard labor and dismissal from the service.

Noyd and other selective objectors who have suffered court-martial because of their moral opposition to the Vietnam war are the type of persons to whom amnesty should be extended. First, there is usually little question about the sincerity and depth of their convictions. In Noyd's case, all of the Air Force officers who reviewed his request attested to the sincerity of his beliefs. The Court of Military Appeals, which upheld his court-martial conviction,[19] observed in another decision that Noyd could not be considered disloyal to his country as he "demonstrated a genuine dedication to the United States as a political entity, but scruples of conscience about the Vietnam war compelled him to refuse to obey."[20] Conscientious objection is no less deeply felt because it is selective, as noted by Judge Charles Wyzanski in a decision holding that denial of exemption from military service for selective objectors is unconstitutional:

> The sincerely conscientious man, whose principles flow from reflection, education, practice, sensitivity to competing claims, and a search for a meaningful life, always brings impressive credentials. When he honestly believes that he will act wrongly if he kills, his claim obviously is not appreciably lessened if his belief re-

[19] United States v. Noyd, supra note 14.
[20] United States v. Harvey, 19 U.S.C.M.A. 539, 544, 42 C.M.R. 141, 146 (1970).

lates not to war in general, but to a particular war or to a particular type of war. Indeed, a selective conscientious objector might reflect a more discriminating study of the problem, a more sensitive conscience, and a deeper spiritual understanding.[21]

Although a persuasive case might be made for extending conscientious objector treatment to selective objectors, the military has not chosen to do so. Therefore, there is no legal right for selective objectors in the military to refuse duty. However, once a selective objector has been court-martialed for noncompliance with orders and has served his sentence, there would appear to be very good reasons for considering amnesty treatment. Amnesty in such a case would not undercut the deterrent effect of the law or military effectiveness. A claim of selective conscientious objection is a very poor refuge for a serviceman who is willing to lie in order to obtain a discharge. It is well known that the military consistently denies requests for discharge by selective objectors. A serviceman with no qualms about fabricating a claim would surely have no difficulty in simply claiming that he was opposed to all wars. The selective objector is often a person who has agonized over his beliefs and who is unwilling to compromise them even in the face of regulations that refuse to accord them conscientious objector status. The conviction of such individuals is troubling in a society that attempts to respect individual moral beliefs and to recognize the demands of conscience.

There is a second reason why amnesty for selective objectors would not be as corrosive of the deterrent effect of the law as in other cases. Until very recently there has been a genuine dispute as to the legality and constitutionality of the military conscientious objector regulations that exclude selective objectors. Several United States Dis-

[21] *United States* v. *Sisson*, 297 F. Supp. 902 (D. Mass. 1969).

trict Courts have ruled that different treatment of selective objectors is unconstitutional.[22] Thus a selective objector could reasonably have concluded, in reliance upon sound legal advice, that the military's refusal to discharge him was improper and would eventually be overturned by the courts. Until the *Hammond* decision in 1968, such a serviceman had to subject himself to court-martial by refusing an order before he could obtain judicial review of his claim in a federal court. Thus, commission of offenses punishable by court-martial was an appropriate legal means of challenging what many considered to be an illegal regulation, a course not inconsistent with the American constitutional tradition that one must challenge a law by breaking it.

In March 1971, the Supreme Court ruled for the first time on constitutionality of the Selective Service and military regulations excluding selective objectors from conscientious objector status. In *United States* v. *Gillette* and *United States* v. *Negre*,[23] it held that the regulations are constitutional. Although certain points are still unresolved, which have led some to maintain that the Court has not definitely rejected the position of all selective objectors, it would appear that after March 1971 it is no longer reasonable for a serviceman to believe that, in the present judicial climate, the military conscientious objector regulations excluding selective objectors are unconstitutional. But for those selective objectors who refused orders prior to that date and were court-martialed, there would seem to be an especially persuasive legal argument for amnesty. Although they clearly have no grounds for reversal of their convictions (a person who challenges the constitutionality of a law does so at his own risk), amnesty after the fact would seem appropriate. The previous uncertainty of the law and the acknowledged sin-

[22] *United States* v. *McFadden*, 309 F. Supp. 502 (N.D. Cal. 1970); *United States* v. *Sisson*, *supra* note 19.

[23] 91 S. Ct. 828 (1971).

cerity of their individual beliefs provide sufficient justification for their records to be cleared without adversely
affecting the deterrence of the law or undermining the
legal process.

3. *Nuremberg Dissenters.* In a few cases in the Vietnam war period, servicemen have refused orders on the
grounds that the orders violated the Nuremberg Principles and therefore claimed that they were entitled, indeed obligated, to disobey them. The most publicized
case of this type was that of Captain Howard Levy, who
was court-martialed in 1967 for refusing to teach medicine to Green Beret troops at Fort Jackson, South Carolina. Levy claimed that the nondoctor Green Berets were
to be trained to use drugs and other medical techniques
among the Vietnamese for political and tactical purposes
in violation of medical ethics and the international law
of war. In a precedent-setting decision, the military judge
stated that if Levy could prove that the Green Berets
were committing war crimes, he could raise a Nuremberg
defense to the order.

Levy's attorneys introduced considerable evidence of
actions by individual Green Berets in Vietnam that constituted violations of the international law of war, such as
unnecessary destruction of homes, improper treatment of
dead bodies, assassination assignments, and torture of prisoners of war. However, the judge found that there was insufficient evidence of officially condoned illegal activities
or evidence that Levy would be required to participate in
illegal activities and therefore ruled that the Nuremberg
defense was not raised. Since the Levy court-martial, a
good deal more evidence of American war crimes in Vietnam has come to light. The 1967 Stockholm Commission on War Crimes (the "Russell Tribunal") and the
1970 Citizens Commission of Enquiry on U.S. War
Crimes in Vietnam (the "Winter Soldiers' hearings"),
although conducted in a highly propagandistic manner,

produced substantial evidence of war crimes resulting
from both individual actions of American soldiers and
official command policies. Finally, the evidence adduced
by the military investigations and court-martial trials of
servicemen in Vietnam, especially the Green Beret murder case and the My Lai cases, have added hard evidence
of widespread commission of war crimes by American
servicemen in Vietnam.

In light of the new and continually growing evidence
of violations of the laws of war by American troops and
policies in Vietnam,[24] there is reason to re-examine the
court-martial convictions of servicemen who relied upon
the Nuremberg Principles in refusing orders. Both military and civilian courts in the early Vietnam war period
summarily disposed of claims by servicemen that their
Vietnam orders required them to participate in an illegal
war or in illegal actions. Thus, Privates Dennis Mora,
James Johnson, and David Samas (the "Ft. Hood Three")
were given three- and five-year sentences in 1966 for refusing to board a troopship for Vietnam despite their
contention that the war was "immoral, illegal, and unjust."[25] Likewise, the claims of Private Luftig[26] and
Private Mitchell[27] that military service and orders in the
Vietnam war were illegal were rejected in federal court
suits. It appears that the evidence is still insufficient under
the law to provide a Nuremberg defense to disobedience
of orders in most of these cases, although further evidence
of war crimes and a court determination that continuation
of the war without a congressional declaration of war is

[24] See D'Amato, Gould and Woods, "War Crimes and
Vietnam: The Nuremberg Defense and the Military Service
Resister," *California Law Review*, 57, 1969, pp. 1055,
1069–97; T. Taylor, *Nuremberg and Vietnam: An American
Tragedy* (1971) pp. 95–153.
[25] *Mora* v. *McNamara*, 389 U.S. 934 (1967).
[26] *Luftig* v. *Mitchell*, 373 F. 2d 664 (D.C. Cir.), *cert. denied*, 387 945 (1967).
[27] *United States* v. *Mitchell*, 369 F. 2d 323 (2d Cir. 1966),
cert. denied, 386 U.S. 972 (1967).

unconstitutional[28] would improve that legal position. But even if there is still inadequate legal support for reversing their convictions, there may be reasons for granting them amnesty now that they have served their sentences.

In a number of the Nuremberg dissenter cases, disobedience of orders was shown to have resulted from a personal abhorrence of the conduct of the Vietnam war and awareness of the legal and moral strictures of international law and the Nuremberg Principles. The shaping of the arguments in legal terms, of course, was generally done by the lawyers, but frequently the moral concern of the individual in terms of the Nuremberg experience seems to have been a motivating force in the disobedience. Amnesty treatment for such individuals would indicate the continuing commitment of the United States to the international law of war and the Nuremberg Principles. This country has come to a belated recognition, as especially evidenced by the public reaction to the Calley conviction, that the Nuremberg Principles create a tremendous dilemma for the soldier who is held personally responsible for his acts and yet who, if he disobeys orders he considers illegal, will be subject to court-martial for disobedience if they are later determined to be legal. The Nuremberg dissenters, unlike Lieutenant Calley and the soldiers involved in the My Lai incident, resolved that dilemma in favor of disobedience, rather than participating in actions they considered immoral and illegal. Their choice may display undue sensitivity to moral considerations and exaggerated legalism, but nevertheless represents, in many cases, a genuinely conscientious decision and deeply personal moral commitment. Although such a commitment may be an inadequate defense under the law, it should be considered in granting amnesty. At a time when there is increased national reexamination of the values and policies that led the United

[28] See *United States* v. *Motolla*, F. Supp. (1971).

States into the Vietnam war and dictated the conduct of
that war, it would appear appropriate to extend amnesty
to those who, early in the war, displayed sensitivity to the
legal and moral issues that lay beneath the surface.

4. *Political Dissenters.* A number of servicemen have
been court-martialed during the Vietnam war for expressing their opposition to the policies of the military and
the government in the conduct of the war. Many of these
men were convicted of military offenses that would not
be crimes in civilian life. Many were also convicted for
relatively innocuous activities that would clearly have
been constitutionally protected "free speech" if they had
been civilians. Thus, Lieutenant Henry Howe was convicted in 1965 of "conduct unbecoming an officer and a
gentleman" and "contemptuous words against the President" for carrying a sign critical of President Johnson's
Vietnam policies in an off-post peace rally while off duty
and in civilian clothes.[29] Corporal William Harvey[30]
and Private George Daniels[31] were convicted in 1967 of
making "disloyal statements" and attempting to cause "insubordination, disloyalty, and refusal of duty" for telling
other black Marines in a bull session that Vietnam was a
"white man's war" and that they should talk to the commander about not going there. Privates Daniel Amick and
Kenneth Stolte were convicted in 1968 of making "disloyal statements" for passing out a leaflet expressing opposition to Vietnam policies and asking other soldiers who
agreed to get in touch with them.[32] Seaman Roger Priest
was convicted in 1970 of making "disloyal statements" for
publishing an antiwar servicemen's newspaper with state-

[29] *United States* v. *Howe,* 17 U.S.C.M.A. 165, 37 C.M.R.
429 (1967).
[30] *United States* v. *Harvey, supra* note 18.
[31] *United States* v. *Daniels,* 19 U.S.C.M.A. 529, 42 C.M.R.
131 (1970).
[32] *United States* v. *Amick and Stolte,* 40 C.M.R. 720
(1969).

ments critical of the military and the war.[33] Captain
Thomas Culver was convicted in 1971 of violating an
Air Force regulation forbidding participation in demonstrations in foreign countries for joining a peaceful presentation of a petition against the war to the U. S. Embassy
in London. The sentences were generally harsh, particularly in the early part of the war. Lieutenant Howe received two years (later reduced to one), Harvey and
Daniels ten and six years, respectively (reduced to four
and three), Amick and Stolte four years each, and all
with less-than-honorable discharges. Priest received a less-
than-honorable discharge, and Culver a reprimand and a
one-thousand-dollar fine.

The scope of servicemen's rights to free speech under
the First Amendment of the Constitution has been stead-
ily expanding during the Vietnam war, due, in part, to
cases such as these. The court-martial convictions of Harvey and Daniels were reversed by the Court of Military
Appeals for instructional error (although convictions of
a lesser included offense were affirmed), and the conviction of Priest was reversed by a Navy Court of Military
Review. Most of these cases—Howe, Daniels, Amick and
Stolte, and Culver—are now in various stages of appeals
or direct attack in the federal courts. However, it is not
certain that the legal remedies will be adequate. Although
the Harvey conviction was reversed because the military
judge had failed to instruct that his statements must be
"disloyal" to the United States and not merely the military
(the Priest case was reversed on the same grounds), other
court-martial convictions for making "disloyal statements"
still stand.

It is a long and a difficult process to attack court-martial
convictions after the fact and even if the attack eventually
succeeds, the serviceman will usually have fully served
his sentence (for example, Daniels spent over two years
in military prisons although the conviction against him

[33] *United States* v. *Priest,* No. 23,937 (U. S. Court of
Military Appeals, August 27, 1971).

that was finally affirmed carried a maximum sentence of
only four months). Even more significant, there is still
insufficient legal authority to attack most of the court-
martial convictions of the political dissenters, since the
Court of Military Appeals has taken a narrow view of
servicemen's free speech rights and the federal courts
have continued to display an unwillingness to tamper
with the military in this area.[34] Thus, although the legal
situation is still in flux and it is possible that cases now
pending will result in an expansion of servicemen's rights,
many servicemen court-martialed for expressing dissenting
views who have served their sentences and been discharged will very likely be stuck with military records
showing criminal convictions (the speech offenses, carrying more than one year's confinement, are usually felo-
nies) and less-than-honorable discharges.

Servicemen convicted for activities that are considered
to be "free speech" in civilian society have an especially
strong claim for amnesty treatment. First, no society that
espouses individual liberties as does the United States can
be content to see servicemen severely punished for merely
expressing their views on political matters. The 3½ million servicemen are voters and taxpayers, and it seems impossible, and probably unwise, to attempt to insulate them
from the winds of controversy and change and to forbid
them from discussing the principal political issues in our
country. Although the courts, military and civilian, have
not yet been willing to extend broader "free speech" rights
to servicemen, amnesty treatment would provide recognition of the sincere motivations that led servicemen to
speak out on such an important public issue. Second, most
of the political dissenters who have been court-martialed
have good prior records, both civilian and military, and
are not in any sense criminal personalities. Lieutenant
Howe was a recent ROTC graduate with no prior rec-

[34] See Sherman, "Judicial Review of Military Determinations and the Exhaustion of Remedies Requirement," 55 *Va.
L. Rev.* 483 (1969), 48 *Mil. L. Rev.* 91 (1970).

ord. Harvey, Daniels, Amick, Stolte, and Priest had volunteered for the service after finishing high school and
had good service records. Captain Culver had served six
years as a legal officer in the Air Force and had received
high ratings throughout his career.

In many cases the dissenting servicemen did not know
that the activity in which they engaged was considered
criminal. The military speech offenses use extremely
vague terms—like "conduct unbecoming an officer and a
gentleman," "disorders and neglects to the prejudice of
good order and discipline in the Armed Forces," "disloyal
statements," and "participation in a demonstration"—
which give little advance notice as to what is covered.
Such vague terms would constitute a denial of constitutional due process in a civilian court,[35] but have been
upheld by the military courts. Furthermore, there is little
case precedent to indicate clearly what is covered, since
these offenses have rarely been used before the Vietnam
war. Thus, Lieutenant Howe, the first of the Vietnam
war dissenter cases, assumed that he had a right to go on
a Saturday to a small, peaceful rally in a park in El Paso,
Texas, and, dressed in civilian clothes, to carry a critical
sign. Privates Amick and Stolte testified at their court-
martial that they constantly heard about the Vietnam war
in the media, had read critical statements by senators,
congressmen, and ex-generals, and thought they had a
right to express their opinions in a leaflet. Captain Culver,
a military attorney with six years' experience, testified that
he had every reason to believe that a presentation of a
petition to the U. S. Embassy was not a forbidden "demonstration" and that his actions were permitted by military law and the Constitution. Thus, the extreme vague-
ness of the military terms, giving military courts-martial
the opportunity to interpret them according to their own

[35] See *Cox* v. *Louisiana*, 379 U.S. 536 (1965); *Lanzetta* v.
New Jersey, 306 U.S. 451 (1939); *Kirkland* v. *Wallace*, 403
F. 2d 413 (5th Cir. 1968); *Baker* v. *Binder*, 274 F. Supp.
658 (W. D. Ky. 1967).

disposition, provides an especially strong reason for considering amnesty for political dissenters.

Finally, amnesty treatment seems appropriate for servicemen court-martialed for expressing opposition to the war because of the very political nature of the offense itself. These servicemen, as much as any individuals in America, can be considered to have been political prisoners. They were court-martialed not because they did not do their job well or because they were endangering the effectiveness of the military (the military courts have generally refused to require a showing that a serviceman's critical speech had any adverse effect upon the military).[36] Rather their crime was the violation of vague offenses and regulations, the legality of which is still in question and the propriety of which is troubling in a democracy. Amnesty has always had an admittedly political objective, being used most frequently in our society when substantial numbers of citizens have been in sharp conflict over fundamental political policies, which has resulted in arrests and convictions. Amnesty would permit recognition that such citizens are not basically criminals and should be returned to society without the stigma of criminal convictions. Those servicemen who have been court-martialed for expressing opposition to the war, whether innocently believing they had the right to do so or knowingly violating the severely restrictive military limitations on speech, are representative of a large number of Americans with similar reservations about the war. Amnesty seems especially appropriate to speed the return of the punished individuals to society and to heal the bitterness they continue to feel over the harsh treatment they received for actions that they considered merely their right as citizens.

5. *Servicemen Court-Martialed for Acts Caused by*

[36] See Sherman, "The Military Courts and Servicemen's First Amendment Rights," 22 *Hastings L. J.* 325, 360–73 (1971).

Special Circumstances of the Vietnam War. A number of servicemen have been court-martialed in the Vietnam war period for acts directly caused by special circumstances of the Vietnam war that may make amnesty appropriate in certain cases. Servicemen have frequently gone AWOL out of frustration with the role they are forced to play in the military, in relation to the war effort. They may not be conscientious objectors nor even have come to express their dissatisfactions in terms of antiwar dissent, but nevertheless they may have been clearly motivated by moral and political opposition to the war. Private Michael O'Connor, for example, enlisted in the Army in 1967 after dropping out of high school.[37] He experienced a gradual disenchantment with the military that was very much related to his aversion to the authoritarianism and brutality he had observed in some phases of military training and to a growing unease about the war in Vietnam. He went AWOL after observing Military Policemen beat a black prisoner in the stockade, and took sanctuary at the MIT Student Center in November 1968. At his court-martial for AWOL, his attorneys introduced the testimony of several psychiatrists that his going AWOL was a psychiatric response to his aversion to the war and certain aspects of military life that had created an "irresistible impulse" in him. However, military law does not provide for such a defense, apart from proof of insanity, and O'Connor was convicted. His case indicates, however, that a number of court-martial offenses, such as AWOL, disobedience of orders, insubordination, and failure to carry out military duties properly, can be directly related to the moral and emotional turmoil within a serviceman over the war. This problem is increased by the fact that the average age of members of the military is now nineteen and that 90 percent of the courts-martial

[37] For fuller description of the case, see A. Yarmolinsky, *The Military Establishment: Its Impact Upon American Society* (1971), pp. 356–57.

in the military are for offenses that would not be criminal in civilian life. The adjustment of young men to military life is at best a difficult one, but when intense personal aversion to the war and one's role in it is added, adjustment may become impossible.

One difficulty with amnesty for such servicemen is that all servicemen have adjustment problems, and amnesty for those whose problems were related to moral or political opposition to the war raises questions of equal protection for the others. Therefore, any proposal for amnesty should necessarily require strong and substantial evidence both of a direct connection between the offense and the individual's moral or political views and of good and sufficient reasons why the serviceman could not have solved his problems through normal channels available to him. It would appear that the number of cases that can meet such requirements would be rather small.

Amnesty is aimed at restoring to society individuals whose moral or political views resulted in their being branded as criminals. In view of the tremendous psychological pressures imposed by a war that is considered illegal and immoral by many, amnesty would seem to be appropriate in such limited cases. It is unfortunate, of course, that servicemen whose courts-martial resulted from other pressures should not also be granted amnesty, but amnesty has always been only selectively applied. There are certainly other inequities in military justice that deserve consideration, but the righting of all injustices is beyond the limited legal and political objectives of amnesty. It has been proposed that there should be a method by which all servicemen who have courts-martial and less-than-honorable discharges on their records could have them expunged upon leading exemplary lives after leaving the service. In light of the severe pressures of military life, such a proposal would seem to be an appropriate concomitant to amnesty for Vietnam war cases.

ALLAN SOLOMONOW

Allan Solomonow, who works with the War Resisters League, also founded Leprechauns for Peace.

The act that landed me in prison wasn't one of C.O. or draft resistance specifically, but violation of that portion of the Universal Military Training Act that makes it a statutory felony to knowingly or willfully mutilate or destroy a draft statement or certificate. During the course of a speech I gave outside a sub base in Connecticut, I simply, gently, severed that portion of my Selective Service registration card that had my signature on it. I put the signature portion of the card in my wallet, the remainder of the card in an envelope, and mailed it to the President.

As it happened, two FBI agents were there. They visited me the next day and I refused to answer questions at that time. I was indicted about six months later. I heard of that indictment through my father in California, who read it in some sort of press release that had been issued by the Department of Justice. The whole period leading up to the trial encompassed only about six months. A few months after that I began serving a year in prison. I voluntarily turned myself in at the Federal Hall of Justice in downtown New York, in front of many of my friends who shared my interest and concern. I then spent a few weeks in the Federal House of Detention on West Street

in New York City, and the remaining nine months of
the year I was supposed to serve in Allenwood Federal
Prison, except for short periods at Lewisburg because I
was a naughty boy at Allenwood.

There are several factors about my situation that certainly color my views on the subject of amnesty. The
first is that I was what they call a "short timer." I served
about half of the normal time in prison that most draft
cases serve. The normal sentences right now are around
nineteen months. My views might have changed had I
been in a lot longer; I might then be more favorable to
amnesty than I am. The second concern, as you know, is
that I am a pacifist and I have a stronger ideological basis
for making some sort of statement. The third concern is
that there is always a problem when talking about this in
the abstract. It's like saying, "Well, I know how I would
have reacted in World War II. I certainly would have
been a pacifist and I wouldn't have lifted a finger against
Hitler even if I heard that my family or my grandparents
were in a camp over there." It's so hard to be abstract
about a problem like this. It's an intellectual thing.

Sitting back now, I say that I would not have accepted any sort of amnesty, just as I would not have accepted any sort of parole or probation. It strikes me that
anything that sets any sort of limitations to your freedom,
any position that allows the security of the state to be
placed over the tremendous moral principles that have
led you to prison, simply doesn't make sense. It's really
saying, "Well, I really have changed, I've decided to play
their game, decided to set my principles aside, to yield to
their whims." I tell myself that I would not have accepted amnesty for that reason.

However, if they had said, "Solomonow, we don't want
you any more, we decided to forgive you, we were really
wrong. Take off!," that would be the harder decision for
me to make. There are a couple of people who have re-
sponded to that, like John Phillips up in Boston, for ex-

ample, who I think is one of the more creative spirits in the Movement. John is underground now. He was the one who put out *PISS*, Prison Information and Support Service. When it came time for him to be processed he refused to be outfitted for civilian clothes and refused to fill out any of the necessary forms. The latter seems to be pretty important to the prison authorities; for some reason it's very sacred that you must have your forms filled out, and you have to be out on your "release day." The guards bodily removed him from Allenwood and took him to Lewisburg, a few miles away. From there, they picked him up in the middle of the night and drove him by car from Lewisburg, Pennsylvania, to Boston, where they left him on the step of his folks' house. He didn't cooperate at any time; he tried to engage them in conversation, but obviously they weren't terribly happy about the circumstance. Marshals have better things to do than drive a kid several hundred miles. This was necessitated because he wouldn't get on any bus or railway.[1]

More recently, Ralph Bertolucci was up as a car thief, but claimed to be a resister had he been given the chance. He is close to the Catholic Peace Fellowship. Ralph was in prison for four years under the Youth Act for stealing a car. They shaved Ralph forcibly in the middle of the night and took him by car to a halfway house in Boston. This was still a few weeks before he was to get out of prison. In theory, he wasn't even eligible to go to the halfway house; it is always something you have to fight for. A few days and a few hassles after he got to the halfway house, he simply left. He just walked out, even though his prison term wasn't done; technically he became a fugitive from justice, and eligible to spend further time in prison because of that. To the best of our knowledge, the FBI is not moving in his case. I don't know why, but he certainly has appeared in public places where they could have picked him up had they wanted to.

[1] Phillips surrendered to federal authorities in mid-1971.

I align myself with John and Ralph. I say that I couldn't accept any parole, probation, or amnesty even if it were given without *any* conditions, because the government does not have the right to say it is sorry for something it should not have done. What it has to do is adjust itself to the problems that have created its vulnerability to such insanity. That is my primary concern.

What does the state have the right to demand? To me, that is not as realistic a question as the personal, individual question, "What do *we* have the right to do?" A state may make demands, but inevitably the execution of the demands of the state and the legitimacy of the state itself depend on individuals and whether their own moral consciences concur with the state's decrees. If you acquiesce to the state, and you believe you should not, whether or not that violates the law, you are saying that it is more important that the state continue and that the state grow, learn, change. I am saying there is a positive individual moral obligation to act as your conscience would have you act, and that is the *only* condition in which states improve, and, indeed, preserve themselves. I think the malaise from which we suffer now is the fact that people haven't *acted* enough. I believe people generally must act because my primary concern is to try to change this country. That, of course, is what led me to prison. But if amnesty had been granted to me while I was in prison, I can't see that it would have had any particular personal impact on *me*. If others want to accept amnesty, it is their decision.

The question arises, "Does this mean that I am advocating total anarchy?" That question is basically silly. No sane individual goes around ignoring the myriad acts of society. Ironically, the most natural thing for a person is to tend to conform, to assume that his parents, authority, the state are right. People are only moved to dissent after tremendous effort, and tremendous frustration is involved. The question is seldom "anarchy" but finding some balance where individuals don't fear the state so much that they decline to speak up when the state is going awry. The state has gone awry in the war in Indochina. The legal, the political, the social quagmires are so vast that my mind boggles just speaking of it.

In the long run, amnesty misses the whole question. Even if people come back to this country, the question remains, "Have either the people who have returned or the legislation helped to create a climate more viable for social change?" Amnesty would be a facile way of appearing to be benevolent, yet continuing to maintain the oppressiveness that leads men to prison and exile in the first place. In fact, those conditions will obviously continue regardless of the nature of amnesty that is involved. Also consider the nature of our people. The war in Vietnam has come about because of a tremendous malfunction in the social processes of our country; the people found it necessary to mount a movement involving millions of dollars and years of effort, in order to get what is now still only a halting step toward the "phasing out" of the war. To most of us who have gone to Canada or prison, the war clearly indicates that things are basically wrong with our society. The time and effort that have been taken to point up these difficulties have been so overwhelming that the only conclusion remaining in my mind is that our society is not open to social change, particularly under crisis situations, when morality is crying to be heard. I want to try to move people to ask themselves what it was that led to this trap.

Regarding legislation on amnesty, I think a lot of people would feel that in granting amnesty we would be "admitting" we were wrong, that we made a mistake. But that doesn't change the circumstances that will make for the next Vietnam, be it in the Middle East, Guatemala, or Indonesia. Amnesty doesn't address itself to those things that have to be changed to avoid the need for another amnesty five or six years from now.

Another question, of course, is how it applies to those of us who have been punished, imprisoned, or gone to Canada. That is not an easy question, simply because I think there is quite a bit of difference between those who have gone to Canada and those who remained in the United States. To those in prison amnesty will arouse varying reactions but little enthusiasm, and surely no great hope or praise. My general sentiment is that those who have gone to Canada and other countries have been less politically keen than those of us who have been in prison in the United States. I suspect that a surprisingly small number of people who say they yearn for the United States would not return from Canada if they were given the option. The primary reason that motivates return, along with loneliness and a desire for friends and family, is a simple economic one. While traveling in Canada, I found a great deal of ambivalence in the exiles, not because they didn't like Canada but simply because they haven't had the time to really assimilate in a creative way with the talents that they have. Some would expect to come back to the United States as conquering heroes, and some would return thinking that things have really changed when in fact they have not. Inevitably, the guys who return will have to face the same circumstances with their sons and daughters.

After you have gone to another country to establish new roots, it would be disappointing to come back to your own country and not see something strong and decisive, something more than amnesty, like some genuine change. I suspect that most exiles will not return for that reason, and that the ones who do return will tend to be the deserters and those who fled out of fear or in unthinking haste. I thought that most of the people I met in Canada were there as individuals and don't want to deal with the exile groups; they want to do it on their own. Amnesty simply *wasn't* a real issue when I visited Toronto and Montreal. Every time we brought up amnesty they said that Congressman Koch was really a very nice guy but by and large their commitment was to become Canadians. They had not come there as temporary dodgers, merely waiting until America overcame its insanity. They came there with the desire to become Canadian and to strike out in a new land.

In theory, because I have committed a statutory felony, I am deprived of "rights." I can't run for public office. I have to petition to be able to carry a firearm interstate. I can't vote in elections (although I do happen to be registered and I do vote). So amnesty probably does affect *all* of the people who have been in jail or fled to Canada, to the extent that it secures the restoration of these rights. Still, I think most of us consider most of these rights rather trivial.

Amnesty remains a "sop" to the liberal; it doesn't require that anyone do anything, save write a letter to their congressman and then, hopefully, all of us guys will feel a little better. What is hard, and what this society has been continually unable to do, is to create people who would be willing to forgo their second cars, their fancy homes, their getting bugged at the Black Panthers and actually getting out and *working* for *gut* matters such as decentralization, abolition of the draft, equal rights in fact, community co-ops, and day-care centers. Amnesty is really a trap that permits people to believe that they have done something "concrete"; it is an excuse because it does not require serious investment on their time, nor does it tap the basic courage needed to build a meaningful society.

It strikes me as being still more perverse than that. If amnesty is granted after this war, what will happen if we get involved in some sort of conflict in the Middle East in two or three years? Then people who are thinking of going into the draft and joining or not joining the armed services have an additional factor to plague their consciences, not a moral concern but a highly political concern; namely, "Maybe history will be with me; maybe I'll get amnesty too. Maybe I won't try to be a C.O." It's a gamble. Amnesty tempts one to think in political terms and set aside the harder issue of conscience. No matter which way you look at it, amnesty is a way of saying everything but "What do I do to change the society in which I find myself?"

I do not believe that there has ever been a full, general amnesty. These matters being highly political, they are always compromised, never neat, never humane. Some people are forgiven, others are not. Some rights are restored, others are not. A full and general amnesty is terribly improbable, and what is the response when it is only partly granted? Politics is like that: "The art of the possible" implies, demands compromise. You come off as rather ungrateful when you win part of your battle (a hell of an achievement *these* days!) and then say, "Forget it, it's all or nothing."

It is that sort of pitfall that the moral stand avoids. But if there are those who still think that amnesty can be a moral achievement, let them first ask those who would "benefit" from it. The amnesty seekers should not think that they are speaking for the resisters, the exiles, and the "mutilators," without first making every effort to understand the sentiments of those who have faced the hard decisions of our day.

PETER STEINFELS

Peter Steinfels, Associate Editor of Commonweal, *has been a contributor to several books as well as the New York* Times, The Nation, La Nouvel Observateur, Concilium, National Catholic Reporter, *and other journals.*

I don't think it is very straightforward to discuss amnesty without stating how one stands on the war itself. I am one of the many Americans who feel that long ago our engagement in Vietnam passed the point after which it could only be properly described as immoral. Furthermore, when my ignorance about the legal status of the notion of amnesty prompted me to page through some law journals and indexes of legal periodicals, I was struck by the fact that though there is virtually nothing written by lawyers about amnesty in the present circumstances, there is a vast literature on the constitutionality of the American war effort, on the question of whether our effort violates international law, and finally on the terrible question of war crimes—in the sense of atrocities—committed both by soldiers and by the policymakers.

There is something ironic, then, about asking whether one group of people, the war resisters, deserve amnesty, when the question might be as pertinently directed toward another group of people, the warmakers.

This is the background to my contention that the call

for amnesty is fundamentally a moderate request. There are many who see it as an extreme position, of course: "You resisted the war. You refused the draft, or deserted the Armed Forces. On top of that, you want amnesty!" On the contrary, I would argue that amnesty is not a radical proposal but a very moderate one involving compromise on every side.

What is amnesty? Historically, amnesty has had several purposes. One of them was simply to bind the wounds of a nation after some kind of civil dispute, a measure to facilitate forgiving and forgetting. Now, on both sides of the present division in American opinion, there are many who question whether it is a good idea to forgive and forget something as important in our history as the war in Vietnam.

A second purpose of amnesty in the past has been to display the magnanimity of a sovereign after he has in some way achieved or consolidated his power: He therefore deigns to forgive those who have opposed him.

A third purpose has been to relieve individuals of penalties they may have incurred in a struggle when, with hindsight, it is seen that their positions in that struggle were somehow legitimate. After the war of 1870 between France and Prussia, the treaty that handed Alsace over to the new German state also included a clause granting amnesty to those former French inhabitants of that territory who had naturally fought on the side of France. It was recognized that they should not incur penalties for this legitimate service. Something analogous to this occurs in labor disputes: an understanding, as part of the settlement, that those who engaged in a strike action will not incur any penalties or discrimination.

It should be clear that these purposes do not necessarily complement one another; sometimes they are contradictory. In one case, amnesty implies a recognition of a certain justice in the cause of those being amnestied. In another case, it implies no such thing, but rather reflects the power and virtue of those *granting* the amnesty.

In short, the whole thing is pretty ambiguous, and many zealous people on the left, perhaps some of the war resisters themselves, can make as good a case against amnesty from *their* perspective as can the conservatives on the right. Amnesty will render certain benefits to both parties in the current profound dispute among American citizens; in the same way, it requires certain concessions from both parties. The call for amnesty is a moderate position in the sense that it recognizes a divergence between what might be best at the level of abstract principles and what might be best at the level of the concrete individuals, the resisters, the imprisoned, the exiles; and it concludes that for the concrete good of these individuals, both parties, left and right, will have to compromise some of the absolute purity of their principles.

Some would argue against amnesty on the basis that it would involve a kind of national confession of guilt on the question of the war—some favoring such a confession, some opposing it. I think there is an element of truth in their belief. On the other hand, amnesty also involves a certain recognition by the people being granted amnesty of the unity of our society and the ties that bind them to it. Accepting amnesty does imply, on their part, a nebulous willingness to get on with business *within* our society, even if that business is only to continue their debate over American foreign policy. Accepting amnesty means risking an implicit admission of the legitimacy of the government that grants them amnesty; it means risking the smoothing out and tucking away of all the unsettled moral and political issues involved in the Vietnam engagement.

I simply stress the risks to point out that they are not only on one side of the dispute but spread between both sides. These risks should be taken. The overriding concern should be the welfare of the specific individuals who have resisted the war. From contacts with draft resisters and deserters in France and prisoners in the United

States, I know they are undergoing experiences in exile and in prisons that are not to their benefit nor to the benefit of any of us. What we have been discussing, what it seems is always being discussed when amnesty is on the agenda, are symbolic questions. Far be it from me to join those who would belittle "symbolic questions"; but I have been trying to point out how ambiguous, how two-edged, the act of amnesty is. What should count in this instance is the suffering and hardening and embittering of more young men. It should be ended.

Objections to amnesty have been raised on the practical grounds that granting amnesty would encourage war resistance in the future. Some advocates of amnesty, of course, see this as an argument in favor of the measure. I suspect that both parties are wrong, and that, apart from rescuing some good people from a bad, dead-end situation, the practical consequences of amnesty are often exaggerated. In some disputes on college campuses, the issue of amnesty has been raised almost to the central question. However central it may be in terms of vindicating one side or the other symbolically, I doubt whether a grant of amnesty weighs very heavily as a factor in terms of the practical consequences, of encouraging or discouraging future disputes or future riots.

I can, however, foresee an exception to this rule. Should the United States ever again engage in a war in which the support of the many is so passive while the opposition is so active and intense, then perhaps the example of an amnesty granted after the Vietnam war would encourage resistance in that future case. The potential of such resistance, fueled in part by the confidence in an amnesty, might act as a check on the government, might make it hesitate to engage in a war without solid popular support. But such an outcome would be healthy in my opinion. Foreign policy is an area that has nearly become exempt from the principle of checks and balances.

The most common argument for amnesty is that of

reconciliation. To my mind, the movement could do with a larger dose of reconciliation and openness toward reconciliation. So could the rest of us. But I do not feel that the notion of reconciliation is as essential to the amnesty question as some people would like to make it. Whether amnesty would indeed lead to reconciliation I can't say. It is an appealing aspect of amnesty, but it is also an unknown element; as such it becomes minor. Again, I think the plight of young people in prison for three, four, or five years or treading water in exile because of the moral demands of our times is the central issue.

When it comes to speaking about either reconciliation or practical consequences, we might consider the experience of European nations after World War II. There, the great question that had to be faced was what to do with people who had engaged in collaboration with the Nazis. Some nations pursued wartime collaborators more vigorously than others; they defined collaboration in different ways. Eventually there were amnesties granted in most of the European countries. The whole question was by no means unimportant. But perhaps, from a distance, we are struck by the similarity, rather than by the differences, in policies toward collaborators and in attitudes toward amnesty—most of the prosecutions were dropped. What is more, none of us would feel very confident in pointing to important practical consequences that flowed from the differing policies followed, or in insisting that much of contemporary European history really depends upon how that question was solved.

The effects of an act of amnesty—political reverberations, reconciliation, dampening of foreign policy criticism, whatever—would depend in large measure on the actual circumstances of the public debate, on who supported and opposed it, on how it was finally implemented. All these things might have a bearing on whether amnesty signified a legitimation of the opposition to the war and a confession that the war was wrong, or whether it implied an openness of the American political system to protest, or whether it implied both. What I would like to see the movement for amnesty stand for, above all, is a sensitivity to the situation of living human beings and a refusal to elevate abstract principles to a position where they become divorced from all feeling for the human reality. Perhaps I stress this because I feel that the war itself springs from this sort of submission to abstractions, this sort of loss of feeling for the reality of the human lives and the culture being destroyed. Such matters weigh very lightly, I feel, in the strategies of our war managers and policymakers. Even the antiwar movement has on many occasions become caught up in abstractions. The regaining of a sense of the concrete human person would be an important thing for it, too.

As for the issue of selective conscientious objection, it can be divided into two separate questions. The first is whether there is a constitutional right to selective conscientious objection. The U. S. Supreme Court has recently ruled that there is not; in fact, it is widely held that all conscientious objection, selective or total, is not a constitutional right but a "privilege" Congress has seen to enact for prudential reasons. There is, of course, a good argument for the opposing viewpoint.

The second question is whether selective conscientious objection, even if not a *right,* is nonetheless a good idea that should be instituted by Congress. Opponents argue that selective conscientious objection would create extraordinary difficulties for the process of raising and maintaining our Armed Forces. My own impression is just the opposite: It is the *absence* of selective conscientious objection that creates and will create in the future extraordinary difficulties for the Armed Forces.

But a distinction should be made between amnesty and selective conscientious objection. Selective conscientious objection provides an institutionalized way for young men to be exempted from service in wars they hold immoral without incurring any penalty. Should an amnesty be granted, those who have been war resisters will have incurred penalties up to the point of the amnesty; further, they have incurred these penalties without being sure that any amnesty would be granted.

Thus the only instance in which amnesty might begin to resemble an equivalent of selective conscientious objection would be the engagement of this country in a war that was so enormously unpopular that resisters were almost 100 percent certain they would shortly be granted an amnesty. Should we really worry now about the possibility that a government might one day encounter a lively resistance to another unpopular war?

The answer to the question of the extent to which a nation can let its citizens pick and choose their own wars, I think, is that we don't really know precisely, but that we have grounds for thinking that a nation could go a good deal farther than the United States has. The experience of most nations in modern times is that they have never had any trouble getting their citizens to fight in even the most questionable enterprises. Unfortunately! Furthermore, some nations like Great Britain have had what amounted to selective conscientious objection and yet never found themselves short of people willing to defend their borders.

Has war resistance spared the lives of some young resisters from injury and death? Yes, I suppose it has in some cases—though at a very high price in personal sacrifice on the part of many resisters. Other young men were spared from injury and death in Vietnam because they were able to stay in school and out of service, because their skills earned them safe jobs in the Army, because they joined the National Guard, or simply because they were lucky. Why death and suffering strike down some people and not others early in life is a mystery to which there is no "answer." But rather than opposing those who have placed themselves in jeopardy in the war to those who have placed themselves in jeopardy through resistance, perhaps we should recognize that both groups in some ways more closely resemble one another than they do the great number of passive and uninvolved on-lookers who have allowed the war to grind on.

We can only plea that suffering be not added to suffering and loss to loss.

JOHN M. SWOMLEY, JR.

John M. Swomley, Jr., is Professor of Christian Ethics at St. Paul School of Theology, Kansas City, Missouri. He has been active in campaigns to desegregate the Armed Forces and against universal military conscription. Working with the Fellowship of Reconciliation, he assisted James Farmer, Bayard Rustin, A. J. Muste, and others in laying the groundwork for the emphasis on nonviolence in the American civil rights movement. He is the author of American Empire, Religion: The State and The Schools, The Military Establishment, *and other books. His articles have also appeared in* The Progressive, The Christian Advocate, The Commercial and Financial Chronicle, *and other magazines.*

". . . it appears to me no less consistent with the public good than it is with my personal feelings to mingle in the operations of Government every degree of moderation and tenderness which the national justice, dignity and safety may permit." From George Washington's proclamation of amnesty, July 10, 1795.

This is a revised version of "Memo to Nixon: Why Not an Amnesty?," by John M. Swomley, Jr., in *The National Catholic Reporter,* January 1, 1969. Reprinted by permission.

The Need for Amnesty

Thousands of young men are either in prison or exile because of military conscription in the United States. Some of these men are sincere conscientious objectors to all war who were not recognized as such by their draft boards. Other young men did not pass the religious test imposed by Congress.

Some men are in prison because they are objectors to the war in Vietnam, but not to all war. Traditional Roman Catholic theology provides criteria for just wars, and hence for unjust wars. Similarly some non-Roman Catholics could not conscientiously participate in the war in Vietnam even though they are not prepared to declare their opposition to all war. They felt they could not maintain personal integrity and participate in a war they believed was unjust or served no defensive purpose.

Other men went to prison because they believed conscription itself to be wrong—a type of involuntary servitude. They refused to cooperate by keeping a draft card or by accepting induction as conscientious objectors. A few ministers who objected to "special privileges" not granted to laymen took this position.

Most of those who went to Canada to take up immigrant status there either felt they could not get "justice" from their draft board or were not prepared to spend a term in prison because they could not meet the religious test or claim objection to all war.[1]

What Is Amnesty?

The word "amnesty" comes to us from ancient Greek, where it meant "oblivion" or "not remembering." It was an intentional overlooking of an offense. Today it means

[1] John M. Swomley, Jr., "Draft Exiles in Canada," *Christian Century*, October 30, 1968.

"a general overlooking or pardon of past offenses by the ruling authority."[2] It differs from a typical pardon in that it involves a whole class of offenders rather than one or a few individuals. It may result in the commutation of sentences of those already convicted, as well as a blanket pardon for those who have not been brought to trial.

The United States Constitution gives the President "power to grant reprieves and pardons for offenses against the United States, except in cases of impeachment." The framers of the Constitution borrowed the idea from England, for this has been firmly imbedded in Anglo-Saxon law for centuries. Amnesties may also be declared by act of Congress, but the traditional and most expedient is by presidential proclamation.

The first recorded amnesty was in about 40 B.C., when Thrasybulus in Athens forbade any additional punishment of citizens for their past political acts and exacted an oath of amnesty so as to eliminate civil strife from legal memory.

There have been a number of amnesties in French history. Probably the most famous was the Edict of Nantes, a proclamation issued by Henry IV in 1598 that put an end to persecution and gave legal status and religious liberty to the Huguenots or Protestants. Napoleon's imperial decree of 1802 provided amnesty; so also were there amnesties after the civil disturbances of 1871 and the Paris Commune.

In English history the best-known amnesties were those after the Civil War in 1651, one proclaimed by Charles II in 1660, and the amnesty of 1903 to the Boers in South Africa.

There have been a number of amnesties following wars granted both to enemies and to a nation's own citizens. For example, France, Norway, Germany, Belgium, Japan, and the Netherlands granted amnesties for persons

[2] The Oxford English Dictionary.

engaged in compromising activities during the Second
World War.

George Washington on July 10, 1795, granted "a full,
free and entire pardon" to those involved in an insurrection in Pennsylvania against the United States. In explaining this to Congress he said:

> For though I shall always think it a sacred duty to ex-
> ercise with firmness and energy the constitutional
> powers with which I am vested, yet it appears to me
> no less consistent with the public good than it is with
> my personal feelings to mingle in the operations of
> Government every degree of moderation and tenderness
> which the national justice, dignity and safety may
> permit.

John Adams in May 1800 granted an amnesty for another "wicked and treasonable insurrection" in Pennsylvania that occurred a year earlier. James Madison also
proclaimed in 1815 "a free and full pardon of all offenses
. . . touching the revenue trade and navigation" in the
vicinity of New Orleans.

During the Civil War, Abraham Lincoln on December 8, 1863, offered a full pardon to those who "participated in the existing rebellion" who were prepared to
take a prescribed oath. Certain classes of persons were ex-
cepted. Lincoln also directed the War Department in
February 1864 to see to it "that the sentence of all deserters who have been condemned by court-martial to
death . . . be mitigated to imprisonment during the
war. . . ."

Following the Civil War Andrew Johnson proclaimed
a partial amnesty in 1865, another in 1867, and on July
4, 1868 a full pardon to everyone who "participated in
the late insurrection of rebellion" except for those under
indictment for treason or other felony. Finally, on December 25, 1868, he granted a Christmas "amnesty for
the offense of treason against the United States. . . ."

President Johnson's first proclamation states his reasons for pardon. He believed that:

> a retaliatory or vindictive policy, attended by unnecessary disqualification, pains, penalties, confiscations and disfranchisements, now as always could only tend to hinder reconciliation among the people and national restoration, while it must seriously embarrass, obstruct and repress popular energies and national industry and enterprise. . . .

There were no general amnesties following World Wars I and II. Woodrow Wilson, who was vindictive and considered critics of the war as traitors, refused his own attorney general's recommendation for commuting the sentence of the sixty-five-year-old Eugene Debs. Only after the Senate ratified the peace treaty with Germany did President Warren G. Harding release Debs from prison. On December 23, 1921 Harding announced that Debs and twenty-three other political prisoners would be released on Christmas Day. He did not, however, grant the general amnesty for which hundreds of thousands of Americans had asked.

Calvin Coolidge on March 5, 1924 issued an amnesty to those who had deserted from the military or naval forces between November 11, 1918 (Armistice) and the technical ending of the war. Franklin D. Roosevelt issued a Christmas Amnesty Proclamation in 1933 for persons convicted under the Espionage Act and conspiracy to violate Section Five of the Selective Service Act of 1917 and who paid the penalty the law imposed on them. This was a limited amnesty, since it did not pardon fugitives from justice or men sentenced by military courts. It was in these military courts that the best-known conscientious objectors or absolutists were sentenced.

Following World War II President Harry Truman was under great public pressure to grant an amnesty. He appeared to comply with the demand while avoiding it, by appointing an amnesty board of persons hostile to the idea. On their recommendation, 1523 of the 15,805 who had been convicted under the Selective Service Act were pardoned on December 23, 1947. In general, Truman's phony 1947 amnesty excluded Jehovah's Witnesses, political prisoners, and willful violators of the law who had walked out of the conscientious objector camps. Earlier, on Christmas in 1945, Truman granted full pardon to all former prisoners who had served honorably in the Armed Forces for at least a year. Former criminals were thus pardoned, but men whose convictions led them to violate the Selective Service Act were not.

Why Amnesty Now?

Amnesty is generally granted only for political or military offenses against a state. In each of the presidential pardons prior to World War I described above, the offense involved actual insurrection or war against the United States, which the Constitution calls treason. The men in prison or exile today are not charged with military action or insurrection against the United States. Their offense is either that they valued freedom too highly to submit to conscription or that their consciences did not permit them to prepare for, participate in, or even indirectly contribute to the war in Vietnam. Americans may rightly differ about the wisdom of their actions, but it is quite clear that their acts in no way involved the destruction of life or armed revolt against the United States. If Presidents could grant amnesty for the more serious offense of armed insurrection, why should amnesty be withheld from men who were apparently motivated by humanitarian opposition to war?

One major purpose of amnesty is to heal the wounds and divisions of war, to restore confidence in government on the part of those who have been alienated by the war. It is obvious that former Presidents of the United States had such healing in mind after the armed uprisings in the

1790s and the 1800s. The division in the United States today is just as real. It is not based on sectional grievances, nor is it confined to any part of the United States. Rather it is chiefly defined by age—draft age—or by the kind of idealism that expected the United States to behave differently from other nations. Still, the fact must be acknowledged that the United States' war in Vietnam has been opposed and condemned by many highly respected citizens in all walks of life and of all age groups. Whatever one may think of the phrase "credibility gap," it does express a loss of faith in their government by thousands of Americans. An act of amnesty now would go a long way toward restoration of that faith.

Another purpose of amnesty is to bring back into useful citizenship those who are now barred by legal restrictions. Many of those sentenced for draft resistance as unrecognized conscientious objectors will be barred by state laws from voting or running for public office. Others may find it difficult or impossible to enter certain professions, such as law, with a technical felony on their records. Needless to say, the thousands in exile from the United States would be valuable assets to American society were they able to return with freedom from imprisonment.

Amnesty would also put an end to the emotional and economic suffering of the families of those who resisted the draft. These families, together with their friends and neighbors, represent a larger segment of the American community than the draft resisters themselves, and in varying degrees are affected by the imprisonment or exile of persons they have known intimately as children and young adults. The renewal or increase of their confidence in government would be a by-product of amnesty.

Amnesty by any government is generally a sign of governmental strength and always a sign of magnanimity. *The Encyclopedia of the Social Sciences* says that "the granting of an amnesty is nearly always a sign that the government feels its position secure . . . and that hav-

ing disarmed its enemy in the field, it may proceed with
the attempt at disarming hatred and resentment by an
act of grace."[3] Since modern limited wars seldom end
in victory for either side, amnesty for those who refused
to participate in the war would be an even greater indi-
cation of the security of the government that proclaims
it.

Prisoners of war are sometimes freed during war and
almost always at the end of the war in spite of their direct
participation on the other side. There is an implied recognition that they did what duty and citizenship required
of them. Governments ought similarly to recognize the
devotion of some of their own citizens to a higher moral
duty or citizenship that makes them disobey an order
for induction or the draft law itself. Amnesty for violators of the draft law would in effect be an acknowledgment by government that in the stress and strain of war
some laws may have been administered too narrowly,
and some boards may have been too warminded to recognize conscientious objectors. It would be an act of humility
and magnanimity to indicate that no government or law
is so perfect that conscious or unconscious injustice cannot take place in its administration.

The Social Meaning of Amnesty

Millions of people in the United States and in other
countries have been taught that forgiveness is a virtue.
Most religions encourage their adherents to forgive those
who seek forgiveness. Some proclaim the importance of
forgiving those who wrong you even if they seek no reconciliation. It is assumed in this latter case that the act
of forgiving is an expression of no malice by the recipient
of the wrongdoing and even a gesture of acceptance of
the wrongdoer in spite of the unacceptability of his deed.

[3] Vol. II, page 36. New York: Macmillan, 1930.

Amnesty is the political equivalent of such a religious act.

To those who understand that God is love there can be no human act or alienation that is unforgivable. Persons alienated from their fellow men and therefore from God are brought back from a fractured relationship into genuine community by the knowledge or faith that they are accepted in spite of any apparent unworthiness. It is the initiative taken by the person wronged that is always to some degree unexpected and therefore the more impressive. Christian theology holds that God's forgiveness is always present for the wrongdoer. Only when persons show by their own refusal to forgive their fellows that they have no faith in forgiveness are they denied forgiveness by their own rejection of it.

In political terms a government that cannot bring itself to proclaim amnesty for political offenses indicates its hardness of heart, its willingness to keep the nation divided in order to vindicate its own partisan judgments. By its own lack of faith in the process of forgiveness it prolongs and perhaps intensifies the resentment of those who could not cooperate with the war in the first place. It is willing to risk a buildup of hostility, perhaps even continued violence, rather than take the step of initiating reconciliation. Only the government can take such a step because it alone speaks for the whole nation and because it has prosecuted or driven into exile, or stands ready to punish, those who are politically dissident.

Amnesty is an act of grace—clemency—by the President, restoring offenders against the draft or the war to their position in society without any legal stigma or impediments. It does not mean that their position has been vindicated. From the government's point of view it is forgiveness for an act that is still legally wrong.

Amnesty changes legal status only. It does not change society's social approval or disapproval of what happened. To some Americans the offenders against the draft are heroes, and to others, villains. Those who view them as heroes will be less able to view amnestied men as martyrs, and those who view them as villains may take some satisfaction from that fact, for they are less likely to be symbols of continuing opposition to government if they are amnestied. On the other hand, amnesty does not silence opponents of conscription or war; neither are they silenced now by penalties already imposed or about to be imposed. For many Americans, Eugene Debs' imprisonment during World War I was a greater reminder of the injustice of government than anything he would have said, had he been free to speak on the outside. Similarly, the fact of "good" men in prison today is a constant prod to many Americans who generally do not have friends or acquaintances in prison.

Americans generally have frowned upon imprisoning men for political reasons. Although violation of a conscription law is technically the same as violating any other law, it is not assumed by most Americans to involve the violation of other persons or personal property that is implied by assault or theft. Breaking the draft law is a political offense in that it challenges a political course of action that the government can implement only by taking away a man's freedom. Those who resist conscription at whatever level are political offenders and constitute the largest category of political prisoners in the United States today. In a sense the test of how democratic any government is depends upon the number of political prisoners it keeps behind bars. In the eyes of millions of people around the world the United States' reputation as a democracy would be enhanced rather than diminished by amnesty for those who are in prison for draft-related offenses as well as for those in exile or still awaiting trial.

There is probably very little public opposition to amnesty for those who resisted the draft by nonviolent means. After all, three-fourths of the American people have, at the time of this writing, according to public-opinion polls, registered their opposition to continuing the war in Vietnam. It is without doubt the most unpopular war in American history. The crucial questions about amnesty, therefore, relate to activity that is harder to explain than mere draft resistance. Such activity ranges from the destruction of government property such as draft board files or offices, to desertion and war-related acts of violence. These actions may seem extreme to those devoted to domestic tranquillity. Yet they can be understood as the result of frustration at the failure of people in general and government leaders in particular to respond to massive and orderly dissent. The nation engages in war not only against combatants but against noncombatant women and children. To some of those sensitive to this injustice, the destruction of property, desertion, and other extreme acts are ways of political opposition. It may be difficult to separate these politically inspired offenses from typical crimes, yet this is essential if there is a governmental intent to wipe the political slate clean and to seek to blot out the divisions and resentments caused by the war. It is assumed that totalitarian nations have political prisoners because freedom-loving or peace-loving people will oppose the regime. One assumption about democratic states is that there are no political prisoners because men are free to say "no" to their governments. The fact that men are not free to say "no" to conscription or to war and thus feel it necessary to resort to extreme acts puts any free society to the test. General amnesty is the way a free society can proclaim its acceptance of political offenders who are no longer "dangerous" to governments because the war that caused or precipitated their actions has been ended. They are not offenders against society or threats to the life and property of their fellow citizens. Their offense was war-inspired and war-directed. Therefore, there is no reason for their continued alienation, unless the nation continues to see itself as a largely war-motivated entity or as justified in punishing its conscientious protesters.

Ernest van den Haag

Ernest van den Haag is Adjunct Professor of Social Philosophy at New York University and lectures in sociology and psychology, Graduate and Undergraduate Faculties of the New School for Social Research. His many books include The Jewish Mystique, Passion and Social Constraint, *and* Education as an Industry. *He has also written for the journals* Partisan Review, Encounter, Transaction, National Review, Esquire, Modern Age, *and many others.*

Deserters, draft resisters, and men who went into exile to avoid the draft are three different classes of people. From a legal viewpoint, a deserter is under military law. He should be treated somewhat differently depending on whether he deserted in battle as a matter of cowardice or whether he deserted as a matter of conviction. I think the three categories of people should be treated differently. I think too that there is a case for regarding them as falling into morally different classes.

Among the draft resisters are people who feel they have a fundamental objection to war and have not been able to persuade the courts to classify them as conscientious objectors. There are other people who resisted the draft because it was inconvenient or unpleasant for them.

We must make these distinctions; but having made

them, I think all of these people should be punished. They should be punished because they took it upon themselves to exempt themselves from a duty that other people had to undergo. It seems to me that if they do not suffer for their failure to perform the duty that falls on all citizens of their age, they are in effect telling the others that they were fools to submit.

As for the punishment, I am not fully informed about the present law, but I think it makes reasonable provisions. Each case, of course, has to be evaluated separately. Suppose, for instance, that a man went to Canada illegally to avoid the draft. Obviously, as long as he is in Canada, he will not be punished. If he decides to return, I think he should be aware that he will be punished. Now, if the court is convinced that he sincerely repents his previous acts, and if he is willing to make reparation as imposed by the court, I should, if I were the judge, be willing to inflict fairly mild punishment. In effect, what I would want to do is make sure that he did not get any advantage from his evasion of the draft, that he is in no way better off than those who performed their duty. But, as I said, if he has sincerely repented, I would not want to be vindictive. On the other hand, if he maintains that he has a right to flee to Canada, then I would indeed assert the law in its full gravity. Any time that he returns to the United States unrepentant, I would certainly want to inflict that punishment on him that the law provides.

Given the events of the past five to seven years, there are many factors that help to explain the refusal of men to go into the service, but there are none to justify it. For instance, if I were a judge, I would keep in mind that many of these young people were encouraged to evade the draft by older people. These men were, in a sense, seduced by people who told them that they had no obligation to serve in this war and, in some cases, that it was their moral duty not to serve. I would regard this as a mitigating circumstance. If a young man came back

from Canada and convinced me that at the time he sincerely believed it was his duty to go to Canada, or at
least not his duty to serve in the Army, and if he sincerely
convinced me that he now recognized that his unlawful
act could not be justified and he is willing to make reparation, I would hold this as an extenuating circumstance.
But I would always want to make the draft evader suffer
a service or activity equivalent to what he has avoided to
make sure he got no advantage from his evasion. The
time he spent in Canada was probably not very pleasant
and, in a sense, he punished himself, but that is his business.

Legal punishment has a variety of functions: to protect society, to deter others from doing what the punished
person did, to try to rehabilitate him, to do justice. If
the act is not punished, we weaken this proclamation
of the law. To put it in practical terms, if a man who
avoided the draft unlawfully is not punished, what we
are saying in effect is that it is acceptable for people to
break the law under certain circumstances. Thus we
discriminate against those who naïvely believed in a law
that compelled them to be drafted. Why discriminate
against them?

I have heard resisters say, "If I am going to be punished, how about punishing as well those who helped
bring us into this war?" There are two precedents for
the punishment of so-called war criminals, Nuremburg
and Yamashita. I do not believe either of them corresponds to our tradition of law. In Nuremburg, we punished people for something that has never been established
to be a crime, that is, waging of aggressive war. Let me
point out that no generals were punished in Nuremburg.
The people punished were political leaders; and it was
not established either in German or in any other law
that the acts of these political leaders did in any way
make punishable the acts of those who simply followed
them, unless the acts of the followers themselves were

contrary to generally recognized norms of international law. In other words, a German general was not punished for following Hitler's orders and attacking France. He was punished if, in attacking France, he also overstepped the normal boundaries of warfare. But that is a different matter. Nor was any German soldier accused of having allowed himself to be drafted or of volunteering merely because the war was regarded as aggressive. Nuremburg, then, as a precedent, is somewhat irrelevant to the issue involved here. And even if the political leaders of America were punishable, that would be somewhat irrelevant to the punishment of draft evasion.

Since Nuremburg, a number of other wars have been fought: Korea, the attack of England, France, and Israel against Egypt, the Sino-Indian War, the Pakistan-Indian War, and so on. As far as I know, no one has been punished, because people have realized that Nuremburg is not a precedent at all. It amounted to the victors executing the leaders of the defeated. Now America has not been defeated in Vietnam. And I doubt that the North Vietnamese will ever be able to set up a tribunal to punish Americans.

I also think the Yamashita precedent was terrible and should be excluded from international law. What happened was that our courts held that even though there had been no evidence whatsoever that General Yamashita was aware of atrocities committed by his subordinates, even though there was no evidence whatsoever that he could have prevented them, he was held responsible for what people did without his knowledge, wish, or control. I think that goes too far because it means that if a policeman in New York City murders someone, the mayor will be responsible for it, even though the mayor neither ordered him to do so, nor knew about it, nor had any way of preventing it. I think the legal principle should be that a man is held responsible either for what he knowingly permitted, or for what, with reasonable care, he could have prevented but failed to prevent. He should not be held responsible for something that was done without his knowledge and which he had no way of controlling.

Therefore, it does not seem to me that American generals should be held responsible for any atrocities being committed in Vietnam, unless it can plausibly be established that they consented to these atrocities, instigated them, tolerated them, or failed to take reasonable precautions to prevent them. That is as far as their responsibility should go.

As for the draftable young man, American law permits conscientious objection, by which we mean that a person who can show that he holds deeply and strongly a conviction that he cannot use violence is exempted from the duty to fight. No law, including American law, however, can ever condone civil disobedience.[1] Civil disobedience means basically, not that a person claims an exemption for himself that the law can, and in America does grant, but that the person says that he's better than the government and the majority that supports it. Now I do not deny that morally this can sometimes be quite justifiable. I am denying, however, that this can ever be legally permitted. Civil disobedience means knowingly to disobey the law. No government that makes laws can permit their defiance. Hence, punishment is necessary in civil disobedience. It seems clear to me that anyone who engages in civil disobedience is saying, "For the sake of my moral convictions, I am willing to accept the punishment the law metes out to me. I am doing it deliberately to persuade my fellow citizens to change the law and I am willing to make sacrifices."

After the war is over, shall we grant amnesties? My answer is no. The punishment should remain the same. Otherwise, we make suckers out of those people who

[1] See his new book, *On Political Violence and On Civil Disobedience*, New York, Harper & Row Publishers, Inc., 1972.

obeyed the law. I am not denying that some of the people who engaged in civil disobedience did so convinced of the morality of their act. I am not taking a position on whether these acts are moral. I am simply saying that the government that makes a law cannot say that this law can be defied by impunity by anyone who thinks it wrong. The law would no longer be a law, it would become an option, a suggestion, that you can either accept or not. It is the nature of laws that disobedience must be excluded.

Nor do I think that amnesty would be an act of healing. Those who have been willing to defy the law should be willing to suffer the punishment. I would, however, make some distinctions. There are those who engaged in civil disobedience in the United States in the hope of persuading the majority to change the law. They refused to be drafted. These people are already in prison or are in the process of being put in prison. They have been willing to accept punishment for their convictions. I think they are in many cases morally admirable, however much I may disagree with them. I would certainly consider what can be done to shorten their period of imprisonment by amnesty or by any other way, or by limiting their time in service. I would have to consider the matter in more detail, but I think these are people who deserve some moral respect. I do not think the government would suffer any damage by amnestying them in some form or other at some later time.

The case of those who fled to Canada is very different. They avoided any punishment. They were simply saying, for moral or other reasons, that they would not be drafted. If they were to return they would have to accept punishment. I would not grant them amnesty.

Some individuals feel there is a higher law, over and above the positive law. St. Thomas More died proclaiming himself the King's good servant but God's first. He felt that beyond the King's rule there was a higher law. Many people today have felt that way. The troublesome thing about this is that no one has been able to figure out when the higher law should take precedence over the positive law. So it is really left to the individual.

Now, if a government makes a positive law, then that government must enforce that positive law. You and I may regard it as wrong. I might indeed be willing to defy the law. In a dictatorship I would find it very easy to do so because I would think that I had no part in making it and had no other way of opposing it except by not obeying it. In a democracy, it is somewhat more complicated because in effect what I am doing by not obeying the law is defying the majority in favor of a minority view. And I am not in favor of a minority dictatorship. But that is what it would come to if I were to win, because my view is opposed to the majority of the lawmakers who are in turn elected by the majority of the public.

Yet even a majority law can be morally wrong. You have to consider all the consequences of your resistance. But there are cases where you might want to disobey. What I cannot see is the demand for amnesty. The men who went to Canada and avoided the draft would be right in demanding amnesty only if they are aware of this implication. They are saying to the American government, "Please repent, you were wrong, I was right." But I don't think the American people feel that way.

As we can see now, I feel that we made a military and political mistake in going into the war in Vietnam—a mistake made by President Kennedy and followed by President Johnson, and which Mr. Nixon is trying to repair as best he can. Now this reparation of the mistake takes a while and it involves further sacrifices. I think that in the nature of the matter, it should not be up to the individual citizen, particularly once he sees that the mistake is being repaired, to resist his legal duty.

I would agree, however, with the war resister who asked, "Would Willy Brandt have demanded amnesty of the Nazi regime?" The point is valid. Can a war resister demand amnesty from a regime that feels what it did was not wrong? The demand for amnesty really must be based on saying to the American government that it had no right to demand from the resister the service that he denied it. If that is not the case then the resister must admit he made a mistake. "I may have been morally right but I still should not have resisted. I am now willing to perform the service I wasn't willing to perform then and to accept the punishment."

A demand for amnesty is not justifiable unless you assume the American people are willing to say that we should never have asked for the performance of this service, that the United States was morally wrong. We made a mistake in Vietnam in good faith but I would not be willing to say that we were morally wrong. And we are doing the best we can to repair this mistake. But it is not up to individual citizens to resist. If every individual served in war only when he wanted to we would lose all wars.

WILLIAM WORTHY

William Worthy has been a correspondent for the Baltimore Afro-American *since 1951. A former Nieman Fellow and Ford Foundation Fellow in African Studies, he has also served as a Special CBS correspondent in the USSR, China, and Africa. In the past he has challenged the State Department's rigid bans on travel to China, Cuba, and North Vietnam.*

After the Vietnam war is ended, amnesty may be considerably more difficult to extract from the government than it was after World War II. This is true because the final stages of the war itself and the termination of the war will throw the country into turmoil. I've felt ever since the mid-sixties that there will be no graceful exit by the United States from Vietnam, given the chauvinistic mentality of many policymakers, and the terror that they must feel at the domestic and international consequences of a defeat for the United States in Vietnam. Americans lack the imperial finesse of the British, who usually were astute enough to pull out of a colony in time to save the furniture.

One domestic consequence would of course be the election defeat of the incumbent President, because there is going to be no way for Nixon (if Nixon is the one in office when the war ends) or any other President to explain away the serious defeat that the United States has suffered at the hands of a tiny, weak nation. On top of that, the extreme right-wingers in this country, with tremendous sums of money behind them, in alliance with military and CIA elements that verge on the fanatic, would be out for scapegoats, gunning for those in this country to whom they could attribute the so-called "loss" of Vietnam or the "loss" of Indochina. Certain people were persecuted after the Communist victory in China in 1949 for having contributed to the so-called "loss" of China. The scapegoats included diplomats and people on policymaking levels in government.

This time, I think the hysteria is going to take violent forms. There was practically no violence during the period of McCarthyism, which ran roughly from 1950 until the mid-1950s. I don't think we are going to be that lucky a second time. I think that whatever the new McCarthyism is called, it will have a violent aspect to it, perhaps an overwhelmingly violent aspect. Therefore, with these domestic complications, plus the enormous loss of face in Asia, Africa, and Latin America that a defeat of the United States will automatically entail, this country, both internally and externally, is going to be in an extremely defensive, touchy, irritable, angry, bitter, exasperated, frustrated mood.

Amnesty implies charity and forgiveness, and I don't think there is going to be much of a forgiving, forgetting, compassionate spirit in the country—even less so if we are by then plunged into a very serious depression. So I think amnesty will be a sort of tangential issue; it will be an issue pushed by small elements of the population. I don't expect it to gather the kind of support that it gathered after World War II, when President Truman was forced by a relatively small but prestigious amnesty committee to grant at least some degree of amnesty. It is going to be a much more complex and probably less hopeful picture after the end of the war in Indochina.

This has special meaning for black people. Several years ago I wrote:

> Afro-American resistance to the draft is widespread. If you visited the Pitkin Avenue draft board in Brownsville in 1967, the heart of the black ghetto in Brooklyn, you would have seen sheet upon sheet of names mounting into hundreds marked delinquent. The situation described is not unique. Local draft board 16, which covers a part of Harlem, recently had a list of 600 cases, most of them Negro, a few Puerto Rican. It is doubtful that many of them will be inducted or prosecuted, and without exception these so-called delinquents have the blessing of the surrounding community.[1]

Why are there so many black delinquents in terms of the draft? A great many black people always answered the call when America went to war. But there is also a parallel tradition of skepticism, if not opposition, to American wars in which there has been a racial angle. In that same *Esquire* article, I quote the Reverend Henry M. Turner of Georgia, in 1900, at the time of the Boxer Rebellion, saying that any Negro who put a gun on his shoulder to go fight China "should find the bottom of the ocean before he got there." The point is that the precedent for Negro opposition to a war involving the United States is more than a hundred years old. Back in Abolitionist period, Frederick Douglass attacked the "disgraceful, cruel and iniquitous Mexican War" and, like today's black militants, demanded the recall of our forces. Fifty years later, during the Spanish-American War, the Richmond *Planet,* a Negro newspaper, declared that the American Negro cannot become "the ally of imperialism without enslaving his own race."

[1] Quoted from my article, "The American Negro Is Dead," *Esquire,* November 1967, in which I discussed the changing posture and possibly changing psychology of a good many black people in America.

The average ghetto kid would know nothing about conscientious objection—even the term, let alone how to go about applying for C.O. status. It's one thing for an educated, articulate minister to make a speech; it's quite another thing for his words to permeate in any practical way a disadvantaged, disorganized, disoriented neighborhood. There's a tremendous gap between platform rhetoric (however sincere) and neighborhood follow-up. I think that people in almost any circumstance have a sense of when they are being used, exploited, and manipulated by their rulers. It's a very understandable reaction just to absent oneself from a conscription process that is formidable, time-consuming, and hostile. There is no gracious, cordial atmosphere at any draft board. It's government at its worst and its most arbitrary. I think it was Shelley who spoke about the crime of murder in a uniform possibly being the worst crime of all, because of the element of servitude in the soldier committing the murder.

So it's difficult for those of us who have had some educational benefits, particularly beyond the high school level, to put ourselves in the role of an eighteen-year-old dropout who is faced with the reality of being ordered to fight and kill people who have never done him any harm whatsoever. He couldn't even locate their native country on a map if he were asked to. Since birth, the ghetto kid has been conditioned to distrust all of the white repressive governmental apparatus. Such a person could almost be expected in many, many cases to take the easy way out— just not to show up for a physical exam, and not to show up for induction, and just to stay on the lam. He would at least know that the FBI or U.S. marshals coming to seek him out would usually get no cooperation from his neighbors.

There is an ancient tradition in any kind of ghetto in which the authority figure meets silence or doubletalk or evasiveness. There is a wonderful passage in *Porgy and Bess* illustrating this point. Catfish Row is in Charleston,

South Carolina. A white man comes there and asks for Porgy. *No one* knows Porgy. Of course, Porgy has lived there all his life, but nobody knows him. Then this man turns to go away and says, "Well I'm sorry, because I came to tell Porgy I had a job for him." "Oh, you mean *Porgy*," and they pronounced his name slightly differently, just as if they had misunderstood the man in the first place. They immediately became open and revealed Porgy's whereabouts.

Another story from *Porgy and Bess* concerns a resident (if you can use such a high-flown word for Catfish Row) who has disappeared for quite some time and finally comes home. Everybody comes around to ask him where he has been, and he says, in a sort of humorous, semiresigned mood, "Oh, the white man done put me in jail, and the white man done let me out, and I *still* don't know what it is all about. That's the way it is."

This kind of knowledge of the arbitrariness of the U.S. judicial system, particularly vis-à-vis minority groups, this very keen awareness would certainly teach any draft delinquent to stay out of sight and in hiding just as long as he possibly can. I'm quite sure that there are FBI men (although I haven't taken any polls!), with families and the normal instinct to keep on living, who wouldn't be too zealous these days about going into a ghetto and knocking themselves out to find some draft delinquents, because it could be distinctly unhealthy.

In fact, there have been several attacks on FBI agents that must give the rest of them pause—one in Brooklyn, I'd say roughly around 1968, maybe earlier. FBI agents went to look for an Army deserter and they found him at home. They were taking him out of the building when his sister leaned out of the window and called to some neighbor. I think she said, "Get the brothers!" There was quite an outpouring of neighborhood people. I don't know if any of the agents were actually hurt, but they certainly had to flee for their safety. This of course was regarded

by Mr. Hoover as an intolerable affront to his beloved
Bureau, and the next day he sent a hundred FBI agents
armed with shotguns into that neighborhood, not only to
find the Army deserter, who I think had gotten away
in the confusion, but also to find those who had come
to his defense.

A similar thing happened in Wilmington, Delaware in
1968 or 1969. Some passersby, seeing a guy in the custody
of federal agents, came to his defense and freed him. Some
of them were caught, and I believe they ended up with
severe federal sentences. My point is that certain FBI
agents know the mood of minority groups today. It's not
a passive mood, certainly for those in the younger age
brackets. It's a mood of reckless defiance, resistance, anger,
and indignation. It isn't like the old days when any white
officer, all by himself, could go into a ghetto and do whatever he wanted to and emerge unscathed. That period
has passed.

The white draft resister, certainly in most cases, can
count on his parents coming to court, providing legal
counsel, and standing by him, even if they don't agree
with his stand. It's a pretty sick parent who would want
to see his or her child go to jail, no matter how hawkish
they might be about the war. With a kid from Harlem
there would not be the problem of parents being hawkish,
because ghetto hawkishness is very, very rare. But
there is a problem of his parents being able to take a day
off from work and to afford legal counsel, and of knowing
where to turn to get unpaid legal counsel, whether by an
individual attorney or by some committee, such as the
Central Committee for Conscientious Objectors.

So who is going to defend you in court? In terms of
getting out of the country—to Canada or to Europe—
who is going to pay the bills for travel, and how are you
going to support yourself once there? All these questions,
which also might be in the minds of quite a few white
draft resisters, would be multiplied if you come from a

disadvantaged ethnic or racial group. You know that Canada is a white country—with all that that connotes. Sweden is a white country. How do you get along with the language barrier? All these factors would be multiplied if you were not white.

Walter Collins came to me several months ago and we talked about his case. It's a situation where a black man was victimized through the discriminating draft apparatus for his political and socioeconomic activity among poor people in the South. He worked for the Southern Conference Educational Fund, and he has been organizing in the South. His draft board didn't like this.

The draft board was unquestionably illegally constituted. The Selective Service regulations call for all draft board members everywhere to live within the county, as I recall, and I think one or two of them are supposed actually to live within the district of the draftees over whom they have jurisdiction. This requirement was clearly violated, and yet the U. S. Supreme Court in a decision (or an "undecision" quite typical of the Court's behavior in ducking the whole war issue) refused to review his appeal. This was a clear violation of the residential requirements cited by his attorneys in their briefs. I believe that Justice Douglas objected very strenuously when the Court declined to review the Collins case.

The U. S. Supreme Court is a very political institution, and the Justices knew very well that they would be opening up a hornet's nest if they reviewed his case and ruled that his draft board was unconstitutionally constituted. Then every person similarly situated in the South (and the North too) could immediately challenge his draft classification. Those already in the Army who had been illegally drafted by these draft board members who didn't meet the residential requirements could apply for writs of habeas corpus to get out of the Army. Those eight Justices were not going to bring the wrath of the military

and the Executive branch down on their heads by so ruling. So they ducked the issue.

This has been the history of the Supreme Court in
every imperialistic war in which the United States has
been involved. When the anti-imperialists, such as Jane
Addams, Mark Twain, and others at the turn of the century, challenged the extraterritorial issue in the Philippines after the United States had wrested the Philippines
from Spain through a forced sale, the Supreme Court
came up with a weird series of decisions that upheld what
President McKinley was doing. This is the tradition of
the U. S. Supreme Court, and those eight men were not
about to change that tradition. So when he refused to
fight, Walter Collins was kidnapped and put in jail.

This is supposed to be an object lesson to people who
go around the South agitating for constitutional rights
and racial equality. Now the difference between Walter
and a lot of other people is that he was open about his
draft resistance. Others, as we said earlier, just do not
show up for physicals and do not show up for induc-
tions, or desert once they get in.

Unfortunately, I doubt that there will be much organized agitation by Walter's friends, neighbors, and as-
sociates. He is in a federal prison now. Whatever anti-
draft, antiwar activity there was in the heyday of SNCC
and CORE in the mid-1960s has just disappeared. There
has been a demoralization of people who used to belong
to those organizations. Many of them have dropped out,
taken jobs, and they rationalize, in one way or another,
their inactivity or much-reduced activity. There are just
not the organized forces to put up much of a fight for a
person like Walter.

The demand for amnesty will come largely from
Quaker circles, other religious pacifists, the Catholic peace
movement, and groups such as that. I don't expect much
of it to come from ghetto areas, where amnesty is not a
bread-and-butter issue. Walter Collins and others like

him are going to be out of sight and somewhat out of mind. This is the great tragedy of people who go to jail in this country. It is such a large country, there are so many issues, there are so many pressing problems, that going to jail almost seems to be a futile act in contemporary U.S. society. It does not stir the conscience of the country. It does not precipitate any wild agitation that disturbs the government or interferes with its ability to govern. It is like a pinprick, and I really have to question not the devoted and dedicated intentions of those who go to prison or into exile, but the practical impact that their sacrifice brings.

I should hasten to add that the Berrigan brothers are an exception, for a combination of factors. Their case has captured popular attention, and they will continue to be in the limelight. Their example will undoubtedly inspire many college students and many youth in general to step up the tempo of the resistance to the war, to refuse to be drafted, and possibly to go out and burn draft records.

The U.S. world empire is under a fundamental challenge all over the globe, on every continent, including Europe, and even within the United States. It may survive another decade, or another two or three decades. Of course there is no way of knowing exactly how long. The point is that those who really run this country, those who really pull the strings of power have their backs to the wall. The brutal, totalitarian, fascist things that have been done in Vietnam, at My Lai and elsewhere, are going to have their counterparts *inside* the United States as the youthful resistance and the racial resistance and the ethnic resistance and the rank-and-file working class and unemployed resistance increases. The brutality, the slaughter, the terrorization are going to come home, as the Weathermen say—even though their tiny underground group is not strong enough, all by itself, to "bring the war home" in any major sense.

But conditions brought about by this worldwide challenge to U.S. domination mean that there are going to be more Kent States, more Jackson States, and more shooting down of workers, such as took place in company towns and at the gates of Republic Steel in Chicago during the New Deal days. When "our" imperial system is on the ropes and in an increasingly desperate condition, I can't see it extending or bestowing amnesty on those who have said "no" to that system, by refusing to go out and get shot and killed in order to perpetuate that system.

It would be like expecting Mafia chieftains to be charitable and forgiving toward someone who had refused to do their bidding at a very crucial point when they were under siege. As others have pointed out elsewhere, imperialism really is a racket, and those who run it *do* have the mentality of racketeers. There can be a certain veneer of civility, of tolerance, of benevolence when there is no serious challenge to the racket. But the chips are down now. The peoples of the world are fighting for keeps—which means fighting to get the white West, and particularly the white United States, off their backs. Those who run the system have passed the point where they can maintain the pose of gentlemen, the pose of civilized people governing without open brutality and terrorization. So what the United States did in Mexico and Cuba at the turn of the century, in the Philippines with the water torture, in countless small "police actions" for all the two hundred years of this country's history—those things that were done *abroad* are now coming *home*.

No empire gives amnesty in a colony at the height of a movement for colonial independence. So no empire such as the United States is going to give amnesty to its protesting citizens at the height of agitation all over the world, including inside the United States, for the end to its domination of all parts of the world. This is a qualitatively different situation from the end of twentieth-century wars in the past, where the United States emerged *stronger* than it had been when the war began.

The United States began to cash in on the crumbling empires of Europe after World War I, and to a much, much greater extent after World War II. The British, French, and Dutch had been weakened seriously, and the United States slowly but surely picked up these remnants of empire in a pattern that is called neocolonialism.

It's a different ball game now. United States neocolonialism is being challenged in as fundamental a sense as when the Indians challenged British rule; the Indonesians, Dutch rule; and the Vietnamese, French rule. At the height of Gandhi's and Nehru's agitation for Indian freedom no one would have realistically expected the British to bestow amnesty on those hundreds of thousands of Indians who were in jail. The same was true when Sukarno and other Indonesian revolutionaries were challenging the Dutch and were being put in concentration camps on malaria-ridden islands. Nobody who was aware of the facts would have expected the Dutch at that point to give amnesty. Nor, short of mass pressure, which is hard to foresee, will the United States give amnesty to those who refused to do the bidding of the empire when the empire had its back to the wall in Indochina.

The Punished

MELDON ACHESON

Meldon Acheson. I grew up on a small farm in Iowa where life was a joyful gift that came from the earth and from the depths of my being. I studied astronomy in Arizona and became involved in several civil rights and peace groups. I was a Methodist then, and I applied for a C.O. classification. But Thoreau, Gandhi, Tolstoi, and Ammon Hennacy, among others, showed me I need not submit my life to the antilife perversions of authoritarian organizations such as governments and churches. So just before I graduated, I returned my draft card. I was arrested two years later and imprisoned on McNeil Island. I have a B.S. degree (which is just that: B.S.) and an E.C. (ex-con), the latter being the more valuable.

McNEIL

McNeil properly began when I was growing up in relative seclusion on a small Iowa farm. My parents were Methodists who took their faith seriously. We always said grace before meals and went to church on Sundays (unless we were snowed in or a cow was sick). When I was old enough, or perhaps before, we would read daily devotions from the Bible. My parents would tell me that if a person is going to call himself a Christian, he should live by the law and spirit of the New Testament: love God and neighbor. They often inveighed against the hypocrisy of a state and a church that called themselves Christian but practiced racism, war, and exploitation of their neighbor.

My parents also had a great respect for all life. We were close to each other, close to the animals and the crops, and close to the soil. I learned not only to be skeptical of institutions but also to love the common things of life.

It's not surprising, therefore, that I applied for an I-O (conscientious objector) classification when I registered for the draft at eighteen. (I had gotten in contact with several peace groups, and I was aware of and attracted to the position of "absolutist," but prison frightened me, having been brainwashed in school as everyone is that prison is the worst of all possible experiences.)

I was then attending the University of Iowa, which exempted me from their compulsory ROTC classes. At the end of the year, I transferred to the University of Arizona because the U of A had a good astronomy department and because I had itchy feet to travel. But the U of A wouldn't exempt me from ROTC. Being convinced then of the necessity and the goodness of "an education," I gave in. I learned why ROTC was called mickey-mouse, and I began to see that "an education" was not truly educative.

I was active in the Methodist Student Movement, and in my second year at Arizona I joined Tucson CORE. I spent more time with these groups and less with classes. I was learning the important things in those groups, the life things, which the U avoided teaching because they would disrupt the process, called education, of turning out morally immature but intellectually brilliant scientists and businessmen for the status quo. The libertarian religious atmosphere of my home life had saved me from believing the lies and delusive assumptions about this "great" nation that my textbooks and schooling had taught, and now I began to understand politically and economically what my parents had taught me religiously.

Shortly after I had applied for I-O classification, my draft board had written that I would be so classified when my student deferment was up. I was content with that for a time, but now I began to see that war, racism, poverty, and the draft were all inherent products of the authoritarian economic system of the nation. Graduation approached; I had decided not to go to grad school; and being drafted, even into alternative "service" (compulsory service is not service but slavery), repelled me. Dissent against the Vietnam war was mounting, and the so-called responsible officials were ignoring, rejecting, and trying to suppress it. The atrocity of the war called for an atrocious act of negation—obviously, words were incommensurate with the onslaught of the irresponsible state—and my inaction agonized me.

Three months before I was to graduate, Johnson announced that the military had been bombing North Vietnam for several months. I wrote him a letter of disaffiliation and enclosed my draft cards.

An under secretary sent them to the Iowa state draft board, and some officer returned them to me with a note saying he understood and he would direct my local board to classify me I-O. I rereturned the cards, saying he didn't understand, that I no longer cared to be a member of his little organization, and that I definitely wouldn't carry the membership cards.

A few months later, my local board sent a I-A classification card, which I duly returned.

I spent the summer with CORE in Louisiana, working on voter registration and suffering angry white fists and firebombs. I returned to Tucson to receive an induction order. I sent that back, too.

That spring I had met Amy, a girl of wild and radical ideas who was disgusted with the meaningless affluence and hypocrisy of white bourgeois existence. We met Ammon Hennacy that fall and turned on to Christian anarchism. Ammon had gotten married without the help of either church or state, and we suddenly realized we could do it, too. On Thanksgiving day, we did.

Amy was still in school, but she, too, was disillusioned with it. She began questioning and resisting some of the discriminatory rules the U had, and four days before the end of her second year, she was kicked out. We rejoiced, and prepared to go to Washington state to work with the Wobblies trying to organize the migrant fruit pickers.

Meanwhile, the draft board had decided to forget that I'd disobeyed an induction order, and they proceeded as though I'd appealed the I-A classification. The FBI investigated me; I refused to appear for a hearing on my old I-O claim; the state board decided that since I'd taken ROTC I was insincere and should be classified I-A. I got another I-A card and returned it.

When the fruit season was over, we bought two bicycles and bicycled to California to spend the winter with a friend. While there, we fasted for seven days, I refused a second induction order, and Amy got pregnant.

In the spring, we returned to Washington to attend Amy's sister's wedding. A week afterward, I was busted.

I pled guilty and was released on my own recognizance. During the summer, the Tacoma Friends befriended us. They helped get free prenatal care for Amy and a job for me.

August came, and with it came my sentencing date. Two and a half years had elapsed since I disaffiliated from the war machine. I walked into the courtroom with Amy and our unborn child. I sat down and smiled at the man hiding behind the heavy robes of a judge of men. He banged his little hammer and said, "Three years." *McNeil* began.

> The State has fatally interfered with my lawful business. . . . It has interrupted me and every man on his onward and upward path.   —Thoreau

There were only two other passengers on the boat the day I was released on parole. They had often talked with me when they came to the island grocery store where I worked. They had been sympathetic to draft resistance, and as we got on the boat they said they were glad I was getting out.

On the boat I sat by myself at a window and watched the waves and the overcast in silence. I was out. I would soon begin to worry about finding a job to bring in what little money my family would need, but for now my mind was languid.

Seventeen months before, when the boat was taking me the other way, I had been anxious about the future. How would I manage when accosted by homosexuals? How would I get along with the guards? Would Amy and our unborn child get along all right? I kept a smile on my face despite my inner fears; I watched the waves then as now. The boat had been crowded then, and the sun was shining. I could see the Olympic Mountains in the distance.

That was the last I saw of them for nearly two weeks. Along with seven or eight other prisoners, I was taken to the basement admitting room where we were given a number and had our personal belongings recorded and filed. Then we stripped and showered, had our body orifices examined for contraband, and were given coveralls and put in A&O—"fishtank." It was a basement dorm with forty or fifty double bunks spaced every two feet. Although there were only about a dozen of us, I felt crowded. Beyond a windowed partition was the day room, furnished with a few chairs, two tables, a TV, and several old Bibles and other books and magazines. On the other side of the day room, behind another windowed partition, was the guard's office.

The two weeks in A&O were mere wraiths of all I once recognized as life. The simple routine and the idleness lacked any of the continuities that characterize life, but neither were there any of the finalities by which one can recognize death. My mind and spirit were paralyzed by the shock of realizing that I was, and for three years would be, indefeasibly in prison.

The lack of continuity prevented the tedium that would occasionally oppress me later. But that austere basement with the high, barred windows and the guard always behind the glass of the small office gradually built up depression like the tobacco smoke that imperceptibly darkened the windows more each day. I began spending more time in reminiscence.

After sentencing, when I stood to be led off by the marshals, I had blown a kiss to Amy and to our unborn son. That image stayed with me the ten days I was alone in a Tacoma City Jail cell. I slept a lot. I was at peace. I felt freer than at any other time of my life. I lived each minute as it came.

Now McNeil Island Penitentiary was all around me like the forest around a somnambulist who has wandered away from camp and has suddenly awakened. Just as suddenly I wanted out; I wanted to be back with Amy; I felt I had become involved in more than I could cope with. Occasionally I felt panic. But I maintained an outward show of bravado. A bank vice president doing six months on embezzlement befriended me. His anxiety for his family and for their future welfare kept me from getting lost in self-pity and melancholy.

I never found out what A&O stood for. While I was there, I was given a physical examination; I was lectured by the chaplains and the culinary officer on the types of food each served up; and I was compulsorily entertained for two evenings by a disdainful youth from the mainland who showed a dozen civil defense movies and told us, "You've already begun your rehabilitation by watching these movies." I found later that someone had neglected to give me and several others certain aptitude tests and interviews that were supposedly mandatory for all new prisoners. A month before I was released, I was called in to take the tests. I was told they would help the education department plan a rehabilitation program for me.

Other cons in A&O told me that my number meant I would be sent directly to the prison farm without spending any time inside the main institution. Only minimum security inmates were sent to the farm, or camp—usually only those who had less than a year to go or who had less than year sentences. (It seemed to be a policy to send all draft violators to camp regardless of their sentences, though a few did spend several weeks inside.) Campers did most of the maintenance work around the island, and they did the farming that made the prison 90 percent self-sufficient. They got extra days good time.

The day the guard told the banker and me to get ready to go to camp was the first day in nearly a month that I felt really joyful. The sunlight on the walk and the buildings, on the trees and grass beyond the fence, even in the air, seemed an extension of the happiness I felt. We rode to the farm and got settled in our assigned bunks in the third-floor dormitory. The view of the Olympics silhouetted against the sunset and the sound of the fountain spraying into the pool beside the dorm ended the day in perfect keeping with the mood that had possessed me.

The camp was located three miles from the main joint. A three-story building contained administrative offices, a chow room, and six dorms that held around fifty men each. Near it was the vocational training building that contained a gym, library, fire station, maintenance shop, wood shop, hobby shop, and several classrooms. Around these buildings was a four- or five-acre lawn in which inmates could spend time when off work. On a hill west of the camp were several barns, and forest surrounded the camp on the other three sides.

Two days after I got to camp, Amy came to visit. She brought two friends who thought they could get the judge to change my sentence to probation. I told them they could go ahead if they wanted, but I was sure their efforts would be in vain. They left, and Amy and I spent the rest of the visit hoping they would be successful but telling each other we shouldn't hope.

After she left and I was back at camp, I suddenly felt hopelessly alone. My mind was engulfed in turmoil. The intensity of these attacks increased with each visit. Months later I recognized that the turmoil came from the conflict between my desire to see Amy again and my loathing of being torn from her again at the end of each visit. At one point I suggested she not visit any more, but we never acted on the suggestion. Other cons apparently felt the same thing because several refused to have visitors. It was too intimate a reminder of the outside.

Each inmate was allowed twelve people on his visiting and correspondence list. Immediate family members were approved at once, but others had to fill out a questionnaire and be approved by the caseworker. Each inmate could have three visits a month. Just before noon, a guard would call the numbers of all inmates who had visitors. The visiting room was in the basement of the administration building inside the fence. Campers were driven in from their jobs. Inmates had to strip and put on a new set of clothes in a side room before they could enter the visiting room. Once in, they were allowed one embrace with their wives before and after the visit. During the visit, they had to sit on one side of a small table and their visitors had to sit opposite them, no touching, no display of any books or documents, no holding of hands under the table. (After our son, Alazel, was born, Amy and I would push the table away to let him crawl and walk between us. Amy was nursing, an occurrence the guards couldn't cope with, and they rather obviously ignored us. We must have broken about every rule they had in that visiting room.) After the visit, the inmates were searched for contraband; they changed back into the first set of clothes; then they returned to their jobs. Visits could last from noon to 3:30 P.M.

Correspondence was limited to "a reasonable amount." According to one form, "It is asked that correspondent's (sic) do not exceed two (2) letters in any one day." Censorship was random, not every letter being read. I had several letters returned because I'd mentioned guards' names, but others in which I mentioned those same names went through. We could have subscriptions to various papers and magazines, and some of my friends got subscriptions to the *Friends Journal* and *The Peacemaker* for me.

All mail from unapproved sources went to the caseworker, who would decide whether to let it pass or not. The camp caseworker let all my unauthorized mail go through, as far as I could tell. I guess he liked me, as much as he could like anyone. Once he told me of all the C.O.s who had been at camp during World War II. Some had tried to get away with all they could, and these he despised. Others were what he called "good cons." He said he thought I was a "good con," and he began telling me about his life and his grandchildren. I feared I had made a mistake somewhere.

He was an old man who was easily excited, who had had several heart attacks, and who thought of and treated most convicts as scum—a suicidal combination of traits. He had begun his career as a guard, and he had worked his way up from obscurity to obscurity. He did what he could to obstruct the efforts toward freedom of all cons except those few he tolerated. It seemed the only ones he tolerated were white. He called me in one time to warn me that my closest friend, a black, was one of the worst cons around and that I should stay away from him: "I know. I've read his record." I thanked him for his concern and added, "You may have read his record, but you haven't read him."

The first three Saturdays at camp I was assigned to

go on the island garbage run, picking up garbage at the various residences on the island. Each Friday night the guard would post a list of those to go on the run, plus a list of alternates. There was a lot of maneuvering done during that night until 8:30 Saturday morning. It always seemed to be the last four alternates on the list who went on the runs.

I got to know the island fairly well on those runs: the road that burst suddenly from the forest and down the hill to the beach; the driveway under the pear tree, where we would fill our pockets with pears. And I got to know some intimate details about the guards and their families from observing their weekly garbage. One always had a case or two of empty beer bottles beside the garbage can. Another would have the garbage wrapped neatly in plastic sacks. Another would always have the can filled to over-flowing and looking as though the attic or basement had been cleaned to get its contents. Later I was able to compare the personalities of the people who produced the garbage with the impressions I got from that garbage. There was a remarkable correlation.

I was put on the orchard crew my first two months at the farm. The weather was warm and usually clear. From the orchard I could see the Olympics beyond the stretch of water separating the island from the mainland. I enjoyed picking the plums and apples. I could work alone most of the time, and I lost myself in the familiar feeling of oneness with nature, much as a child who has been away from home for a long time will clutch his favorite toy for hours on end.

We worked about six hours a day. We would load up on the crew truck at eight o'clock, but after being counted, riding the few miles to the orchard, and getting our picking gear together, it was eight-thirty or nine o'clock before we actually started working. Our lunch hour likewise was spread out to an hour and a half. We often stopped working around three-thirty. It wasn't especially hard work, although the week we were pulled out of the orchard to harvest the quarter-mile-long patch of potatoes was miserable: three days in the heat and dust; two in what seemed like near-freezing rain and mud.

After the four-thirty dorm count and supper, the evenings were free until the nine-thirty dorm count. While it remained warm, I usually went outside and sat on the grass by the fountain and pool and wrote voluminous letters to Amy. I said nothing of value in the four pages I covered with words each evening: It was therapeutic writing. In the middle of September I wrote Amy, "I just put down a bunch of words—like eating and eating and eating, unable to stop, because I really only want a glass of orange juice but don't have it. I want to hug you and kiss you and cry on your shoulder and snuggle up to you at night—but I can't, so I just write tons of words as an ineffective substitute." I was overstating everything, attaching important meanings to every triviality, and forcing one interpretation after another onto my prison experience as if by encompassing it in words I could somehow rid myself of it. In one letter after another I would tell Amy that I seemed to be adjusting, that the shock was wearing off, that I wasn't shook any more; only to follow each such letter with one detailing a new period of depression, anxiety, and nostalgia. As a result of this extreme introversion and intellectual hallucinating, I made few friends and missed or avoided many things that would have helped me do easier time.

There were several tame deer on the island that would come onto the camp grounds and eat food the inmates would offer them. A lot of raccoons came around, too, but they were more wary. I would often step outside at night to look at the stars. There were no bars, but we were expected to stay inside our dorms after lights-out at ten o'clock. Each dorm had a TV room that stayed open until midnight, and each inmate had a pair of earphones that he could plug in to one of the two jacks by his bed and listen to whatever radio station the (elected) inmate in charge of the radio room would select.

Once a week we could go to the commissary to buy fruit, ice cream, candy, cigarettes, toilet articles, and magazines. The limit was twenty dollars a month per inmate, purchases being deducted from the inmate's account. Inmates weren't allowed to have money in their possession (though there was a lot floating around). Cigarettes were the usual medium of exchange among the convicts.

During the first months I was approached by homosexuals. There are few true homosexuals in prison, but quite a number of what were called "ass-hole bandits." Several ingratiated themselves into a rather friendly relationship with me before ever mentioning anything about sex.

They would give me things—pens, razor blades, a pair of sneakers—which I unknowingly accepted. I returned the favors. We would occasionally talk and play chess. Then they began to approach me oftener and to waste my time with inane chatter, most of which was about sex. They made themselves increasingly more annoying.

I hesitated to cut them off. The summer before, I had become fascinated with all the talk about hippies—the idea of being gentle, of doing one's own thing. I was trying to project such an image, but it was entirely superficial. The result was that I failed to understand the situation I was now in, and I was too tolerant, letting them do their thing at the expense of mine. I began seeing potential threats, and I soon got very uptight about it.

I hung around with four Jehovah's Witnesses. Whenever I mentioned homosexuals to them, they would give me such angry advice as making a date with one of the homos and beating his head in with a pipe when he showed up. They also said that I should have nothing to do with the homos, that I shouldn't say so much as hello to them, and that I should never accept a gift from them. I rejected the advice along with the contemptuous attitude it belied, the situation continued as uptight as before, and I became suspicious of everything that was said to me and of everyone who looked at me. That only kept away those few people who genuinely wanted to help me.

After several weeks, a con who had just been transferred up from Lompoc took upon himself my "prison re-education." He talked with me a lot, telling me to get myself together, and forcing me to see that the way I was acting wasn't authentic. He told me I should get a circle of friends and stay within it. I should keep busy, and I should work out a schedule and follow it. That would make time go faster, and if someone came around I didn't want to talk to, I could use the schedule to excuse myself gracefully. He pointed out several musicians who would get together several times a week for a jazz session. There was a lapidary shop and a weight-lifting room. One could take up painting or knitting or some other hobby-shop activity. One could take correspondence courses or attend the school courses that teachers from the mainland would come over to teach. Many inmates studied law to fight their own cases. He said that prison was a waste unless I used the time to learn. He didn't mean the school classes but something deeper and more basic: Awareness. Dignity. Survival. I finally snapped to it, and that very night I told the homos not to speak to me again. They didn't.

Just at this time our baby was born. On the way in from the orchard one stormy noon, the orchard boss told me to see the camp caseworker's secretary, that "a little boy wants to talk to you." I guessed what that meant immediately: Only the day before I had written Amy teasing her about tomorrow being Friday the thirteenth and that both our families had a history of Friday-the-thirteenth births.

The secretary called the hospital and let me talk with Amy for three minutes. Sometime during the walk to the office my mind went numb. I remembered nothing of Amy's and my conversation, only the secretary saying,

"Your three minutes are up," seemingly before we'd said hello. I was suddenly filled with an unspeakable rage and plunged into the worst depression I had had in prison. Amy had had her baby and I wasn't there to hold her hand. I kept thinking, "He was born fatherless."

I went back to the orchard and picked apples, very slowly, getting some grim satisfaction that the storm was mirroring my rage. I delighted in the rain whipping across my face and through the trees; in the waves breaking and frothing white in the sound; in the apples being shaken from the trees to bruise or burst on the ground. I wished the storm on to greater deeds of devastation in a blasphemy against life. I seethed with hatred for prison, for the guards, for the judge, for the whole society that perpetrated prisons, wars, and poverty upon men.

For three days I raged in the depths of dejection before I calmed the surface of my mind. The rage beneath never died out completely. The wound torn in my being that day never healed.

Shortly after it turned cold, toward the end of November, I was reassigned to work in the island store stocking shelves. I was glad to get in out of the rain and cold. When the civilian boss learned I was a vegetarian, he let me eat all the fresh fruit and vegetables I wanted. (They served plenty of vegetables at camp, but all were over-cooked, and fresh fruit was scarce.) We got along well together; his wife would often bring over some cake or cookies for me. I caught him talking behind my back a few times, telling someone how he couldn't understand my radical ideas, but he never spoke condescendingly or contemptuously about me—or any con—as several guards would do. (Some guards felt that cons and niggers had no feelings, and they would stand around the cash register and tell each other that, paying no mind to me standing among them.)

The guards often came in the store just to talk over what was immediately on their minds. Most of them were painfully provincial. They talked racism and advocated one solution to any and all conflicts in which things seemed not to be going the way they would have it: the force of overwhelming violence.

One guard came in the store one day with a new variation he must have just figured out: "What we oughta do 'bout Vi-et-nam an' China an' Korea is ta line up all the SAC bombers in the Pacific an' then git on the hot line an' call up Khrushchev an' tell 'im we're comin' through whether 'e likes it or not, an' just fly 'em over Korea an' China an' Vi-et-nam an' drop H-bombs on 'em an' wipe 'em off the map."

The usual attitude among the guards was that of putting in their eight hours as quickly and as easily as they could so they could hurry home to occupy themselves with more pleasant activities. "If you're going to escape, don't do it on my shift." Someone had forgotten to tell me the rules while I was in A&O, and I learned what they were by being told I had just broken one. There were rules posted in each dorm—faded papers behind a dusty frame to one side of the bulletin boards—but none of these rules was enforced. The ones that were enforced weren't posted. The guards seemed quite casual about the rules, so I never worried about them either.

One rule was that cons weren't to take food from the dining hall. Cookies, meat, sweetrolls, cereal, drinks *were* taken with only cursory attempts to conceal it. Now and then a new guard would come to camp when the shifts changed who thought he was supposed to enforce that rule. He usually came to see that it didn't hurt anything, that it helped keep the cons happy, and he'd start letting it go.

I found some mint plants, and I dried the leaves over the steam heaters. Before going to work, I'd put some leaves in a jar of water and set it atop the heater. That night I'd enjoy mint tea with my sweetroll. One guard came out who thought the rules had come from Mount

Sinai, and he confiscated my mint. He thought it was
marijuana. He confiscated a lot of the other cons' little
pleasures, too. No one liked him. He once confided to a
friend of mine that he was afraid to go home: His sons
smoked grass, and he had threatened to bust them himself if he ever caught them. They in turn told him they'd
kill him some night in his sleep. He was a very lonely
person.

But the contact with the guards when off the job and
with their families helped counteract a growing tendency
to view them as unhuman machines, caring only to do
their job, totally lacking in feeling, totally brutalized and
depersonalized. They seemed to share in part the fate of
the convicts that the rest of society treated them as pariahs.
They did time, too, but whereas the convicts were deprived of freedom by locks and bars, the guards were
deprived of it by keys and by choosing to take up those
keys. I had learned that while still in the Tacoma jail:
After picking up my lunch tray one noon, the guard for-
got to lock the door to my cell. It remained ajar while I
read several chapters in a book I had. Another guard
finally discovered it. He looked into the cell, then he
slammed the door, locked it, and shook it to make sure it
was locked. About every fifteen minutes after that, he
would come by, look in, and shake the door again. I continued reading; the door meant nothing to me. But he
was tied to that door more than any convict could be. His
key was his imprisonment.

This contact with the island people also kept me in
mind of the outside world. Thus the prison environment
never seemed quite as total, nor the outside world quite as
unreal, as it did to many other convicts.

The store hours were from nine-thirty to six o'clock,
four days a week, plus Saturday mornings. I now had an
hour or more to myself of mornings and one entire day
when everyone else was away from camp working. Except for the few noises made by the janitor, the often

uproarious dorm was silent. I began to do some yoga exercises regularly and to spend thirty to sixty minutes daily in meditation.

Evenings were too cold now to sit by the fountain. I retired to the library to write and to read. It was a better library than I had expected, but none too extensive or up-to-date. It had subscriptions to several daily papers and to about two dozen magazines. There were two to three thousand books, two-thirds of which were fiction—mostly Westerns and mysteries. I found several books by Thoreau, Whitman, Merton, Tolstoi, Camus; several books of modern poetry; and college-level textbooks in various sciences. There were a dozen or so astronomy texts, much to my surprise and delight (astronomy was my major in college). I was told that several years before, a con had become interested in astronomy and had managed to cut through the red tape enough to get those books in and to get a kit from which he made a telescope. He would get permission on clear nights to take his telescope outside and look at the stars.

I read a lot, still wrote four-page letters, and was fancying myself a poet to boot. But I was finally beginning to settle down and to get a pattern established. Although an occasional day went a bit slowly, in retrospect time seemed to have flown. I was finding that I didn't have enough time to do all the things I wanted to do. I was learning how to do time.

I became comfortable in the routine I'd established. The days, the weeks, the months passed almost unnoticed. I was very reluctant to get involved in anything that would change my routine in the slightest. I never had more than half a dozen close friends, though some would leave and others would take their place. But even with them I spent little time. I had always preferred to be alone, and I now became very possessive about my solitude.

In the middle of November a man inside the main joint drove a truck through the fence in an attempt to escape. Guards in three gun towers shot at him and killed him. There was a small item in the next day's paper. It became just another incident for the guards to joke about; it added another flame to the fires of bitterness and hatred in the convicts.

Christmas went by, marked by a huge feast and a bag of candy that the institution gave each inmate. Christmas cards began to arrive in December, and by the middle of January I had received nearly a thousand. "Solidarity cards" I called them. I was overwhelmed. They filled those months with expansiveness.

In the spring two resisters arrived doing six months on two-year split sentences. One had been overseas for several years with his family, which had been involved with the CIA. He characterized the CIA agents as a bunch of "snivelers" who used treachery and deceit to accomplish their objectives. The daring and romantic people were the gun runners the CIA agents would shoot in the back.

As the year progressed, more resisters arrived, and the number of J.W.s passed a dozen. In April, a resister with two years came in and got a bunk beside mine. A&O was nearly full when he came through, and he had been beaten up a couple of times. We became close friends and spent much of our time on our bunks.

He was an artist and got paints through the hobby shop. He put in a request to have an art book sent in to him, but it was denied: "This book not necessary for your incarceration." Inmates were allowed to receive one package at Christmas in which two books could be sent, so he got the book the next Christmas. But it was otherwise nearly impossible to get books in other than textbooks for a course one was taking. The same was true of guitars, which several of us tried to get: The few guitars at the camp were old and warped and falling apart, but the aged caseworker wouldn't give us approval to get new ones.

I applied for parole in April and went up before the June board. They gave me a flat denial. But on the third of August I received a form granting me parole in five months. It was then that I stopped doing time and began waiting.

During those five months a certain bitterness and anger settled in me. My outlook on the world became marked with cynicism and a degree of futility. I still had periods of depression, but they became, as it were, standardized. I took them in stride, along with the bitterness, as mere facts of existence. The idealism I once took for granted I now often laughed at.

"Funny how a man can screw up his courage to walk in the face of death, but somewhere along the road something in his soul gets lost and he winds up wanting to die —what the hell, just get it over with," I wrote Amy toward the end of August. "It's so easy to forget. . . . The bi-weekly visits are completely parenthetical, like the Sunday movies or the nighttime stars I never see any more for having no reason to look up. . . . Dreams and illusions soon die, you see it like it is, and you laugh (perhaps a bit wistfully, certainly bitterly) at them. And you cease to see beyond the encircling beach; the words 'natural' and 'real' grow hollow—center rot gets them; and it gets easy to forget."

But I did look beyond the beach, and the bitterness only served to enhance my love for the natural beauty of the earth. Early in the summer I began walking the mile from camp to work. The road went through a patch of forest, and I reveled in an intimacy with the trees and occasional deer. The road emerged from the forest at the top of a steep hill, which plunged down to the harbor and the store. From atop the hill I had a magnificent view of the small island in the harbor on which lived a herd of harbor seals and of the blue water of the sound stretching out several miles to Fox Island. Salmonberries and blackberries were beginning to ripen, and I occasionally skipped lunch to eat my fill of berries on the way back to work at noon. After two or three weeks of this, one of the guards who was friendly but hung up on rules stopped me from walking: The rules said cons weren't to walk outside the camp.

Still it was a pleasure to ride around the island on the crew truck. My favorite spots were a winding road along the lake in the middle of the island and the coast road, from which I could see the sound and the other islands in it and the mainland. On clear days Mount Ranier would command the view entirely.

Three times that summer I was put on a crew that went to the mainland to unload flour and fertilizer from boxcars for the prison. We would ride over on the boat or the barge at eight o'clock and return at three-thirty. After being confined to the prison atmosphere, the boat ride and the hours spent in the small town gave respite and solitude. Here were houses in which families lived together, where there was privacy and love, where people didn't have to be wary every minute. I felt removed from the tension created by having someone always watching me, always snooping into my activities, always treating me as a despised animal. I could regain my dignity without having to hate and to reject another person in order to make room for it.

There was one convict at camp who would spend days by himself, talking to no one. Then suddenly he would become very aggressive and bellicose and get drunk on "pruno"—home brew he would make in some hideout. I was able to talk with him quite a bit. I watched these oscillations increase in intensity and gradually tear him apart. The guards were aware of his condition, but there was no effort made to get him to a psychiatrist. The responsible authorities just ignored him.

Sunday morning, September 1, he had an altercation in the dining hall with an old con who refused to steal sugar for him to make his pruno. That evening he stabbed the old man with a knife in front of my dorm. I went out seconds afterward and followed the pools of blood up the stairs to the control room, where the night guard was calling for the ambulance. The manic-depressive roamed the halls and dorms for about an hour before they took him to the hole. The old man died a few hours later. Few survive prison without some scars; some don't survive it at all.

When I first came in, I had felt a rather intellectual solidarity with the other cons, but as I grew to know them more this developed into a love for them as an oppressed people. Convicts are considered the lowest part of society. But as in a house, the lowest part is the foundation, and it is deserving of special love and care. A man who neglects the foundation of his house, and a society that turns its back on the needs of some men, prepare their own downfall. I've heard that Muslims consider the poor and the outcast to be God's representatives because they bring the opportunity to do good. But then we're a Christian society.

I developed some sympathy for the guards, but I was never sufficiently close to them to gain any greater understanding of them. I overheard a guard and another con talking one day. They had come to the island the same day. The con had two years to go before his release; the guard had eight years to go before retirement. The guard said he would have little more to show for his time when it was over than would the con. Though I saw that the only difference between the guards and the cons was that the former had keys (some of the biggest thieves on the island were guards), I felt quite a bit of antipathy toward them for being keepers of men.

In October I wrote Amy, "I've been using the slogan 'I'd rather fight here than there' more and more. And meaning it not entirely nonviolently. What happened to gentleness and compassion . . . ? What happened to the gentle hippie? The unmitigated evil and injustice of this society finally appeared in his awareness, and in the resulting nausea he threw up his gentleness as well."

The cynicism I developed seemed to clear my vision.

I didn't day-dream as much as I formerly did, nor did I spend as much time in reminiscence. I saw the poems I'd written for the silly things they were and threw out most of them. I spent a lot of time drawing floor plans for a house we hoped to build some day as part of our plans for a self-sufficient homestead independent of the capitalist economy.

Questions of direction began to confront me with greater depth and insistence. I heard that several resisters were being taken around a second time after their first case was over. I questioned the wisdom of going to prison a second time, and I doubted Amy's and my ability to endure another siege. I wrote her: "It looks fairly certain that we'll have the opportunity of going around twice if we want to . . . Canada looks more inviting, especially since we've planned more or less to homestead there anyway. So the question becomes: How long do we want to stay in the battle here: We seem to be getting ever more disillusioned with protest . . . and I think my 'faith and hope' in this country ever surviving the disease is nearly gone. So why stay in a burning house spitting on the walls? Let's go build a new home." Later, I got more to the heart of my trepidity: "I'm ready to face a firing squad, but not life imprisonment."

I questioned the value and efficacy of much that was done in the movement, but I was still strongly attracted to it and saw no reason to repudiate it. I had just come to see it in the light of American revolutionary tradition, and I often spoke of carrying the American Revolution to its logical conclusion. I felt there was no hope for the country as a nation, but that the individuals living in the country might be able to regain their sovereignty as their ancestors proclaimed in the Declaration of Independence and to make the country truly a land of freedom. I was torn between a desire to devote myself full-time to resistance activities and a desire to build a homestead. After years of trying to be an organizer and agitator,

I realized I hadn't the personality for it. I felt that protest per se was fruitless, that it had to arise out of a person's total life-style to be meaningful. The only needful
thing, perhaps the only meaningful thing, was simply
for each person to turn his back on the Army and the
state and to devote all his efforts to living as he saw right.
If the state came to beat his head in, he should be ready.
But he needn't go looking for a fight. In this view, all the
noise and scuffling in the streets was a diversion and a
delay of the revolution. I was more convinced than ever
that our homestead plan was right for us, but I still questioned it as being the luxury of a hermitage. Yet what else
were we to do? Perhaps I was thinking too much in terms
of an either-or, whereas our plans allowed more for a
synthesis of the two ideas. I thought of the Wobbly slogan: Building the new society within the shell of the
old.

Just before Christmas, a con inside escaped. He had
a record of four previous escapes. There was an eight-
foot fence topped with three strands of barbed wire
around the prison except for the front gate of iron grill-
work by the administration building. After it was dark
one night, this man and four or five others got into the
ad building and ran out to the gate. He climbed over the
gate, ran across a narrow road, and jumped over an em-
bankment onto the beach before the guards in the gun
towers could get their guns out. He disappeared into the
dark.

A second con tried to climb over the gate and was shot
and wounded. The others ran back into the ad building,
only to meet a guard coming out to see what the shooting was about.

"They're shooting! Someone must have escaped!" they
told him.

"Well, go to your cells. We'll sound the alarm," the
guard replied.

After they had gone, he realized that they must have

been in on the escape, but he couldn't remember who
they were.

The boat was returning from the mainland, and it
turned on its radar in case the escapee had arranged for
a boat to meet him. The radar was clean. A search party
set out to track the man. They reportedly found a pile of
prison clothes on the beach and footprints leading into
the water.

The temperature suddenly dropped below freezing
and it began to snow.

We were confined to camp for six days while search
parties with dogs combed the island. We heard that the
man had been sighted on one of the hills. Supposedly,
police and soldiers from Fort Lewis were searching the
mainland. Finally, the warden called off the search,
saying that the man had frozen to death on the island or
had tried to swim and had drowned.

A week later they found a prison stretcher with canvas stretched over it awash on the mainland north of Mc-
Neil. Apparently, the man had hid or had someone hide
food, clothes, and the stretcher and canvas somewhere on
the island. He had concealed himself and had waited until the search was called off. Then he fashioned a raft
out of the stretcher and canvas and made his escape good.
As far as I know, he's still free.

My second Christmas in prison came with about half
the number of solidarity cards as the first. I got my dress-
out clothes, said goodby to my friends, got my things together, and suddenly the day of release was at hand. I
was alone on the boat taking me through the gray water
and the gray overcast to that unreal land beyond the island. Amy and Alazel would be waiting, but my waiting
was over.

In prison I saw society at its worst, wreaking vengeance
on a few scapegoats, not with open hatred, which can
be understood and resisted, but with unconcern, with a

cutting off of recognition, by depriving these men of any meaningful life and forgetting them. There is no hope for such a society: That unconcern is the seed of its own destruction. A society is composed of all the individuals in it, and to cast out any of those individuals in unconcern wounds the entire society, just as a man cannot cut off a finger or a toe without it hurting all of him. I learned that without love, without concern, a man shrivels and becomes a creature of bitterness and anger and cynicism. And this is a rot at the center of society.

I learned that prison reform was a delusion. An article in a paper one day told of a prison in which the inmates had their own cottages with their own keys, worked only four hours of mornings, had a "main street" lined with cafes where they would throw parties to which girls from the outside were invited, and could have their families visit and stay with them in their cottages five days a month. I showed the article to another con. He read it: "Yeah, but there's just one thing. It's still a prison." I became an advocate of tearing down the walls.

I learned that prison is "dead time" only if a person makes it so. Prison is an intimate and personal thing. It's different for each individual. It exposes your weaknesses and forces you to overcome them or be overcome by them. You are totally on your own. You are totally alone. You make your time what it is. But this may be said of life. In prison you only have fewer opportunities than on the outside to hide from yourself and from the more vulgar side of life. The challenge of life is just as immediate in prison as on the streets. One's freedom is limited in prison only a few degrees more than in the world. The struggle to live meaningfully and existentially continues unabated. The necessity of freeing one's mind, of becoming human, is not diminished, regardless of one's situation, so long as one remains alive.

Tom Cornell

Tom Cornell, co-chairman of the Catholic Peace Fellowship, is now a staff member of the Fellowship of Reconciliation. He is co-editor of A Penny a Copy: Readings from the Catholic Worker.

A Draft Resister's Story

A very long time ago—in November, 1965—I burned my draft registration and classification certificates in Union Square. The Peace Movement had been agonizing over the war in Vietnam—writing letters, parading in the streets, blocking draft-board entrances and exhorting young men to noncooperation with Selective Service. No one paid us much mind. There were a few young men in jail for refusing military service, but there are always a few men in prison for that, most of them Jehovah's Witnesses. People started noticing the protest movement during the summer of 1965, when thousands invaded the Capitol precincts in an illegal, highly disciplined, nonviolent Assembly of the Unrepresented. That October, David Miller burned his draft card, and a few days later others of us did the same. Not even the Justice Department could refuse us notice that time (I had done it several times before—and had had to request replacements cards —but they had chosen to ignore it), so I was indicted, prosecuted, convicted and imprisoned for five months* for burning two small pieces of paper, while some of my contemporaries won military decorations for other kinds of incendiary activity in Vietnam.

The crime of punishment has been described in detail by professionals in many fields, by Dr. Karl Menninger in a book of that name and by Myrl Alexander, director of the Bureau of Prisons, in The Times. I will attempt a more personal approach to what I saw and did and felt in a community of imprisoned draft resisters at the Federal Correctional Institution at Danbury, Conn.

There were only a handful of draft resisters at Danbury. Most such offenders in the Northeast were sent to the Allenwood Prison Camp, a minimum-security prison farm near the Federal penitentiary at Lewisburg, Pa. There are perhaps 130 Selective Service violators at Allenwood, 80 of whom are Jehovah's Witnesses and 30 of whom identify with the resistance movement. About 2,500 other young men who have refused induction for reasons of conscience are at various stages in the process of indictment, prosecution and appeal or are awaiting imprisonment.

At Danbury were the slightly older draft resisters who might be thought of as potential organizers. Peter Irons had been an assistant of Victor Reuther and an organizer of the Student Peace Union. Earl Jenkins is a Black Muslim leader. Ed Oquendo was head of Blacks Against Negative Dying. Edmund Champlin Kittredge was

* The average sentence for draft refusal is 3½ years; the maximum is five. My sentence was lighter than most because at 31 I was beyond draft age, having won official classification as a conscientious objector five years before; because I was married and a father, and because my previous record was "respectable."

prominent in the New England Resistance. I serve as co-secretary of the Catholic Peace Fellowship. There were a couple of less political resisters and a few Jehovah's Witnesses, who are a type of their own. We made common cause with some other young men of similar background who had been caught with a little marijuana or a borrowed car before they'd had a chance to refuse the draft.

Much of what happens in a prison is so trivial that it cannot bear translation. Youths starved for any kind of stimulation, full of life and fervor, are penned in a sterile environment by men who in almost every conceivable way are their inferiors. Guards are difficult to characterize charitably. Theirs is an easy job, and overheard conversations give even the naive prisoner a sense of the abysmal level of human awareness that informs the personnel, professional and subprofessional.

It is not so much that our wardens set out to degrade us, to make us miserable, not so much that they are evil men. They are stupid and petty, but that is not a moral failing, just a fact of life in a society such as ours. The men employed by the Bureau of Prisons are what might be called marginal employables. Many have served a few years in the Army and liked its security but couldn't really make it, even there. So they are filling out their time for Government pensions by serving as guards (hacks) in the prison system. The professionals—with the exception, in our case, of the doctor—are also from the lowest drawer.

During orientation lectures, the warden, who had worked his way up from hack, told us: "Joy is for children. When you grow to maturity you find that contentment is the best you can hope for." He now adds the admonition that manifestations of individuality are also signs of immaturity. The education supervisor was characterized by his staff as the dumbest s.o.b. in the compound. He succeeded in reorganizing the library by burning about one-third of the old books (old, old, dirty, burn!), which were not really much of a loss. Many a familiar bookbinding was destroyed. The rest of the library's volumes were divided and distributed to the cellblocks and dormitories, along with some good paperbacks bought by the pound, and the library was turned into a "learning laboratory" by the addition of plywood dividers on the tabletops, resembling those found in college library stacks. The supervisor viewed the denuded library and sighed, "Not a book in the place!"

The captain, chief of the custodial staff, was a man of learning who wore a tie clasp in the form of miniature handcuffs, rather like a prostitute sporting a tiny phallic symbol. Since the education supervisor had his doubts about an inmate's request for a Chinese grammar, it fell to the captain to decide whether the common good would be served by admitting such a book onto the reservation. "Why do you want to learn Chinese?" the captain queried, "English is good enough." The authorities might have feared that the request was part of a plot. They refused The Catholic Worker for a while because, the educator explained, "I thought it might have been Communistically inspired."

It is difficult to organize in prison. Most of the inmates are beyond apathy. They have become convinced by the pattern of failure in their lives that they are losers, that nothing they can do for themselves, alone or together, will avail them anything. They failed in grammar schools, which were also prisons, in the slums and ghettos of overcrowded cities. The experience of failure repeats itself so often for ghetto dwellers that they project their lives in the pattern set for them by failure and go on to fulfill their own bleak prophecies. So they scoff at any suggestion for concerted action.

A riot is another matter. We didn't have one when I was at Danbury, though it seemed close for a while. The Puerto Ricans were talking about having a riot on Labor

Day weekend in revenge for the beating of some of their number. The goon squad, as they were called, the most sadistic of the guards, had beaten two Puerto Ricans who had been confined to "administrative segregation," known in prison jargon as "the hole." Rumors that the men had been handcuffed and beaten were circulating around the compound. Some of the stories were obviously hysterical overstatements, but one inmate whose job it was to take meals to the men in the hole got to know first-hand. The hacks neglected to forbid him entry to the hole after they worked the Puerto Ricans over, so when the inmate orderly saw their condition he had to be put with them so that he could not report what he had seen to the rest of us. By Friday night the situation had grown tense and there were real indications that something might blow, probably in the dining room. Racial tensions were high, too, so I was glad that I worked in the scullery, where I might duck behind my dishwashing machine. If violence were to erupt it would surely degenerate into a mindless melee in moments. When it was announced that a special movie would be shown on Monday to celebrate Labor Day, the riot was called off. It's hard to organize anything in prison.

The lives of men sentenced for resisting the draft do not differ from those of the rest of the prison population. They are isolated, not only from family, friends and work, but from each other. The authorities have learned, as they must, that to assure tranquillity in their institutions they must keep the men from organizing, they must keep the inmates separated. This they accomplish, at least in part, by rigidly enforcing a Byzantine complex of arbitrary and useless regulations. Infractions are penalized by loss of "good time," the time taken off the original sentence one must serve. This system has established an atmosphere that fosters back-biting, pettiness and paranoia so that men's frustrations never find their proper objects in focus.

Perhaps the cruelest aspect of prison life is the loss of identity with friends, family and work—the erosion of identity. One knows after a few months that he is changing, and he suspects that those who are waiting for him are also changing. Fear grips him that friends and family and self, even the world, are growing away from each other so fast and so irreversibly that re-entry may be impossible. Whatever self-confidence a young man might have gained is eroded. Some, after a couple of years, become "institutionalized." They fit into the system; in a way, they get to like it. It is so frightening to think of release into a world where your laundry is not taken care of, where there is food to be bought and prepared, where there are women who attach themselves to you and have babies which need things or they die. . . It's horrible. One of the boys at Danbury who has reached a level of institutionalization once asked me, half seriously, "Why would anyone want to leave? Plenty of booze, plenty of dope, plenty of sex!" Some people don't like the quality of booze, dope and sex available in prison, I reminded him. But this young middle-class white, jailed for one silly offense before he could be prosecuted for draft refusal, actually fears expulsion from prison.

Plenty of booze, just the way we used to make it in college: fruit with its juice left to ferment. There were gallons stashed away for Christmas before I left. Plenty of dope, but there wasn't much marijuana. I smelled it only once in the compound. I was told that there was a little being saved up for the holidays, but I doubted the ability of most of the men to delay their gratification, even for reasons liturgical. There was plenty of "speed," though. Amphetamines were procured through the hospital, where one of the medical technical assistants, something less than a registered nurse and more than an orderly, was on the take. One of the prisoners who had friends and money on the outside let the M.T.A. know it,

and the M.T.A. had on the inside what the prisoner
wanted: speed.

The one professional on the prison staff at Danbury
who can be called a man of sense and sensitivity is the
doctor, but he is only one M.D. and there are 750 inmates. He cannot work around the clock, seven days a
week, so he has to depend on M.T.A.'s. They examine all
prisoners who register a complaint. They thump and listen, read the vital signs and then call the doctor if they
deem it necessary. They do not like to appear incompetent,
so they turn most complaints aside with a knowledgeable
dodge. Like almost all the other employees of the Bureau
of Prisons, these men would have difficulty finding work
elsewhere, and they are glad of the underpaid job with its
security.

Many of my friends, and especially their mothers, ask
about sex in prison—whether there are gang rapes and the
sort of abuse we have read about. This is not a problem
at Danbury or Allenwood or any other Federal prison
where draft resisters have been held. At Danbury the law
of supply and demand seems to work out to everyone's
satisfaction. I'm either innocent or unobservant, but I did
not catch on to what was happening around me for a long
time. One of the men who came in with me to Danbury—
"Auntie," let's call him—took on 29 men the first day we
were there, but I didn't see a thing.

There is one area of the compound where we were
allowed to sit on the grass and to take our shirts (but not
our shoes) off in the sun, a very small area known as "the
Park," "the Pool," or "Muscle Beach." We used to read
each other there: "Born to Lose," "Born to Raise Hell"
and often, with bunting and cannons, "Death Before Dishonor." There were the more prosaic "Mom" and "Dad"
and girl friends' names as well. One half of Muscle Beach
was given over by custom to the hippies and beatniks, soft-
drug users and draft resisters with a common background

and general outlook. We called this section "Needle Park."
Across the Pool was "the Meat Rack," where the muscle-
freaks (weight-lifters) took their "girl" friends for some
gentle spooning.

Officially, of course, homosexual activities were strictly
forbidden and the more flamboyant queens were housed
together in the same building as "the hole." In fact,
though, the officials had to ignore a great deal of what was
obvious homosexual activity in the games and flirtations
on the Meat Rack as well as in the laundry, which on
Saturdays was a regular orgy. "Auntie" held office hours in
the laundry john on weekdays, but on Saturdays the
laundry was like a gay Candy. Somehow a syphilitic got
through the medical screening we were given on entering
Danbury, and 12 men had syphilis in no time. That's
nothing compared to the reformatory at El Reno, Okla.
The boys transferred from El Reno to Danbury told of the
gonorrhea epidemic there that infected one-tenth of the
population. Sixty men reported to the infirmary in one
day with clap. The officials had to declare a grace period
in which prisoners were assured that they would not suffer
sanctions for homosexual activities if they reported their
illness by a certain time.

Triangular love affairs generated a certain amount of
tension, and knives were hidden in case of eruptions. In
prison the slightest altercation can end in murder. One
of the men transferred out of Danbury while I was there
was killed over a pair of boxing gloves.

Boredom and isolation are among the hardest things to
bear in prison, and the blandness of the environment.
"High on a naked bluff overlooking Candlewood Lake,"
said a recent newspaper article. Claptrap! We never saw
a naked bluff nor Candlewood Lake. That "country club"
sobriquet is straight out of William Randolph Hearst and
Westbrook Pegler. Yes, there is an eight-hole golf course
on the reservation, for the hacks. For us, an extremely

small quadrangle taken up largely by a baseball diamond.

And canned mashed potatoes! That is symbolic of the whole place, canned mashed potatoes. I have lived at the Catholic Worker House of Hospitality on the Bowery, and I can assure you that we ate better; the meat wasn't so good, but we ate freshly begged vegetables. The food at Danbury produces fat and flatulence; that is all. I could not eat anything much of the time. Macaroni Milanaise, they call it. A fancy name is supposed to make it taste better, and salmon croquettes. Beyond tolerance. I was in pain much of the time and had a scrip for belladonna. The doctor said—and he was probably right—that I had gas, no matter where in my trunk it hurt. I preferred the pain most of the time to the belladonna and ate corn chips and ice cream, sometimes for three meals. I gained 10 pounds. The canned mashed potatoes and the pale green paint, just off white, peeling from the walls inside the compound, the yellow paint in the dorms, all of a piece.

I got only about five hours of sleep a night. Most of the prison population got up to report for work at 8 A.M. But I had been placed in the scullery—because of my educational background, no doubt; an M.S. is a great advantage in washing dishes. I had to get up at 5 or 5:30 A.M. That was all right with me, but I couldn't get to sleep before midnight because I was housed in an open dorm, an honor dorm at that. I should have been pleased. Lights went out at 10:20 and the television at 11:30. It took about half an hour for people to stop flushing toilets and discussing the T.V. movie so that anyone could get to sleep. That is, when there wasn't any speed around, in which case, greet the dawn! I am too frail of constitution to play with amphetamines, and the noise of the others would keep me awake. I asked the captain very nicely for either a change of dormitory or a change of job, explaining to him that five hours of sleep was not enough for me, that I was actually suffering. He smirked and put me off.

He suggested that I didn't really want to work. I admitted quite frankly and realistically that I did not find any jobs in the institution desirable or appropriate but that I was willing to work and in fact had an excellent work record. I told him that I wanted time to read. "To read? What for?" I suspect that they wanted me right where I was so that I would stay exhausted, too tired to get into trouble.

I had been writing about 2,000 words a day to my wife, letters concerning my memory of the development of the nonviolent-action movement and its antecedents as I learned them from A. J. Muste and Dorothy Day and other fellow workers. They knew it and couldn't do anything about it. And I am an organizer, which is probably the reason I was sent to Danbury rather than Allenwood in the first place, so it was better to keep me fatigued.

Toward the end of my talk with the captain he tried to engage me in polite conversation, as many of them do, to indicate that he, too, is a man of some achievement and to bolster his self-image. The captain explained that there are six types of people in prison. He simplified, not to bore me with sociology: "Really, there are three, basically, if you break them down. There is always a small minority, and it is very small, of persons like yourself, men of intelligence and education, men who order their lives by some sort of code, like tax dodgers." (That was supposed to win me.) "Then there is another minority, not as small, but still definitely a minority, who just can't seem to make it on the outside. They are model prisoners once they get here, they're quiet, don't get into trouble, work all right. They just can't live on the outside. But most of the men, the great majority, are just bums. That's all they ever were and that's all they'll ever be, just bums."

The motto of the Bureau of Prisons is emblazoned upon the bureau shield, mounted grandly in the mess for all to see: "If you treat a man as he is he will stay as he is. But if you treat a man as if he were what he ought to be and

could be he will become what he ought to be and could
be.—GOETHE." This hypocrisy was sharply poignant to us,
treated like bums because the captain and all the hacks
thought of us as bums and treated us as they would bums.
When I worked on the Bowery we never used that word,
the word that society gives to derelicts and winos and that
is applied by extension to various kinds of undesirables
(by society's standards). We called them "Ambassadors
of God," and tried to see Christ and ourselves in every
one of them. The guards saw us as bums. This is one
major reason why the prison experience is so degrading
and humiliating and why it generates so much anger.

Corn chips, ice cream and belladonna from the doctor
kept me going at my dishwashing machine and the
"grinder," or garbage disposal unit, with Kittredge, the
draft resister from Providence who played chess into the
night, worked differential equations by day and learned
formal logic from the Encyclopedia Brittanica. We spent
much of our time in the scullery in "clarification of
thought." I would hurl a revolutionary maxim at him and
we would analyze it. Kittredge lacked, in my judgment, a
well-developed sense of class consciousness and had insufficient revolutionary zeal. We would attempt to gain a
sounder approach together by studying the thought of
Peter Maurin, Che Guevara, Lenin, A. J. Muste and Dorothy Day. More of this would go on as we were freed from
our chores, during afternoon breaks and in the evening,
with the rest of our group, perhaps 11 members at the
core. We discussed the news of the Movement and followed the political conventions closely. Chicago gave us a
lot of meat. The soft druggies would join us and we would
have antiestablishment seminars which shocked the mid-
dle-aged embezzlers, who are very patriotic and remember
Pearl Harbor, and the Appalachian bootleggers, who are
the nicest guys around.

Sometimes these discussions would so shock and
scandalize the naive convicts who casually dropped by

that I feared reprisals or at least strong antagonism when
the others got wind of what we really felt about America.
But nobody gave a damn. There was a time when political and religious draft refusers might arouse patriotic hostility from 100 percenter gangsters. Not any longer. Not
at Danbury, anyway. The Johnson Administration has so
confused and disheartened the populace that hardly the
dumbest scoundrel seeks refuge in patriotism any longer.
Still, the vitriol of some of our conversations, especially
from the Leninists, made me fear ostracism that never
came.

One of the hacks, the supervisor of a work detail, came
up behind one of our men—a gentle, Armenian and in-
stinctively Christian soul who wore his hair long, as long
as he dared—and took a big slice out of our friend's scalp
with a pair of pruning shears. Our man was furious at
this intrusion and expressed his momentary anger. The
hack was elated. He saw in Tony's anger a sign of life,
the kind of life that he understood. "Get mad, kid! Yeah,
hate is good for you. You're wising up." That brought
Tony back.

But the hack had put his finger on something. The
anger, the hatred, the fury that I felt—often, that we all
felt—can be good. It can keep you going, too angry to
die. Much better, it can be sublimated and directed, not
at individuals like the warden and the hacks, who are
doing rather bad time themselves in a prison of their own
device, but at corrupt institutions that maintain and promote slavery, racism, exploitation and war. If anger provides the energy for the destruction of these cancers, then
it is worth being angry.

There are 800 "prisoners of conscience" in America's
jails and military stockades, with perhaps 2,500 more in
the docks. And the number will probably rise sharply in
the years ahead. The Allenwood Prison Camp was es-

tablished under the McCarran Act for the detainment of
subversives. The prisoners of conscience held there keep
it in good running order should the nets be flung wider
in some recurrence of the McCarthy syndrome which
grips the country every so often. The political defeat of
the United States in Vietnam might precipitate such repression.

The men serving sentences for resisting the draft are
not marginal types or the sons of marginal types. They
are, for the most part, sons of the middle class. They are
usually a little ahead of their contemporaries academically
and have excellent prospects. They are, many of them,
the moral leaders of their peers. America puts these men
in prison at her own peril. The blacks have more experience of prison than the rest of us, the class structure of
America being what it is. They have known what to do
with prison time. The edge of black militancy was honed
in jails throughout this land. The Black Muslims and the
Panthers recruit in prisons. Eldridge Cleaver's "Soul on
Ice" and Malcolm X's "Autobiography" are prison classics.
We will learn from our black brothers.

If jail for the poor is a college of crime, we middle-
class, educated and favored draft resisters will make it
for ourselves a graduate school of revolution. The anger
that I was taught I will never forget. The bitterness in
my mouth will never lose its sting. I pray God to keep the
fury burning in my heart so that I might never fall prey
to the blandishments of this society and drug myself as
my fathers did, "whose god is their stomach." I know that
these sentiments are not mine alone.

No matter how angry and alienated the young men
who have resisted the Vietnam war might have been, they
will be angrier and more implacable when they experience what society has in store for its "offenders." They
will be able to experience the quality of life that is for
niggers, at least in part and at least for a while. Nothing
tells so much about a society as the way it treats its chil-

dren and its prisoners. Some will attempt to transform their anger into the power of nonviolent revolution, aiming for the liberation of the hacks as well as the more obvious victims, to make our frustrations and humiliations give birth to righteous wrath, as did Jesus cleansing the Temple, if you will. Others will simply lash out. And who has taught them better?

I did good time. I have a wife and two children, a wife who came to see me as often as possible and who wrote daily. The first reason for my relatively easy time is my wife and her fidelity. She shares with me what brought me to Danbury. And faithful friends, especially at The Catholic Worker and the Fellowship of Reconciliation. I was able to relate to a number of very fine young men whom I taught and who taught me. We shared something painful but precious. Of course I would do it again, and I think almost every one of us would say the same. We did not want to go in the first place and I certainly do not want to have to go to prison again. I hope it will not be necessary. Nonetheless, there is in prison an opportunity to grow. Moreover, Christians believe that the greatest power is somehow in the weak, the despised; the paradoxes of the Beatitudes come to mind. If there is hope for the future it may well confound the world that it is in jails.

Arthur Egendorf, Jr.

Arthur Egendorf is a Vietnam veteran, having served in Military Intelligence in Saigon.

Art Thou Really so Different from Anyone Else?

> Wie viel bist du von andern unterschieden?
> Erkenne dich, leb mit der Welt in Frieden.
> Art thou really so different from anyone else?
> Get to know thyself, and live with the world in peace.
> from Goethe's Faust

"Hell no, we won't go." First it sounded silly. Then embarrassing. Finally that cry became an outright threat. Spilling their guts out in protest over an issue that could only be decided by heads of state, they refused to recognize how ludicrous they were and how futile their indignance. Just kids, incapable of accepting what they were, they demanded a voice they didn't deserve. That made it harder on others their age who were engaged in the struggle to be recognized through achievement rather than disruption: a vague but growing pressure to take some stand when there wasn't enough information or understanding to decide. What made them so certain of their course when there were probably good arguments on all sides? In rejecting so much, what sustained their sanity in the midst of anomie and disbelief? There was the faint suspicion that they knew something that the rest of us didn't. But all that I, a nineteen-year-old college student, could say of them for sure was that they were different. That was 1964.

"Why don't you tell them to shove it?" was a friend's question when notice from my draft board arrived three years later. A full answer was impossible; only, "Because . . . I can't do that." With college over, graduate school didn't have any immediate appeal. Europe did. Going away entailed certain risks with the draft, but they could be handled, like anything else. The notice followed me to Germany, after almost a year of my being abroad. The clamor over the war at home was less than a distant rumble, since an energetic study of French and German had left me no time to read American publications. My goals and reactions were unchanged from what they had been years before. There was an indulgent family, bent on respectability, that had to be pleased, a well-ingrained drive for accomplishment to placate, and a yearning to fit into a proud tradition in which men of honor pit themselves against fate without wincing.

Going to jail was out of the question, permanent exile unthinkable. The thought of using influence or subterfuge to avoid service reeked of dishonor. While the arguments supporting the war had already become dubious, it was impossible to believe that a great nation's leaders could be altogether wrong. And although the prospect of being in the infantry was extremely distasteful, it *had* to be that the Army needed men with talent and initiative for constructive purposes. It was these thoughts that I had in mind on the way to an Army recruiter in Munich. I enlisted, signing up for a total of three years, in order to guarantee my placement in the Army Intelligence "Area Studies" program.

The military provided a flight home to begin Basic

Training. It was the summer of 1967. During the first few
unpleasant weeks, solace came from my belief that those,
like myself, who were courageous enough to withstand
the ordeal of duty in troubled times would eventually be
rewarded. There were many for whom the Army was the
first brush with life outside of school. I felt stronger than
they, having already been away for a year and accustomed
to loneliness. The realization didn't come until sometime
later that the toughness was also a drawback. It made me
resistant to a new, upsetting thought, one that others
seemed to have understood from the outset. Many of the
men in training were there by default. It was not something they wanted to do, but they had simply not taken
the trouble to avoid it. The resisters on the outside were
still another breed. Yet their distinctiveness was no longer
so ineffable. It became clearer with time that they were
the fortunate few who had developed a commitment to
their own ideals when others, like many of us in training,
were still in doubt.

Intelligence school was an unexpected shock. What had
been advertised as "Area Studies" was actually espionage.
It was too late to back out. I had made a commitment.
But inarticulate instructors, simplistic lesson plans, and an
incredibly dogmatic approach to history, politics, and human behavior made it all seem like rank idiocy. Our in-
structions for finding good agents: "Get the man who is
ideologically motivated, hates Communists, has a healthy
fear of American power, and wants to get in Uncle Sam's
good graces. But make sure he's beholden to you too. Get
him to take your money and your booze, or else you'll
never be able to control him." And it was through these
means that we were to collect the information on which
sound policy was to be based.

It appeared that I had allowed myself to be deceived
into joining an effort that was inevitably doomed to failure by its own distorted and preconceived version of
truth. Suddenly, the radical rhetoric that had been so

easy to dismiss as misguided and irresponsible years before, provided the only logic adequate to deal with this
new situation. Reading newspapers and magazines assidu-
ously, I cheered each new demonstration and case of draft
resistance. Theirs was the more difficult ordeal. Belief in
some eventual reward for dutiful submission palled before an increasing awareness that rewards were absurd:
The resisters were simply right.

Friends outside the service wrote occasional letters. It
was hard to understand their reticence and distant tone.
In private thoughts, I could concede that my initial decision to join the service was based on misconceptions. The
Army experience was senseless. But I revolted at my
friends' vague indictments of my complicity. Only excuses and consolations came to mind: I was the class
radical; I at least could speak from first-hand knowledge
and not from mere speculation; I had an obligation to fulfill. Those reactions grew out of a new sense of vulnerability and precariousness. If I acted on my true feelings,
the Army might remove me from the comforts of the Intelligence corps and send me to the infantry, even to jail.
Once let loose, the desperation might even lead me to become a lifelong fugitive. And so, in spite of what I felt,
self-preservation became the abiding concern. They could
make me a spy, but I would do them one better. To save
myself, I would dissimulate and hold my real self in
abeyance.

A year in Saigon destroyed the last remnants of doubt.
Intelligence knew none of the answers to the important
questions. Gruff, haughty American officials living with
their concubines in Saigon villas, disdainful G.I.s, and
massive resentment among the Vietnamese for the clumsy
and disruptive foreigners shattered any hope that we were
there to help them. Inside knowledge of intrigue, cor-
ruption, and a tottering regime founded on repression
devastated the myth of our building a viable, representative political structure. Only the claims of a few honest

men in the military, that we were there to maintain our
control of the situation, rang true. And that admission
simply bolstered the polemics of the enemy. We were
fighting a nasty, aggressive, imperialistic war. How disappointing that I had to go so far to find out what others
had known long before without ever having been away.

"If I were Vietnamese, I would be with the Vietcong."
It didn't matter that I said those words to Army officers,
who were willing to stake their lives on the fight with the
enemy, or to Saigon aristocrats, some of whom I genuinely
liked even though I knew they were likely candidates for
V.C. assassination. I still spied for a cause I couldn't believe in, with the relish of a successful double deceiver
delicately balancing conflicting loyalties. There were men
dying not too far away, and I didn't want to be with
them. There was also the year left to serve after Vietnam
to consider. Only a good performance could win me a
place in another safe haven, so I did the job better than
most. The calculation worked. Returning to the United
States in April 1969, in the midst of a crippling colitis
attack, I was given a privileged job in Washington.

A few months afterward, I met and talked for a few
minutes with a man I knew. But I couldn't place him. It
took three days to remember who he was, that he had
taken me to lunch several times in Saigon. Other names,
places, and events were even harder to remember. The
forgetting seemed almost purposeful, and with that sudden insight, the dam cracked, without breaking. At work,
I was supposed to read reports from spies using American
companies for cover (always with the consent of the company president). There was advice to give: whether a
fifty-year-old agent should seduce a twenty-year-old Jap-
anese teletype operator so that he could force her to
supply him with the information she transmitted at her
job. And a constant demand for shrewd deception: How
can official records throughout the government be put to
better use, altering some to make our agents' cover more

convincing, and appropriating others for leads to more "human resources." I tried to have nothing to do with it all. Ideas and slogans culled from underground newspapers at night became the rhetoric for the next day's conversations at the office. They couldn't send me back to Vietnam, so there was no fear in telling everyone what I felt. Yet I stuck it out, going to work every morning and taking my pay, in spite of the conflicts.

Ever since I enlisted, the only plan for what to do after the Army was a return to Europe. In Washington the basis for the plan changed. It was no longer to go back to something I had started, but rather to get away from the nightmare I was in. "Why go to Germany?" asked an uncle. My answer: "That's where the Nazis are . . . I'm a Nazi, and that's where I belong." Yet the day the Army released me in May 1970, I couldn't leave the country. The upheaval and disruptions of the previous three years had developed their own logic, and I couldn't escape it. An emotional breakdown followed. After months of putting the pieces back together, I found my way to Vietnam Veterans Against the War.

As monumental change follows unsettling change, new pat answers replace the ones discarded . . . up to a point. After time and reflection on the latest shift, doubts return, to the point where the flux appears clearly rooted in a few inescapable truths. From the time I entered the military, it became increasingly obvious that the heroes of this war were those who fought it in the streets of American cities, or in the courts, or in jails, or by leaving the country rather than lend their support. Certainly there are distinctions among them. Men who went to jail or left the country because of their public stand faced different consequences than the ones who used a psychiatrist's diagnosis to avoid the draft. But the distinctions are irrelevant. Whatever the personal cost, all of them, exiles, deserters, and resisters of every stripe, answered the call

to fight in a senseless war with the most appropriate response—an outright refusal.

It is hard to imagine any dissenting minority that has
been so dramatically and unequivocally vindicated by the
course of history as those who refused to fight in Vietnam.
If the legal authorities in the United States cease to persecute the resisters, so much the better. They will only be
recognizing the absurdity of punishing individuals for the
foresight that was so clearly lacking within the government and major sections of the larger society during a
period of meaningless suffering for millions of Vietnamese
and Americans. Those who said "no" to the war should
receive an apology, not just a pardon; they should be
granted a place of honor, not amnesty.

While that conclusion is indisputable to me, it was only
reached through anguished reflection. In fact, this essay
is extremely difficult to write. There is a strong urge to
forget past pain, to gloss over personal shortcomings, and
to carry on as if the war didn't happen and I had taken
no part in it. What comes to mind now are vivid recollections of the distressing process through which an ex-
Army spy eventually began to face his own bitter errors
in judgment head on. The realizations came very slowly
at first, followed by an anxious groping for some understanding of why different alternatives hadn't been chosen.
But it was only after the struggle made its impact that the
hidden despair, once brought to light, began to subside,
and I could start feeling whole again . . . braced with a
cautious hope that I wouldn't make the same mistaken
choices again.

Given the trauma experienced by one man, it is unlikely that the wounds caused by an entire society's errors
will heal in any simple fashion. Historians claim that the
nation has not been so divided since the Civil War. It is a
time when people judge others and themselves more by
their allegiances than by personal qualities. And the
greater the polarities, the greater the desire in many of us

to bridge the gaps and obscure the issues that separate us. But there is no way to escape the judgment that the war has been a colossal mistake. Whatever ruse people may employ to hide from the past, it is certain that many others, here and elsewhere in the world, and especially the war's victims, the Vietnamese, will not forget.

A mistake of such proportions is a crime. And the crimes of a nation that calls itself democratic are the responsibility of all its citizens, a notion that the resisters have embraced most fittingly. But that the war has dragged on in spite of their efforts indicates that the responsibility is shared unevenly. Ultimately, it resides with the Presidents, their advisers, and military officials who have had the power to end the war or substantially alter its course had they chosen to do so. But that still doesn't exonerate the individual voter and soldier.

As a young man I look forward to the day when passions will subside and the war in Vietnam is relegated to history. Toward that end, amnesty must be reserved for the true criminals, the principals in the crime and everyone associated with it. I am thinking of amnesty in the largest sense. There is a need to establish a new consensus on which citizens can accept each other and come together, after which it is no longer necessary to defend past roles in order to live in the present. *But the forgiveness can only follow a clear understanding of what and whom there is to forgive.* First, an entire nation must come to grips with the painful lessons that the war has to teach.

Hopefully, more people will come to realize that unquestioned deference to higher authorities has been a self-serving cop-out: The deferent have been able to avoid answering troublesome questions for themselves. In the end, it has also been self-defeating. We have delegated responsibility for the life and death of millions to men who gained power through unrelenting attention to their own self-interest, with the delusionary expectation that once in office, they would act with the wisdom of philosophers. The most perceptive and sensitive individuals can be trapped by a need to preserve their tenure in office, incapable of correcting mistakes even after they are recognized. In Vietnam, what began as a measured display of U.S. force, a military exercise for limited political objectives, has become the longest war in our history. Three times as many explosives have been dropped, and almost half as many men called into military service as during the entire course of World War II. And through it all, the bulk of Americans have been waiting in silence until the men whose job it is to decide call for an end.

It is not enough that military tribunals sit in judgment of men like Lieutenant William Calley. His conviction, based on the ruling that he acted as a sane and free agent at the time of his crime, is more of a reflection of our own perverted standards of normality than of any real justice. Such trials are travesties when a case involving the murder of a Vietnamese spy is dismissed for fear of disclosing espionage *modus operandi,* and of bringing embarrassment to the government; and when the misfeasance of the highest officials has yet to be brought seriously into question.

Nor is it reasonable to expect our legal system to deliver a lasting verdict on the guilt or innocence of those who initiated and conducted the war, for it has stubbornly refused to rule on the legality or the constitutionality of the war itself. Many legal technicalities have been raised that even cast doubt on the appropriateness of the Nuremburg decisions as a precedent for war crimes trials after Vietnam. But there are other questions yet to be answered before proceedings based on the Nuremburg precedent could convene. Did the original trials actually lead to a greater understanding of the moral issues involved? Or was their usefulness canceled out by the resentment they evoked of the unjustifiable self-righteousness of the adjudicators? After Vietnam, what party or individual has the jurisdiction and the "clean hands" to set itself up a judge? In any case, there can be little doubt that legal judgments alone cannot convey the essential message, for even the lessons of Nuremburg were lost on one of the principal parties to its decisions, the United States.

The most crucial postwar task entails more than removal of the officials responsible for the war from office, and the assignment of guilt. The widespread attitudes that made the war possible must change. A substantial portion of the population presently favors the men on trial for atrocities, not because, as some maintain, they did not bear ultimate responsibility for their acts, but because they were only doing their duty. Some of those same people do not see the war as a hideous error, but as a worthwhile cause subverted by elements within the United States. It is difficult to imagine that such minds will be changed by making martyrs out of misguided leaders. And any effort to try war criminals on a massive scale will undoubtedly be misconstrued as an attempt to establish pacifism as a national creed, undermining the institutions that enable a nation to defend itself.

There will inevitably be more investigations and trials. So there should be. But they must be conducted in such a manner to make clear that the judgments apply to more than the limited group that can be brought under scrutiny. There should be no illusions that the evil throughout society is expiated by punishing a few individuals. Nor should there be any support given to the idea that a few scapegoats have to be sacrificed to pacify the most rabid faction. The indictments must indicate how sincere, conscientious people, in and out of office, can be blinded to the implications of their acts . . . by fear, by intimidation, and by their own struggle to maintain the tenuous security afforded them by a restricted vision that excludes intrusive, disturbing truths. When that lesson is understood, when the citizenry at large shows a willingness to accept their share of responsibility for a national catastrophe, it will be time to open a new chapter on amnesty.

In the lines at the head of this essay, the goddess of truth says to a headstrong and immoderate Faust, "Art thou really so different from anyone else? Get to know thyself, and live with the world in peace." In the aftermath of an unjust war, the greatest imperative is not to decide whom to punish or whom to pardon. Rather, it is contained in the goddess' exhortations to Faust. The insensitivity of this willful and excessive nation has shielded it from the suffering caused to others by its efforts to transform the world according to its own fantasies. Now its people, and particularly its leaders, must learn to develop the self-knowledge, the sense of shared interest with all human beings, to live with the world in peace.

Richard Gooding

Richard Gooding is a twenty-five-year-old war resister and free-lance writer now living with his wife in Montreal. A native of Chicago, he was drafted and refused induction in August 1969 while working for the New York Times. *There followed a year underground in the United States before going to Canada, during which he wrote "An Exile in My Own Country," published by* Look *magazine in February 1970.*

Going Home and Never Going Home

> I wondered really whether I counted at all in this . . . I fell asleep in the end on the question, in my own private night like a coffin; I was so tired from walking so far and finding nothing.
>
> Louis-Ferdinand Céline

I have never been very good at going home. There was Christmas 1969, an underground Christmas, four months after refusing induction and eight before exile. I remember promising to be there the weekend before and not arriving till the weekend after, passing up a free ride and canceling several plane tickets, straining to offer some plausible excuse—in the meantime, having nothing really to do, spending Christmas alone, having nothing really to

keep me where I was. It was just so damn hard to make
myself go, so damn hard to *face going*.

Then the next time. It was six months later. Connecticut. Early June. Susan and I over coffee, each waiting
for the other to say it. She did. Finally. "You're restless,
aren't you, you want to get going?" "It's that obvious?"
"Uh huh." Then: "It's all right, though. I can fly back
tomorrow night for school. You can stay home till the next
week and drive back." "I don't know why . . . it seems
important now, somehow . . ." Her smile stopped me.
When we're close, her smile does that. "I understand.
Really. I think I'm just as anxious."

Driving all night, vacant tollways to Chicago. Pale.
Tired. Coming unannounced, Sunday morning, seven
o'clock. Waking my parents. My father at the door in
pajamas, momentarily confused, his hair tossed from sleep
but looking tanned and strong, just back from the Green-
brier. My mother at the top of the stairs, shaking her head,
mock scolding, "What the dickens are you doing here?
You *know* you shouldn't startle us like this." Then laugh-
ing, composed: "Let me get a robe on, I'll make you kids
breakfast."

They'd never met Susan, only heard me tell of her;
we were going to be married (we were home to tell them
that). And it all went quite well then. Relaxed. Warm.
Cheerful. It all went as it is supposed to: *coming home
with the girl I loved* (as if this were the only thing in the
world that mattered, as if nothing else anywhere touched
our lives). It seemed a very special thing.

It was a quiet wedding, virtually alone and on the run,
a hasty courtroom in Michigan, with none of the family
around, none of them even aware.

Four days later, an overheated summer weekend. The
lake cottage. Our sanctuary in central Indiana. My parents
and hers, converging on us, meeting each other for the first
time. Celebration, a transplanted reception. Re-enacting

festivities. Cakes and presents. Pictures and dressing up. Susan and I assuming the role, everything there, all the appearances, *carefree newlyweds,* everything but the kind of feelings that can be spontaneous only once. Smiles and laughter, everybody very friendly, joking, even gracious. Getting along better than anyone expects, everyone wanting, perhaps straining, to get along. "Seems we've known you forever." Nothing phony really, just pressing, really trying very hard. Hectic as hell, everybody in on every act, each parent wanting so much to do everything for us, getting in the way, unable to let us be hosts, even to rest, and yet nothing really unnatural, nothing that couldn't have been foreseen, predicted, nothing that couldn't be allowed, just this once, for their sakes, hang our sakes, we have a long time. This was for them.

But there was something else. Something that surpassed the smiles and the laughter. Something that was quite unexpected. That couldn't be ignored. I don't know just when it began. It had been happening all around me, it had been happening almost from the start, yet it took a while to surface, to see clearly, begin to understand. It was something really very serious. Something really very complex.

There was my mother with Susan's mother. The two of them talking, off alone, talking quite a bit. My mother doing most of it. Telling her about me, about *my situation,* their side of it, about all she and father had gone through, *all I had put them through.* Then telling her about this lawyer. My father had seen him. "The best draft lawyer in Chicago," it was said. "He knows how to talk to these boys," it was also said. There were alternatives, it seems, there was the possibility of a compromise: I would turn myself in, repent, apologize to the authorities, the court; they would grant me a reduced sentence, at worst, a chance to serve, at best. A I-A-O, of course. Noncombatant. And there was more talk. About how this would be so much better for everyone, so much better for Susan, how we could stay in the country, wouldn't have to go so far away, wouldn't have to run forever. How this whole thing, *this whole miserable thing*, could be over, no longer hang over our heads, no longer keep people awake nights. No longer anything.

It all sounds very cynical, I suppose. It was all so remote, so indirect, so behind my back. It sounds almost sinister, working around the triangle, isolating us, playing on sympathies, still fragile relations. But no. I don't suppose it was really that way. I don't suppose it was really anything more than my mother going to whomever there was to help, to resolve this thing, *to do what she thought right*. It was desperation, *survival*. Removing the weight. And it did open up some later. That was Sunday morning. Susan and my mother. Susan at the end of her bed, listening, saying little, crying a bit. My mother laying there, with a headache, one of her rather frequent migraines. She too, crying. Repeating mostly. A few new things. How I have changed since meeting her, "The old Rick is back, he's like he used to be, so much happier, he's mellowed, not so solemn," how good Susan is for me, how things can be better now. Then about the lawyer, the compromise. About how it could avoid jail, *how jail must be avoided*, "I don't think either of us could stand that, I don't know how we'd live through that." About how we could have a normal life, "You could teach near his base, you could be together, you wouldn't have to leave the country, you wouldn't be so far away." That kind of thing. And how Susan must think of herself, "It's your life, too," how it is too important to be left to me.

And there was my father. With me. Sunday before breakfast. Coffee and cigarettes. Alone. (Everyone else sensing seriousness, picking up the cue, fumbling some, disappearing.) My father. Being very thoughtful, very understanding. Struggling to rationalize the whole thing, work it all out. "I agree with what you did, I really do agree totally," leaning forward, elbows on knees, hands folded, a bit nervous, "but this is different now. I think you've made your sacrifice, you've made your statement, now I think you should consider ending it, consider beginning a more stable life, for you and for Susan." Staring ahead, eyes away from me. "I think this compromise is the most realistic option you have." Leaning back, quiet, perhaps relieved that it was over, that he had gotten through it without interruption. Passing to me: a rather halting comeback, tentative, not the time for too much honesty. Giving him the day.

They were leaving then, my father hugging Susan, saying how much he thinks of her, turning to me, "Remember, you have her to think of now, not just yourself." Driving off, waving, hopeful.

Susan and I stayed up most of that Sunday night, long bouts of frantic talk, much holding and much calm, and finally the only thing that ever needed to be said:

"They're ignoring the most important part of this. They think I can talk you into this compromise, and maybe I could, if I cried enough, threw a fit, I don't know. But what would happen if I did that? It would be against everything that is you, everything that I fell in love with, you would be doing it only for my sake, and then we'd be lost. I couldn't live with the knowledge that I changed you that way, and I couldn't even live with you, because you wouldn't be able to live with yourself. It would change you, and how could I love you after that?"

We both tried our best to tell them. Me in my own way, and Susan in her own way. We tried to tell them as gently as we knew how.

Although there never was a gentle way to destroy hope. Although I may never feel certain that it was gentle enough.

[It] had been a sacrificed generation. Those who left Spain never really knew it, and never really came

back to it, however they might dream. And those who
stayed always knew something had been taken from
them.

Barbara Probst Solomon

There is reality and there is myth, everyone wants to
forget, no one wants to admit, there is a desire for roots
and there are no roots, everyone wants to turn back and
there is no turning back, there is not even anything to
turn back to, everyone wants to choose and there are no
choices. There is reality and there is myth, and the two
exist side by side, sometimes blending, mixing, more often
oblique, ignorant, neither having much of anything to do
with the other, not touching, not feeling, not seeing or
being seen, knowing or being known, not anything really,
just cluttering, confusing, robbing each other of individual worth, and everyone wants it to be one way, no one
allows it to be another, everyone wants to hide and there
is no hiding.

I had always thought of myself as a terribly average
kid, an upbringing like any upbringing anywhere, but I
suppose now that there was a good deal more to it than
that, and that, anyway, "average" is hardly sufficient to
describe it. Perhaps the environment was the base of it.
A town of some ten thousand people, a midwestern town
that wanted very much to be just a small town in the
American tradition of small towns, another stop on the
railroad going west, not any kind of world-beater, only
some place very special for those few folk who recognized
what it *really* was, and who coveted it as their home. But
that was all illusion. It was not that at all. It was really
just a suburb of Chicago. One of the *nicer* ones, to be
sure, and at first a distant one, although after a while it
would be much closer than anyone ever knew to fear. It
was a residential community, with quiet, tree-lined, increasingly ranch-style streets, and it was becoming a bed-
room community, with most all its men working down-

town, *in the big city,* working if not for themselves then at least very close to whoever was. And all the women were at home. A house to run, the shopping, the clubs, parties. And the family. The kids. Two or three. Off playing, in the yards, the parks, the pools. Or coming and going from school. The schools with their allotted intervals for their allotted learning, the teachers with their allotted concern. And all the while, all the way back, as if ordained, careers were being planned, were being prepared, mapped out, the chosen career for the chosen child, the child who still nursed pimples and suffered a tall frame and a weak rebound. The child who had not yet discovered a breast other than the one he had suckled.

It was pleasant enough in its way, I suppose, the permissiveness was not really of the sick kind, and there was nothing about it that was ugly or grotesque, or overtly hateful. It was all very *homelike.* With all the right things, in at least the right quantity. I certainly wasn't mistreated, not at all. I don't even remember feeling unfulfilled, not at the time. It was just so damn boring, so awfully dull and awfully sheltered, in the way only American suburbs can be. And so unnaturally anti-intellectual, in the way only the Midwest can be. Then the worst of it. The thing most destructive, most disillusioning to those of us who grew up there with our innocent dreams and our one-time bright faces, those of us who later sensed the necessity of going home and searching out our roots (not so much for settling, no, the idea never was to stay on, it was only to discover something of ourselves, the beginnings of awareness). The worst of it was this: *We found nothing there,* nothing of any use to us whatsoever. Only platitudes and vacuous stares. Only roadblocks. We found a place all but devoid of tradition or values, or the continuity of wisdom nurtured and solemnly passed from one generation to the next. A place all but devoid of interest or creation, all but devoid of passion. Most of all, I think we missed passion.

I was rootless. Alone. The only place I knew as home was empty. I searched elsewhere.

Montreal. Summer again. 1971. A full year of exile. Trying to imagine ever going home again, and finding little to imagine. *Amnesty. Going home.* It is not something that is really happening (there is nothing for my feelings to fix onto, embrace, nothing but limbo, they resist). *Amnesty.* Not now. *It does not exist.* It is something less than real, illusory, something more like myth. It is something elusive and scattered, awkward and painful. Almost farcical. Yet something nevertheless loving.

The other may actually be easier: *never* going home again. I've been through that. It may be inevitable. It may even be possible.

BARRY JOHNSON

Barry Johnson has worked for Clergy and Laymen Concerned About Vietnam and is now serving as coordinator for several social service agencies in Grand Rapids, Michigan.

SEMINARIAN IN "THE RESISTANCE"

On September 5 my draft appeal board voted unanimously to reject my request for classification as a conscientious objector. Instead it classified me 1-A, which means that I will soon be called to fight in Vietnam. My conscience will not allow me to go. I have no desire to go to jail or to embarrass my friends and relatives. I am twenty-five years old, and I would like to remain with my wife, Carol, and our child which she is now carrying. I would like to continue my preparation for the Christian ministry. I could easily have achieved these objectives by re-enrolling at Union Theological Seminary, thus regaining my previous 4-D deferment status. But my conscience would not permit it.

The refusal by my appeal board is only an anticlimax in a lengthy series of events and decisions which by late

August had convinced me that cooperation with the draft would be not only unpatriotic but a gross misuse of my Christian freedom. I do not consider my stand to be particularly liberal, radical, revolutionary or "hip." No matter what label one puts on resistance to the Selective Service system, the reasonableness of that resistance has become quite apparent to me.

When I graduated from Eau Claire State University in Wisconsin three years ago I did not anticipate arriving at such a position. My years there and at Luther College in Iowa were lacking in any form of political concern or interest. There were, however, two important influences during those years that initiated the process that led late last August to my decision for noncooperation.

Of paramount importance was a personal struggle during my sophomore year with the apparent inconsistency between loving my enemies and killing them. I finally decided that a C.O. classification would more honestly reflect my personal position than a student deferment (2-S), which implied that I would participate in military service if I were not a student. At that time my request for C.O. status was refused on the ground that I was a Lutheran, and that Lutheranism is not a pacifist religion. I thought this reason for refusal questionable but did not pursue the matter because I was not sure I was an absolute pacifist.

The second influence was my summer work. I spent each summer during my college career at a New York City Mission Society camp for children from New York's ghettos. That experience stimulated a concern for the poor of this country which in turn led to my decision to live in East Harlem while attending Union Theological Seminary, rather than on campus.

Carol and I spent our first year at the seminary in an East Harlem intern program directed by George Webber. I had a secular job administering a dropout program, and I spent my spare time trying to find out what was going on in the city, especially in East Harlem. Some important changes in my orientation toward our country have taken place as the result of two years of living in East Harlem and one year of field work in Newark, New Jersey. I have developed a realization of the huge gap that yawns between the claims set forth in our Constitution and Declaration of Independence and the living reality for the hundreds of thousands who live in our ghettos. I have also learned that discrimination and racial hatred are not southern issues but national catastrophies.

Since I have always considered our national claims worthwhile, my natural response to awareness of the disparity between claim and reality has been a desire to change the reality. The more I have come to realize how great is the disparity between the two, the more fundamental and serious has become my conviction of the need for change. I am convinced that a sincere desire for fundamental change represents an effort not to debase our country but to help it realize its claim.

In the fall of 1966, while an increasing number of young men from East Harlem were being called to serve in Vietnam, I became a full-time student at Union. I was bothered by the realization that my seminary deferment (4-D) discriminated unfairly in my favor against other young men, just as my student deferment in college (2-S) had done.

Though in theory the 2-S deferment may not be discriminatory, the fact is that its unavailability to young men in East Harlem results in discrimination against them. For example, in order to enter college, one must have an academic diploma. Benjamin Franklin High School, with approximately 3,000 students, is the only academic high school in East Harlem. In 1965 only 34 students out of a potential class of over 800 received academic diplomas. That year more than half of the high school students in New York were Negro or Puerto Rican, yet only one academic diploma in 19 was awarded to a Negro or a Puerto Rican.

Thus the young men from Benjamin Franklin High School are the last to get good jobs, the first to be called upon to kill and die in Vietnam. It is true that many young men from East Harlem enlist; in response to expressions of concern about the disproportionate number of Negro deaths in Vietnam the authorities are always eager to remind us of the high rate of Negro re-enlistment. What that means is that for large sections of our minority population the prospects in civilian life are so fraught with despair and hopelessness that military service is seen as the only viable avenue for self-improvement, dignity and security. High Negro re-enlistment is actually not so much a compliment to our military as a condemnation of our society.

As a result of such realizations I asked my draft board for some classification other than 4-D or 2-S. It was refused.

During the 1966 fall semester I began to read more about Vietnam. From the history of our involvement and from the way we were executing the war, I came to believe that our fight there is both illegal and immoral. It dawned on me that after supporting French colonialism against a Vietnamese struggle for independence, we set up Diem in order to have someone to whom we could commit ourselves; that we bypassed the U.N. and the Security Council's right to determine aggression; that we ignored procedures for collective decision-making within the SEATO treaty; that the Geneva Accords of 1954 fell by the wayside as we refused to support elections in 1956 and maintained an illegal military buildup from 1954 on. It is plain that this misuse and defiance of treaties and agreements have led to our involvement in a civil war in which our conduct reflects lack of both constraint and respect for international law. We callously use napalm, antipersonnel bombs, gas and defoliating chemicals in areas "suspected" of containing Vietcong. These actions, along with "free zone" bombing, mass relocation of civilians and mistreatment of prisoners, are certainly not only illegal but inhuman.

As my concern grew, I found concentration on my studies becoming more difficult. I felt I had to do what I could to stop the war. In January 1967 I went with a few hundred other seminarians to Washington, D.C., to attend a National Mobilization sponsored by Clergy and Laymen Concerned About Vietnam. The articulate yet humble concern of the 2,500 people in attendance impressed me very much. Finding myself in agreement with the position paper and projected plans, I decided to drop out of school and go to work full time for the national committee of Clergy and Laymen Concerned About Vietnam. My wife and I talked over this decision as we had my decision to reject 4-D or 2-S classifications. The 1-A classification, merely a possible outcome of the first decision, would become a sure thing if I were to quit school. I planned to apply for C.O. status, but I knew the chances were slim. If refused, I would be called to fight in Vietnam and I knew I could not go.

The 1-A classification came promptly. I applied for C.O. status and asked for a personal appearance before my local draft board, in Rice Lake, Wisconsin. In my application I indicated that I could not participate in this country's organized military operations for three reasons: (1) I cannot reconcile loving and killing my enemies. (2) The nature of war itself has changed from the time when armies could fight without great harm to civilians. In earlier days attacks on noncombatants did of course occur, but they were seen as acts of terror and repudiated. Today the machinery of war is so enmeshed in the society at war that acts formerly seen as terrorist are now considered matters of military necessity. (3) Any organ-

ized military effort of our nation has the latent potential
of beginning World War III.

In order to make it clear that I was not an absolute
pacifist I concluded my application as follows: "I am not
saying that there will never be a time when I may choose
to kill a man or to fight with all I have against that which
I see as evil. To say that would be to overestimate my
own self-control and self-awareness, and to deny the very
freedom I claim in the victory of Jesus Christ."

After driving 1,200 miles for a personal appearance
which my draft board had refused to guarantee in advance, I found myself on the evening of last June 12
with three men who had not thoroughly read my application, who displayed a lack of openness toward anyone's right to be a C.O. and who even refused permission
for my hometown minister to appear as a witness on my
behalf.

The board members asked questions which had clearly
been answered in my paper, and asked none which even a
cursory reading would have prompted. The degree of the
board's openness to the C.O. position was to be measured
by a number of questions; one: "Some of us fought in
World War II, and as a result life has been pretty good
for you. What do you think about that?" I was asked if I
thought communists were behind the summer riots in the
cities, and whether I knew of any communist cell groups
in East Harlem. One member was sure that "there must
be some organizing force behind it all."

It was a foregone conclusion that the board would refuse my request. When it did so, I appealed to the state
board. While waiting for its decision I tried to determine
how I should respond. If it accepted my appeal, I could
try to find an alternative service job both worth while and
acceptable to my local board. But as my conviction grew
that the C.O. classification is also very discriminatory,
I began to question whether I could accept the very clas-

sification for which I had applied. If the state board refused my appeal, I had a number of options. I could appeal to the President, try to obtain legal help to get my case into a civil court, re-enroll in seminary, refuse induction and face trial, or go to Canada.

Emigrating to Canada had never appeared as a very live option for me for two reasons: (1) Since I believed that I could possibly exert constructive influence in this country, I felt that I had a responsibility to try to do so. (2) I did not think that from two to five years in prison would have too detrimental an effect on either my wife or me, or on our relationship.

It is sad but understandable that many sensitive and concerned young men who cannot fight in Vietnam do leave all behind and go to Canada. Perhaps they no longer harbor any hope that they can be of influence in constructive change; perhaps a long prison term appears to them unbearable. I feel that we should not judge these men harshly. The serious consideration and anguish of conscience over our national policy which undoubtedly precedes most of these decisions is alien to thousands of irresponsible citizens who do not critically seek out information on our involvement in Vietnam. We owe this kind of critical evaluation to our country as citizens; we owe it to each man who dies in Vietnam.

Consideration of options other than emigration to Canada prompted me to inquire further into recent developments in regard to the draft, and into the powers and influence the draft is exerting on our society. What I found was discouraging. In the discussions before the extension of the draft law efforts were made in Congress and by various religious bodies to obtain improvements in the law or actual termination of the draft. These efforts were ignored; we now have a draft law which is as bad if not worse than the old one.

Inequitable and seemingly impervious to change, the

Selective Service System has been given powers that are both misplaced and misused. With no theological expertise whatever, the system has the authority to define what is and what is not "religious." So bolstered it stands in judgment over individual consciences, basing its decisions on its own quasi-religious terminology, which in the present "Form 150" (the C.O. application) discriminates against the semiliterate or less articulate poor, against anyone who has a contextual theology and refuses to make blanket statements about an unknown future, against all whose personal beliefs allow them to say only that they will not participate in a particular war they believe to be unjust. Surely one must question the right of the Selective Service System to stand as the final arbiter over another man's conscience; and there is no doubt in my mind that it is incompetent and discriminatory in its dealings with the consciences of young Americans.

The Selective Service System is an instrument of power in yet another way. Since the National Security Council, with its military advisory board, decides which occupations are "in the national interest," the Selective Service System could become (if it has not already) the agent for using the draft as a club, and deferments as a bribe, to channel young men into occupations which directly or indirectly support and expand the military establishment. As parts of our war-defense machinery, the National Security Council and the Selective Service System are anything but neutral in deciding which occupations are "in the national interest." Besides, "national interest" jobs and 2-S deferments and the C.O. classification are discriminatory because they are unavailable to young men miseducated in the de facto segregated, grossly neglected schools in the urban ghettos. The basic education necessary for entrance into college is a minimum necessity not only for any "national interest" job but also for being able to understand the alternatives and to prepare a C.O. application in such a way as to establish even the most remote chance

of acceptance. This kind of basic education is being denied the Negroes and Puerto Ricans of our ghettos.

At length I realized that I could not cooperate with an
inequitable and discriminatory system which is conscript-
ing disproportionate numbers of the poor to fight in an
undeclared, immoral, unjust war. To remain silent, or to
cooperate with an unjust system because I am not a victim of its injustice, would represent irresponsible, self-
indulgent and unpatriotic acquiescence in the widening
of the gap between our country's claim and the reality,
as well as rejection of the life and teachings of Christ,
who challenged injustice by subjecting himself to it.

It is crucial that the citizens of this great country face
up to the inequities in our society, to our self-righteous
paranoia about communism, to our outrageous actions
against the combatants and civilians of Vietnam. We must
face these critical issues without the self-deceptive desire
to balance our inequities and misconduct against those
of other nations; we must balance them rather against
our own proclamations and responsibilities, both at home
and in the world community.

It was my own attempt to face up to the demands of
the Christian faith and responsibilities as a citizen of the
United States that led me to join The Resistance. The
decision to opt for noncooperation was very agonizing
for me; I am deeply concerned about order and the obligations of citizenship. But I realize that order is not self-
justifying, that it is not order itself but the positive influence of that order in the lives of individuals within the
society that is important. A harsh dictatorship can ensure
order—but who would advocate that road? When a given
social order, in spite of its claims, perpetuates inequities,
when it arrogantly and destructively imposes its will on
others, the plea for order must stand second to the demand for justice.

On October 16, 1967, I joined with twenty-seven students from Union Theological Seminary and 1,200 other young men across the nation and returned my draft card, with a letter explaining why I can no longer cooperate with the Selective Service System. Those of us who will not go to Vietnam and who will not accept deferments which discriminate against our brothers have joined together to form a movement called "The Resistance." We feel that if a war is unjust one should resist its continuation, that if the Selective Service System operates inequitably one should resist its operation. Thus members of The Resistance encourage others to resist; they set about creatively disrupting the smooth flow of that which is deemed unjust; they call attention to its injustice. They hope to challenge people to face the draft, the war and tragedies at home. Information, stimulation and organization may lead to a movement with potential for change.

What Carol, the child to come and I face is highly uncertain, though the hope continues that I can resume study for the ministry sometime in the future. Uncertainty, of course, is often frightening; that is why we are frightened about the future of our children, the future of U.S. involvement in Vietnam, the future of our country whose disparity between its claim and its reality is becoming a burden too heavy to bear.

Raymond J. Pontier

Raymond J. Pontier is the minister of the Allwood Community Church in Clifton, New Jersey.

To Suffer as a Christian[1]

> None of you should suffer for being a murderer, or a thief, or a criminal, or for trying to manage other people's business. But if you suffer because you are a Christian, don't be ashamed of it, but thank God that you bear Christ's name.
>
> (I Peter 4:15–16)

I have a concern. I share it with you this morning because I can preach no other sermon until I have preached this one. It is about my son Glenn, and conscience, and the fellowship of the church—the fellowship that affirms,

> We share each other's woes,
> Each other's burdens bear.

Yes, I have a concern. My son may go to prison because, for reasons of Christian conscience, he refuses to take part in the hurt and hate and killing of war.

[1] This piece is a sermon, "To Suffer as a Christian," delivered May 16, 1971, at the Allwood Community Church, Clifton, New Jersey.

My son may go to prison because, for reasons of Christian conscience, he believes that it is wrong for him as a person to cooperate further with a Selective Service System that is an instrument of making war.

My son may go to prison for up to five years because he believes, as a Christian, that human life is sacred, that people are called upon to heal and not hurt, that Jesus is indeed the Prince of Peace, and "Blessed are the peacemakers."

My son knows that he may spend those years in a federal penitentiary because he believes that no government or ruler can compel an individual to violate his conscience by taking part in something that is evil and wrong.

Because he believes that war and killing are wrong, he has chosen to take his stand at the point of refusing to cooperate with the Selective Service System. Because he will not kill or aid and abet a system that compels others to kill, he was arrested by the F.B.I. and indicted by the government. Have you ever seen a federal indictment? It reads: "The United States of America vs. Glenn R. Pontier." When I think of the uneven odds, I could weep.

You may disagree with Glenn's particular expression of conscience. Possibly you do. But I do hope and ask that you understand and respect his convictions, his conscience, his integrity, his courage. I do hope and ask, even if you disagree, that you uphold him and stand with him as a son of the church in his right of conscience.

Mrs. Pontier and I, of course, support him completely. When we called our daughter, Sharon, to tell her about her brother's arrest, she said immediately and spontaneously, "I'm proud of him!" At the time Glenn and his wife Kim were married they promised in their vows "to have and to hold . . . in prison or free." To be sure, you might expect us to support him. He is one of our own, part of the family. Perhaps you do not expect us to be proud of him. But we are. We know Glenn, and he has the normal human quota of strengths and faults—but we know him best as an intelligent, reasonable, concerned, dedicated person.

None of us wants to see him go to prison. I wish he could find an easy way to oppose the inhumanity of war. It is tempting to say to him, as Peter did to Jesus, "No, Glenn, this need never happen to you! Not five years in jail! Find an easy way out, go along with the system, do alternate service, take a deferment. Lots of guys are doing it." Slither through—for this is approved.

But Glenn has chosen to confront the system of war. If he wanted to, he could have had an easy "out." As a seminary student he is entitled to and could have received a 4-D exemption and never have to think about the draft again. That would be easy. But he has refused to evade, avoid, dodge, or run away from it. He is standing up to it. Out of conscience he is saying "no" to a whole system and pattern that perpetuates the hurt, the brutality, the destruction, the killing of our time. We do not want to see him go to prison, but neither do we want him to or ask him to be untrue to himself or his convictions. So we are not ashamed of him, but, on the contrary, we are proud of him. The tragedy lies in the senselessness and cruelty and waste of sending someone to prison, not for the bad of hurting people, but for the good of affirming the sanctity of human life. To suffer for the sake of Christian conscience has, of course, the firm approval of Scripture, and it was Peter who wrote, "But if you suffer because you are a Christian, don't be ashamed of it, but thank God that you bear Christ's name."

It is significant, I think, to realize that Glenn's faith, convictions, ideals, and conscience were taught and nurtured in the church. The frightening thing is that he has believed what was taught. He has taken the church and gospel seriously. Here he learned about the Jesus who incarnated love and compassion and caring. Here he was taught the commandment, "You shall not kill." Here he heard that the greatest commandment is to love God with total commitment, and to love your neighbor as yourself. Here he was told that "You shall love your enemy," and that the high conscience of those who say, "We must obey God rather than men" is to be exalted.

Shall we tell him now that we didn't really mean it? Have we been playing phony little games with religion? Go to church, Glenn, say your prayers, sing your hymns, read your Bible, pay your dues, attend your meetings— but, for heaven's sake, don't be so serious about this brotherhood and love and peace and conscience bit. Did some Sunday School teacher or minister tell you that God and conscience come first? Forget it, for they really meant that nation and conformity are first. Taking us so seriously is quite embarrassing; it's bad for business, and we may lose money and members. Sure, we know Paul went to prison for his convictions. So did a lot of early Christians. But times have changed; we don't do things that way any more.

No one is really saying that. At least, I hope not. But there are many, I know, who are distressed and upset by his decision of conscience. If he had come home from war in which he obeyed orders to kill and bomb and destroy, he might receive a medal and perhaps be welcomed to speak to a meeting or from the pulpit. When Lieutenant Calley was convicted of killing at least twenty-two civilians, women, and children, massive hysteria developed. Petitions were circulated for his release, Legion posts rallied in support, the President intervened, and Governor Maddox said, "Thank God for Lieutenant Calley and people like you." There is something obscene and blasphemous and sick in all that, that says something about the American character.

Free Calley! Give him a medal. But, horrors—here is a young man who says "no" to killing and war. And he said it decisively, out loud, for all to see, by refusing to go along with something that produced a Calley, that has killed fifty thousand American boys, that has scored vic-

tories by "body counts," that has killed a million or more
Vietnamese, that has laid waste the countryside. He has
said a loud "no" to all of this—and so four F.B.I. men
came to New Brunswick Seminary on April 19 and arrested this dangerous young man who believes in peace.
James Kunen in *The Strawberry Statement* writes, "Isn't
it singular that no one ever goes to jail for waging wars,
let alone advocating them? But the jails are filled with
those who want peace. Not to kill is to be a criminal.
They put you right in jail if all you do is ask them to
leave you alone. Exercising the right to live is a violation
of law. It strikes me as quite singular."

"The United States of America vs. Glenn R. Pontier."
The tragedy of our time is that we have come to a point
when Glenn may be numbered as one among thousands
of political prisoners in this nation, prisoners for conscience' sake, jailed for having exercised their basic right
to follow their convictions, imprisoned for refusing to
participate in man's inhumanity to man. These prisoners
are men and women who could add immeasurably to
the good of our nation in terms of its social ills, men and
women who seek to correct human hurts, who are dedicated to service. But the compassion and imagination of
the nation has not gone beyond sending them to jail for
their refusal to kill. That is what the war in Indochina
has done to our own souls. You may not agree with them,
you may not choose their course—but they are not to be
cast out or castigated as draft-dodgers or cowards. It takes
a high degree of conscience and courage to stand up for
what you believe, and to be prepared to take the consequences.

Courage on behalf of conscience is in short supply. A
prominent clergyman was asked why he did not take a
lead and speak out against the war, and he said, "If I had
said what was in my mind I should have been in prison a
week ago." Several years ago, William Orchard, an Angli-
can minister, told a group of seminarians, "Gentlemen, I

am sixty-five years of age. I have never been in prison; I
have not been burnt alive, or shot at dawn, or stoned by a
mob. You may guess that I have been playing my cards
very carefully." Then he added, "Every good man today
has to explain why he is alive."

In this time when the phrase "law and order" is so
often mouthed, there are some who may believe, ab-
stractly at least, that obeying the law, any law, is the
highest good. Well, law is good, and no one should be
careless in ignoring or defying it. A society without law
can soon become a society that is a jungle. But law, in and
of itself, is not the highest good—especially to a Christian. The highest good is to be obedient to a conscience
that has been exposed to Jesus Christ, and when man's
law and Christian conscience collide, then the choice becomes obvious. When Martin Luther stood against church
and state, he cried, "My conscience is captive to the Word
of God." And that is where it belongs.

The United States of America may not be ready to
honor this. But does the church? The Particular Synod
of New Jersey, at its annual meeting, rose to its own faith
when it approved a resolution that said, "In consideration of the Biblical injunction that a person's conscience is
subject to God, and in light of the many statements of
the General Synod supporting the priority of conscience,
we therefore express our support to those who choose to
make their witness through refusal to participate in war or
the Selective Service System because of their conviction
that such participation violates their obedience to Christ."
And the Synod went beyond a general resolution to particular support when it said that "We as a Synod express
to Glenn Pontier our support of his right of Christian
conscience, embrace him in Christian love, and promise
to maintain the fellowship of Christ to which we are
both committed." And even beyond nice words, it em-
powered the executive committee of the Synod to file an
amicus curiae (friend of the court) brief on his behalf,

and established a synodwide Legal Defense Fund. Where the local church stands, however, remains to be seen.

And what is the good of all this? Why risk going to jail for a principle? I have no easy answers. But I know that I find faith restored by people like Jesus and Paul, Francis of Assisi and Martin Luther, Gandhi and Martin Luther King and the Berrigan brothers—who took risks for love and justice, who went beyond talk to action. When the apostle Paul was in prison he wrote to the Philippians: "I want you to know, my brothers, that the things that have happened to me have really helped the progress of the gospel. As a result, the whole palace guard and all the others here know that I am in prison because I am a servant of Christ. And my being in prison has given most of the brothers more confidence in the Lord, so that they grow bolder all the time in preaching the message without fear." (Philippians 1:12–14) Father Daniel Berrigan, in his book *No Bars to Manhood,* writes: "Now, when a man consents to live and die for the truth, he sets in motion spiritual rhythms whose outward influences are, in the nature of things, simply immeasurable." And in speaking of Gandhi, he says, "Out of a virile disregard for personal danger and stress, he wished to make it possible for others to live—to be conscious, to be freed of demons, to welcome their brothers. The point for Gandhi and Jesus is not that men would agree with them, or do the same things they did. The point is that others would come to a deepened consciousness; that their sense of existence and human issues would be sharpened to the point where they would 'do their thing'—a good thing, a human thing, as they were doing theirs."

I do not ask, I do not expect Glenn to do what he is doing, for I do not want to see him hurt or to suffer. But he is doing it—and I stand with him, I respect him, I am proud of him. Because he is doing it, I imagine I will be doing "my thing" in a different way . . . and I suspect that others will be turned on to do "their thing" for humanity and peace. And deep down I continue to hope that this church, and other churches, will examine the meaning of its own witness and fellowship because of the stand of one young man—and uphold him with pride.

"The United States of America vs. Glenn R. Pontier." I'm in your corner, Glenn—in prison or free. I believe it is the Christian corner, and with Peter I say, "If you suffer because you are a Christian, don't be ashamed of it."

JOHN JACOB PHILLIPS

John Jacob Phillips recently surrendered to federal authorities and is now in prison.

JUDAISM, THE DRAFT, AND ME

*How a prison rabbi restored for me
the meaning of my Jewish heritage*

For many years, I reluctantly identified myself as Jewish. I was Bar-Mitzvahed in an unusual synagogue (established by my immigrant grandfather and his friends) in which the functions of a rabbi were delegated to the members of the congregation, and educated in a Yiddish school operated by the Workmen's Circle ("Arbeiter Ring"). Thus given the impetus to nonconformity at an early age, I was soon alienated from the traditional forms of religious practice. The Zionist phenomenon frightened me, and I was disgusted with its national chauvinism and its emphasis on militarism. In addition, I was preoccupied with the need to discover my individual identity, and shunned all labels that might define me in terms of a larger whole.

My decision to oppose the war in Vietnam and to refuse military service was a personal decision, in which social and psychological pressures were an important fac-

tor. It was also, of course, an ethical decision, but not one
defined within the framework of the Judaic religion
(which appeared to be at best neutral on this issue).
Buber's writing, especially his conception of "I" and
"Thou," had important influence on me, but hardly
seemed a typical Jewish conception. Tolstoy and Thoreau
became equally relevant to me, and Gandhi would have
been if I had studied him. I could not discover many
other Jews who shared my point of view or the intensity
of my concern. My politics at this time were a translation of my ethics: communitarian, libertarian, antimili-
tarist, anti-exploitation. I summed it up by calling myself
a pacifist, and became involved in nonviolent direct action against the war and the draft.

On the day when I refused to submit to induction—
June 14 (Flag Day), 1966—an aging man approached
me and introduced himself as "one who knew my grandfather and my father." Suddenly, he looked very sad, and
he exclaimed, with obvious bitterness-mixed-with-anxiety,
"Always the Jews have suffered for the others!" He was
half-reproachful and half-mournful as he went on to
paint the gloomy picture of a vengeful government that
would single out the Jews as scapegoats if they became
prominent in the opposition movements. I determined to
avoid falling into this sort of trap (which paralyzed potential activists), which I couldn't help identifying with
mainstream Judaism, a heritage that seemed able to bind
people to the past and prevent them from accepting the
reality of change. In so doing, I felt that I was withdraw-
ing even more than previously from my identity as a Jew.

When a prominent Jewish lawyer offered to take my
case without charge ("We have to look out for each
other"), I turned him down, partly because I was convinced that a court of law could not, by its own definition,
acquit me (since I had deliberately violated the law), but
partly also because I was reluctant to make the issue a
religious question. In September of 1966, in federal court

in Boston, I was convicted by jury and sentenced to three years in prison by the judge, Charles E. Wyzanski, Jr. I was immediately taken into custody and removed to begin my sentence at the federal prison at Petersburg, Virginia. Shortly after I arrived, I received word that the judge had reconsidered my sentence and reduced it to eighteen months. I began to write on a regular basis to him, for he had taken such an obvious personal interest in my case. I wanted to convey as well as I could in letters (which to him were exempt from censorship) the impressions I was encountering "behind bars," both good and bad, that he might in this way come to have a better understanding of what prison meant for the people who came before him as defendants. At Hanukkah, we exchanged greeting cards. Later, when my parole hearing was held, the judge urged the Parole Board in Washington (which had power over my case) to release me at "the earliest possible date"; but the Board was not about to let a draft resister off so lightly. When I was released, after spending fourteen months in prison, I was invited by the judge to come and talk together, and I accepted his offer. I discovered that I had greatly overestimated the effect in improving our understanding of each other that my letters had achieved, and felt greatly disappointed.

I felt a similar disappointment about my relationship with my father. From letters, I had gathered that the impact of my imprisonment had been instrumental in his own political development. When I returned home, he greeted me with the news that he had learned to share my pacifist beliefs. But I could not reconcile his claim with the attitude that I had "fulfilled my obligation" by serving a term in prison, and his stern demand that I "take my [proper] place" in school or work—as though my convictions were no longer relevant to my style of living, but matter for the family scrapbook! I felt that in some ways, my father and I were farther apart than ever before.

Two incidents that occurred at the time of Hanukkah

during my imprisonment had an enormous impact on my feelings and identity, and served to revitalize my "Jewishness." The first was the arrival of a greeting card from Tel Aviv, and a letter that followed from the same person. The sender introduced herself, in English (apologizing for her awkwardness although she handled the language very well), as an Israeli pacifist (!) who had received the names of American war resisters in prison from the local war resisters group. Not satisfied with sending a card, she had written in the hope that we could establish regular correspondence as "fellow pacifists." It must have been lonely to be a pacifist in Tel Aviv; she mentioned that she also had been "detained" because of her outspoken views against militarism. I thought to myself, as I came upon the words "fellow pacifist," that without realizing it, she had written to a "fellow Jew" as well. (The regulations at Petersburg prohibited my corresponding with her, but I managed to smuggle out a reply. Afterward, I lost contact with her.) My sudden reidentification with Judaism surprised me, but I dismissed it as more a response to her feminine appeal than to a genuine characteristic of myself.

At about the same time, I found myself summoned to the chaplain's office, along with other Jewish prisoners, to accept a special visit from a rabbi who had sort of a "circuit riding" ministry in that area of Virginia. I went to see him reluctantly, and only in order to fill our ranks (together, there were six of us) so that the rabbi would agree to see the other five. He really made us feel that his visit was a big favor to us, not his obligation. A local colleague of his had refused to accept the prison ministry on even an occasional basis, because there were "too few to bother with," and of course, because we were a source of shame to the "respectable" Jews outside. In the course of introductions that day, the rabbi made it plain that he viewed "Jewish conscientious objectors" as a contradiction in terms. It seemed hopeless to try to draw some distinction between Jewish C.O.s and Jewish war resisters in his thinking, since both groups were to him contemptible, but had I succeeded I am sure he would have placed me in the category of "beneath contempt."

For my special benefit, the rabbi embarked upon an elaborate defense of the U.S. involvement in Vietnam, using the occasion of Hanukkah to draw parallels between the dedication and courage of "our boys" in Vietnam who were winning the hearts and minds of the peasants (by waging war on them) to liberate them from totalitarian control, and that of the Jewish resisters memorialized. His analogy proved too preposterous for me to accept in silence, as I had resolved to do. Suddenly, I found myself launching a rebuttal. The ensuing debate lasted for hours, and by its end I felt that I had made a satisfactory case for my own interpretation, in which the partisans had more in common with the National Liberation Front, and the examples of resistance in the face of certain death were an inspiration for our own resistance to oppressive government policies such as conscription for war. It had been a very lively exchange, and it had given me an opportunity to renew my own consciousness of the war issue, which I had sublimated in the routine of prison life. Afterward, I was not so shy about bringing such matters into discussions with other prisoners. Of course, the rabbi's view remained unshaken, but I had been drawn out of my "protective shell" and sought new opportunities to regain the momentum of political involvement. I realized, too, that the rabbi had unintentionally crystallized a Jewish consciousness that I could regard as authentically my own: Despite my intentions to the contrary, I had been engaging in a vigorous defense of Judaism and Jewish history as a relevant source of inspiration for my involvement in the social struggles of our time.

I have not attempted to remold my own activity in terms of such a "Jewish consciousness." Rather, I have been able to accept my roots as "legitimate," and even indulge in a sort of ethnic pride so long as it does not become a barrier to communication with others (both Jews and non-Jews) or an excuse for unexamined action. When I realized, then, that I was to be the only Jewish member of the group that planned to destroy Chicago's draft files, I felt sincerely that my presence was in some way "representative" of Judaism as I conceived of it. I was consciously stating, as I am with these words, that this is the sort of thing that Jews (as well as others) could and should do.

Why a nice Jewish boy decided to help destroy draft files in Chicago

I emerged from fourteen months of incarceration slightly embittered, but more determined and more confident in my resolution to return to "movement work." Adding Mark Twain and Diogenes to my list of mentors, I set about the task of employing humor and guerrilla theater as the media for my opposition to war. My prison time had convinced me that the struggle against exploitation must be extended to every area of human interaction, and that prisons are themselves as intolerable as armies in a truly free society. As I encountered larger numbers of young men who had chosen to resist the draft, I realized that the proper focus of my energy and imagination was in disseminating information about my own experience to those who would be risking imprisonment. I began to realize, too, that the biggest and most important task lay in reaching people to whom the prisons were a complete unknown, to bring them to realize the part that prisons play in pressuring our choice of action, to shatter their misconceptions of what prisons were like, to foster the understanding that the men and women behind bars —for whatever reason—were the victims of a brutal, dehumanizing system that could only produce more harm to the society it "served." Together with others who had "done time" (at first, exclusively draft resisters), I launched the "Prisoners' Information & Support Service," which published a newsletter irregularly, arranged public speaking for former prisoners, made counselors available to people facing prison, and served as a link between the prisoners and the movement "outside." There was much work to be done, and few of us to do it. My feeling for the work was so intense that I left my job to do it full time, surviving on the basis of contributions from our newsletter subscribers.

For a year and a half, I devoted my energy to this work, and began to feel that it was having a good effect. At the very least, it aided the about-to-be-incarcerated by giving them a concrete idea of what was ahead of them, so that they could respond to that situation more creatively. It was hard to persuade even the most ardent movement workers that the threshhold of imprisonment, far from being a threshhold of death, was merely the entrance to a different institutional structure where our ideals and insights would continue to determine our behavior and where we had a responsibility to experiment in terms of our commitment to social change, however limited the opportunities seemed to be.

My activity along these lines satisfied my desire to remain involved and relevant, for some time. But as the months passed, I could not help becoming painfully aware of its limitations in the context of the massive preparations for continued war on the part of the government, and in the face of the seemingly endless void that we were trying so hard to fill by our little efforts. It was a normal frustration, but I began to watch for an opportunity to become involved on a different scale of activity, one that would satisfy me as a direct and effective action to stop the military machine or its corporate partners.

Although at the outset, the destruction of draft files seemed unsatisfactory to me as that sort of "vehicle," gradually I came to see in such an act a meaningful, symbolic, and practical way of undermining the deadly process of conscription. I turned the proposition over in my own head many times, and came to the conclusion that the objective, and the technique required to achieve it, were not in essential conflict with my own convictions and my commitment to nonviolent direct action. It was a militant proposition, and presented drastic consequences for those who took part. Two ideas came together in my final decision to act. In putting a Selective Service office out of commission by destroying the only "evidence" they had by which to select cannon fodder for the war, I would be striking out against that part of the military complex that had made it necessary (given my commitment) to be imprisoned. This thought made the matter a personal one as well as a political issue. The other was the realization that my previous experience as a prisoner had uniquely suited me for activity in which the risk involved was that of being sent back to prison. Although I was fully aware that the quality of life and the opportunities for creative involvement outside of prison are far better than those inside, I had begun to discover how to transform the prison experience into a medium for self-development and for organizing. The prospect of a new term, while undesirable, could not hold for me the terrors that I had imagined prior to my first incarceration, for I had been trained to deal with the situation.

The symbolic value of such action appealed to me, apart from its obvious practical results (which would be slim and temporary in most cases). Although the draft board raids could not bring about lasting social changes by themselves, yet in the context of a vital and multidimensional movement, they could answer the need for assurance that the system we confront is not beyond our power to affect it, and the desperate need to discover models of personal dedication and collective organized action that has been carried through to its objective. Moreover, the action presents a challenge: first, to those who might be inclined in the face of the growing intensity and violence of the struggle, to resign their efforts from despair or a fear of being drawn into violent modes of involvement; and, second, to those who have been sucked into the whirlpool of mindless slogans and paramilitary (and futile) gestures against the system. To both groups, the draft board "raids" offer an example of an alternative response in a desperate situation, and generate some hope of creative action of other kinds in the wide range that remains relatively unexplored between the two poles of resignation.

[On May 25, 1969, I and fourteen other people of various religious and social backgrounds and temperaments and life-styles came together in Chicago and invaded the Selective Service offices located in the South Side. "The Chicago Action Community" destroyed an estimated forty thousand 1-A files and cross records, forcing the local boards affected to cancel draft calls for the next several months.]

Murray Polner

18-Minute Verdict: Military Justice & Constitutional Rights*

William Harvey and George Daniels have much in common. They are both black, twenty and ex-marines. Today they are also both in the U.S. Naval Disciplinary prison in Portsmouth, New Hampshire. Fifteen months after enlistment they were found guilty by a marine court-martial and sentenced to six (Harvey) and ten years (Daniels), plus dishonorable discharge and forfeiture of all allowances for violating catch-all Article 34 of the Universal Code of Military Justice (UCMJ) and "making statements with the intent to interfere with, impair, influence the loyalty, morale, and discipline of a member of the USMC."

In the summer of 1968 both Harvey and Daniels were charged, tried and adjudged guilty—in Daniels' case in eighteen minutes—and given extraordinarily draconian sentences. Yet, this was not an uncommon ritual. The military services like to deal with their own almost *in camera,* without the attendant publicity and hoopla of civilian trials, not because they have anything to hide but rather because for them it is a kind of continuum,

* This article originally appeared in *Commonweal,* March 28, 1969, pp. 40-43.

another link in the hoary shibboleth that the armed forces always act with dispatch and efficiency. In spite of the introduction of the UCMJ in 1951, the military have nearly always acted as masters in their own homes, rarely countermanded by civilian courts, arbiter of the destiny of millions of conscriptees, and firm in the belief that this arrangement was the best for all concerned.

Normally, then, the court-martial is held and that's that. A few cases are thrown out by higher military appellate courts but in the vast majority the original verdict, if not always the sentence, stands. The Harvey and Daniels case was no exception. It was overlooked by the press (black and white) and TV until Harvey got word out to the American Civil Liberties Union and its chief counsel Melvin Wulf. Even now the ACLU has been unable to interest anybody except Andy Stapp's miniscule American Servicemen's Union.

The reason for this is not hard to find. The educated public is not yet aware of a poorly hidden dispute about to surface within the military establishment and which can be traced directly to the turmoil of the 1960s: should the Bill of Rights and the First Amendment in particular include the man in uniform? Can enlisted men and officers be forbidden the right to discuss among themselves and even publicly the merits of Vietnam, the ferment in the cities, the oil depletion allowance, subsidies, race, indeed things that anyone outside the services can talk about freely?

"Now the question is being raised," reports the Workers Defense League, an organization active in defending servicemen in court martials (and which includes among its National Board members Daniel Bell, Ossie Davis, Michael Harrington, Nat Hentoff, Murray Kempton, Dave McReynolds, Bayard Rustin, Joseph Rauh, Roy Wilkins and Al Shanker of the UFT), "of whether or not civil liberties are feasible within the military structure and whether or not men in the armed forces have constitu-

tional rights that are not superseded by the UCMJ." Put
another way, is the old system out of date? If they were
ever right, are they justified today?

Observers like Army General Counsel Robert E. Jor-
dan III have started to question the old notion that the
unique character of the military always limits an army of
conscriptees' opinions. "I personally reject the view," Jor-
dan has written, "that those who enter military service
perform in an enclave where the Constitution—including
the First Amendment—has no application."

For William Harvey and George Daniels it all began
on a hot summer afternoon in late July, 1967, in Camp
Pendleton, California. A group of marines, mostly black,
sat under a tree eating, talking, arguing and listening to
a record player.

Exactly what happened there (and later that evening,
after chow) on July 27th is a matter of dispute. Marines
dropped by on both occasions, spoke their minds or simply listened, and then casually drifted away. For many
of them, as their testimony at the court-martial later revealed, it was of no special significance, just another bull
session. One Pfc. thought it was a hootenanny. Others
disagreed and said more serious matters had been discussed. But to the Marine Corps it was perfectly clear:
Harvey and Daniels, they charged, were guilty of breaking Art. 34.

The official allegation was that in the two gatherings
both men had described Vietnam as "a white man's war"
that no black man could in good conscience support while
their own people were suffering in this country. The
Corps also charged that they encouraged other marines to
avoid service in Vietnam.

To all this Harvey and Daniels answered yes. They
did make certain statements as charged but with this one
crucial difference: Everything they said in Pendleton was
in "open discussion," a right they held as American citizens. These opinions, they declared, were a natural ex-

pression of concern about matters which meant very much
to them, but in no way had they ever tried to persuade
others to disobey orders.

During their trials several witnesses also remembered
Harvey and Daniels urging them to "stick together" and
"request mast," the latter an official method of jumping
the normal marine chain of command in order to see the
commanding officer about a pressing personal problem.
One need not reveal to any superior except the C.O. the
reason for the request, nor can one be punished—at least
not publicly—for making one.

Nonetheless, the Corps was already watching Daniels
closely. A graduate of Andrew Jackson High School in
Queens, he began turning toward the Black Muslims at
boot camp in Cherry Point, North Carolina, and by the
time he arrived at Pendleton he was marked as a bad
penny, an agitator suspected of preaching black separa-
tism and opposition to the war the Corps was called to
wage.

On the other hand, Harvey was an anonymous graduate of Brooklyn's Boys High School. He enlisted in
June, 1966, met Daniels, thought a great deal about
"events" and by July 27th had made up his mind. The
next day, a Friday, he reported to Company Headquarters and told S/Sgt. William Melton he wanted to "request mast for personal reasons having to do with fighting
a war." Apparently he also told Melton that "about fourteen" others also wanted to see the C.O. Melton, by now
growing concerned, asked who they were.

Late the same day a few more black marines fell out
to ask for mast. Afterwards, at the trial, some of them
said they had been "encouraged" by Harvey to do so.
One Pfc. testified that he told him "It was a white man's
war . . . and that the colored man had no right to go
over there and fight and then have to come back here and
fight." Still another added "He (Harvey) was going to

request mast and refuse to go to Vietnam and fight the white man's war."

Harvey himself was called in for an interview with another non-com, S/Sgt. Waymon B. Wilson, whose job was to screen all requests for mast. He had Harvey write out a statement but failed to tell him at the same time that he was already suspected of breaking military law. Nor did he warn him that he had a right to call for a lawyer. As a result, the remarks were excluded from the trial. Reproducing it here offers a guide to Harvey's thinking at the time and the confusion it caused. Harvey told Wilson that: "On or about July 28, 1967 . . . [I] . . . realized that I will not take part in wars or conflicts against other people while right here in the United States injustice is being committed against my own. I am being suspected or accused of mutiny (sic), that I am not guilty of, because of helping a S/Sgt. save time."

Very soon after he was called in again, this time to headquarters to be questioned by an ONI investigator, Byron Taylor. He carefully informed Harvey of his legal rights and then asked him for a statement. Taylor, it seems, had seen a copy of Wilson's interview but says he never used it. At the same time, however, Harvey thought Taylor was there to look further into precisely that statement, was prepared to comment on it, and kept "wondering where it was and if he would ever pull it out."

Suspicion and Alarm

At this point Harvey asked for and received a lawyer. Then, when the interrogation resumed and completed, Taylor asked him to sign all the pages of his testimony. Harvey agreed and even initialed the typed corrections. But he soon grew suspicious: ". . . what was in that statement was not my own words; those were his words . . . he kept saying things I wasn't saying at all."

He also grew alarmed. What he and Daniels had intended originally as a private act of conscience was now mushrooming into a nightmare. Taylor pressed him to sign the final draft but Harvey turned him down. Neither he nor Daniels ever denied making statements about war and race. But the entire matter, they would continue to maintain, was an expression of personal judgment. The persuasion of others was not on their mind.

The trial transcript would tend to substantiate this. One of the witnesses, Pfc. Johnson, disclosed that while he had overheard Harvey twice say—"We should stick together."—he also added he had never heard him advise anyone to disobey orders. And of the sixteen or eighteen marines who requested mast, only five or six of them said they might balk at Vietnam duty, but if they did, the choice was theirs alone. Two of the men explained further that they hadn't come to see the C.O. for anything political, but only to ask for hardship discharges. Several others said they had come in to request changes in their military assignments. Not one said he had been swayed by either Harvey or Daniels.

The court's severe decisions and penalties will do little to resolve the knotty problem of where free speech ends and military security begins. Harvey and Daniels were sentenced in August, 1967, but in the ensuing months a still small but otherwise vocal and growing number of servicemen has taken its own stand of conscience. Within the past six months, for example, at least three "GI Weeks" have been held, and several more are promised for the spring.

Who's Afraid of Conscience?

In the weeks before last October's San Francisco parade of protesting servicemen the military tried hard to pressure GIs from attending. An unclassified Defense Department memorandum, dated 28 August 1968 and sent to "Headquarters, U.S. Air Force Communication Cen-

ter" at nearby Hamilton Air Force Base, has been declared the real thing by antiwar groups throughout the
country and widely distributed. Aimed originally at an
Air Force Lieutenant who had helped set up the demonstration it allegedly stated: "Strongly believe this demonstration should be quashed if possible because of severe
impact on military discipline . . . particularly in view of
the political climate of the day."

In one case, the trial of a soldier named George Downis,
the court ordered a four-year sentence which included
dishonorable discharge and forfeiture of all pay and allowances. During the proceedings the prosecuting attorney spoke some remarkable words that tell us a good deal
more about the hunters than the hunted. He would not,
he said, care to challenge the sincerity of Downis' views.
But there was something far more vital, indeed far more
invidious in his act of disobedience. "Crimes committed
as matters of conscience are in a sense more serious than
crimes committed as matters of passion or greed, because
crimes of conscience *strike at the heart of our system*"
(my emphasis).

What is really happening is that "participatory politics" is reaching the military and threatens to punch holes
in its formidable defenses. The sudden appearance of
folk-singing, brainy coffee house hostesses instead of bar-
room whores has stunned the military as have Trotskyite
draftees, articulate graduate students in uniform, fly-by-
night newspapers whose circulation has reached into the
thousands, conscriptees who hate the army and the war
and often contemporary America as well, ministers who
allow themselves to be chained to protestors, and in general, any act of moral protest that defies regulations.

The traditionalists are therefore worried. Like all weak
men asked to govern wisely in confusing times, their first
response has been to fall back on the power of authority
and their privilege to punish. Security, they insist, demands total obedience and order, even when alleged in-

fractions are unrelated to military security. Politics, they repeat, must be kept out of the military; they point with horror at Latin America and with pride at our own historical subordination of the military to the civilian.

General Jacquard H. Rothschild (Ret.), former Commanding General, U.S. Army Chemical Corps Research and Development Command, has defended restrictions on free speech in the military on the grounds that what is good for civilians may well be disastrous for the soldier. "The military cannot tolerate this ferment. The unrest will cause a breakdown in morale and discipline." He cites the example of the Korean War: Marine Corps and Turkish Brigade POW's (both groups of traditional unquestioning discipline) had virtually no collaborators among them. These particular prisoners were living evidence, he has argued, that "the purpose of fighting for freedom of speech is not for the satisfaction of the individual, but for the good of the country."

Unfortunately for this position, the most recent study of POW's during the Korean War indicates the opposite: more than twice as many Marines as ordinary soldiers were suspected of collaboration; the Turks were a poor comparison group inasmuch as the Chinese had no Turkish-speaking "brain-washers;" English presented no such barrier. And as a sharp critic pointed out, drawing on several new behavioral experiments, "It may be the people who are used to questioning and challenging 'established' truths who can also question and challenge enemy ideologues; the man who is trained to accept authority blindly will accept that of his captors in the same way."

Moreover, is the military ever really neutral? And are politics excluded from the military? Information and Education officers are free to defend any aspect of government policy in their lectures but heaven protect the errant I&E man who raises the wrong questions or who says the wrong things. Certainly every military parade down

every Fifth Avenue is in essence a pro-Administration
policy. When that navy nurse, Lt. Susan Schnall, was
asked why she had turned out for the San Francisco
march in full uniform she replied: "Well, Generals wear
their uniforms when they speak out in favor of the Vietnam war, so why can't we?"

The Pentagon's brass have challenged and at times
openly defied civilian authority. To be sure, potential
men-on-horseback must have their public statements carefully screened. But every test of the applicability of the
First Amendment would have to determine whether or
not there was a captive audience (as in General Walker's
case), whether there was a dialogue or a lecture, and
whether the remarks made were a call for immediate action or a general exhortation. If junior officers and enlisted men do not threaten clearly to disrupt military discipline and security then there does seem to be a case
against censuring opinions.

This kind of change will not be easy for a class as cautious and conservative or as uninclined to wrestle with
civil liberty issues as professional officers. If it does come,
it will be on a case-by-case basis. It will also have to take
into account the sentiments of two young Vietnam veterans they never heard of. Steve Wilcox, a twenty-eight-
year-old former Political Science instructor at Tuskegee
Institute, has described the UCMJ as historians have lam-
pooned the Holy Roman Empire. "Neither Holy nor Roman nor an Empire" has now become "neither uniform
nor just." Wilcox and a former chaplain's assistant, Carl
Rogers, have been trying to set up a group called "Link,"
which is aimed at trying to explain the peace movement
to GI's and vice versa and, more significantly, to attempt
to bring pressure to reform the USMJ. They think it's
possible and believe that as the word spreads to the new
educated classes and the families of millions of veterans,
a freer code of justice will evolve.

Certainly the entire problem should be re-examined in

the light of the past decade. Ten years ago Frederick Bernays Wiener wrote in the *Harvard Law Review* that while it was true the Founding Fathers never intended the Bill of Rights for the servicemen, the Constitution is, after all, a flexible document and has to change with the times. Sooner or later, in Maitland's phrase, "every age should be the mistress of its own laws."

The first step toward reform would be for Congress to enact new legislation indicating what is allowed and what is not. Grievance procedures should be scrutinized. When the Inspector General system was introduced it was hailed as a means of redressing complaints. It can and does work but anyone who has ever served in the armed forces understands the courage it takes even to bring his complaint to the attention of the I.G., let alone survive recriminations on the remote level of the company or platoon.

Surely we shall also have to wrestle with other ambiguous articles in the Code, such as Art. 88, which declares that any officer who "uses contemptuous words" against many government officials, including the Secretary of the Treasury, may be punished. Conceivably a bitter comment by a Negro officer about say, a racist who happens to represent Alabama or Mississippi in the House, may be grounds for prosecution.

Art. 88 has been employed only once since its initiation in 1951—in the Howe Case—but the frequency of its predecessors' past use whenever the services had to rely on mass conscription, means that it is far from moribund. And when Art. 88 is not applicable, as for example in the case of a Fort Lewis private who publicly condemned President Kennedy in 1961, then the military can fall back on the general articles. One of the allegations brought against Lt. Howe was conduct unbecoming an officer and a gentleman. While parading off-duty in civilian clothing he had carried a placard which read on one side, "Let's have more than a choice between petty

ignorant Facists (sic) in 1968" and on the other, "End
Johnson's Facist (sic) Aggression in Viet Nam."

The Perils of Military Poker

It has also been claimed that Art. 88 is aimed only at
"public" pronouncements, but here again a patchquilt of
confusion has evolved. In 1953 a federal court ruled that
a poker game among GI's in which many points of view
were expressed was not "strictly private." At the same
time the same judicial opinion declared that a meeting of
officers in perhaps an annual get-together, might be private. Thus non-coms or draftees playing poker and bitch-
ing about the world and politicians in a day room had
better watch their tongues. General or flag officers, the
only ones in the military who could conceivably ever
challenge civilian authority, could meet in a downtown
Washington hotel ballroom and defend or attack aspects
of foreign and domestic policies and still be immune from
prosecution. It is as clear and as reasonable as that.

Meanwhile, Harvey and Daniels languish in prison,
awaiting their appeal to reach the various appellate courts.
In a letter to a friend at home Harvey wrote, "It's the
people's turn to protect me. Only they don't have to pick
up rifles, just pens. Hang petitions in the candy store,
Herman's, the Center, and every place you can think of
because it's your turn."

The courts may very well reaffirm their sentences and
validate what is legal and, but not necessarily, what is
just and right. "Folly is not felony" a legal scholar once
said. To find two young Negro marines guilty for saying
in private conversations no more than what was on the
lips of tens of millions of civilian Americans condemns
the Marine Corps for its parochial and authoritarian man-
ners. It was hardly a case for a general court-martial and
certainly not at all for so harsh a sentence.

Of course the courts may also come up with unexpected variations: reduction of the sentence to time already served, re-trial, or even acquittal. But surely they also have a remarkable opportunity now to consider calmly and dispassionately whether or not the armed forces any longer have the right to transform all of their members into instant third-class citizens, as well as a growing number into felons. If the courts cannot bring themselves to re-think the entire situation, then Congress must.

The Court of Military Appeals ultimately set aside the convictions of Harvey and Daniels, found them guilty of a lesser included offense of solicitation, and reduced their sentences each to four months. They were both immediately released from custody and are now civilians. The ACLU is appealing Daniels' conviction in the federal courts.

A CONVERSATION WITH
MR. AND MRS. X

Mr. and Mrs. X are the parents of a twenty-three-year-old son now in exile in Canada. They are both high school graduates and are active members of the Ethical Culture Society.

MR. X: Bill had been going to the University. He knew that when he graduated he would get his draft notice. Up to that time, he had had a student deferment, so he had plenty of time to give it a lot of consideration. There was plenty of preparation in his mind and ours.

MURRAY POLNER: *Was he very much antiwar?*

MR. X: Very much so. He first started to think about it seriously during his junior year. When the draft came closer, he began talking about going to Canada.

MRS. X: He came home one weekend to talk to us about it. He had been getting draft counseling at college. He knew just exactly what he wanted to do. He had been to the Canadian consulate and had taken their examination to enter as a landed immigrant and had been accepted. He had also applied to York University in Toronto and had received a fellowship and was pretty well set. He told us he would not go to war under any circumstances. Not this war anyway. It was quite a shock to us because at that time we hadn't thought too much about it. To leave this country was just terribly shocking. Still, when I began to think, I realized what the alternative was.

MR. X: We agreed with him on the general principle of not serving. Our only difference was his manner of carrying out that opposition. My original idea was that he should take his chances on being called and then hope for a 4-F status. And even if he was called, perhaps they would never send him into combat. I may have been wrong then, but his decision to go to Canada saddened us. We knew it meant he would never again be allowed to return home.

He was already in Canada before he received his notice to report for his physical. I called the draft board and spoke to a very sympathetic woman who advised me to tell Bill first to apply for a change of city of registration for the physical. For instance, Buffalo, which would be more convenient for him. As she put it, that in itself would delay the whole process perhaps three months or so and then if he was accepted, he could apply for C.O. status, which in itself takes another year, as I understand it, just to get through the paperwork. In all that time he would have had the privilege of coming home. Bill just wouldn't do that. He felt it was going back on his principles to cooperate with the Army.

His principles were strictly antiwar, particularly this war. He never joined any organization or actively protested in any way. He was completely nonactivist, nonpolitical, and has lived that way in Canada. He hasn't joined or visited with any resisters' organizations there.

Above all, he feels this war is morally wrong. That's the ground on which he stands. He will not veer right or left. He only sees it in that one way.

M.P.: *What is the reaction you get from people you work with?*

MRS. X: I'm a secretary. There is one mother, a coworker of mine, whose one son had been in Vietnam. He had a very rough time and she is very unwilling to accept what my son has done. She just turns off whenever I mention Bill. Another coworker has a son-in-law who is a professional Army man stationed in Germany and she too is rather cool every time I mention my son. Otherwise they are very friendly. The rest of the people in my office are very sympathetic. They ask me about him, they want to know when we are going to see him and what he's doing.

MR. X: I work for a large organization with probably one thousand people in my office. I have only mentioned it to one person who has been unsympathetic and actually opposed to what Bill has done. The others seem to be sympathetic even to the point of really backing up that kind of thing and saying their sons would probably do the same thing if they were of draft age. In our general circles, both business and social, we have usually found acceptance.

M.P.: *Can you tell me something about Bill's life in Canada?*

MR. X: Most of his friends are Canadians or people from other countries—other than the United States—who have settled in Canada. The only exception that I can think of is one boy who he knew casually from college who also went to Canada. I don't think there are any other Americans that he knows there. In that sense he has been assimilated completely.

M.P.: *What does he do there?*

MR. X: He works for the public library. He also goes to school to take courses toward his master's degree in English.

MRS. X: He and his colleagues at the library are also teaching high school dropouts. This is volunteer work that they do every day when their working hours permit. The Board of Education there has agreed to give these dropouts credit for the courses in which they pass their examinations at the end of the year. Bill has, moreover, been planning to take another master's degree. His preference is folklore and there is only one university in Canada that gives that course, the University of Newfoundland. If he doesn't get accepted by them, he'll take a second master's in library science.

M.P.: *What prompted you to organize a group of parents whose sons were in exile?*

MR. X: Only the feeling that I was anxious for my son to be able to return home. I believe there is only one strong possibility for amnesty, and that is if the parents of boys in the same position organize and throw their weight behind the drive for amnesty when the time is right. I realize it probably couldn't happen before the war is actually over and the draft is ended, but I felt that the parents, particularly in a country like this, where parenthood has always been held in such high esteem, would have a greater weight with Congress or the President, being nonpolitical and having no other ax to grind but the hope for the return of their children. I therefore set about trying to locate parents of boys in similar situations.

It was and still is extremely difficult. There is no really good way of getting these names. I started out with a letter to the New York *Post* and also to the New York *Times* stating my plans and asking parents who were interested to get in touch with me. The *Times* would not print the letter, explaining that they do not print letters of that nature calling for any specific action. The *Post* printed the letter and we had very few replies, something like four. The biggest help that I did receive was from the "Clergy and Laymen Concerned About Vietnam," who gave us the names of about twenty parents in this and other areas, most of whose sons were deserters in Sweden.

These, plus the few that I got from the *Post,* were the people we solicited to join us in some type of organization. We had our first meeting with five couples. That was the best response we had. Since then, we have had more meetings, attended by fewer people each time until the last meeting, which was attended by three people besides ourselves. We are pretty discouraged about any future action, unless something happens and we can get a large and new group of names of people to contact. I have also made various other efforts, which included an advertisement in the *Village Voice,* paid for by the five couples who met at the first meeting. Printed announcements of the second and third meetings were distributed to various resistance organizations, YMCAs, colleges, and other organizations. Letters were sent to all draft resistance programs in Canada, to the American Civil Liberties Union and the American Friends Service Committee. An advertisement was placed in *Amex,* which is a newspaper put out by draft resisters in Canada. I also made a personal visit to the office of the Toronto Anti-Draft Program in the hope of getting names from them. But they either would not or could not give me any names of the people they had there. My efforts actually resulted in obtaining the names of very few people, and those we did contact were rather unenthusiastic.

M.P.: *Why do you think there has been so poor a response?*

MR. X: I don't know, I guess the families felt rather hopeless about it.

MRS. X: Some of them were also afraid of reprisals. A few of them wouldn't give their names. They voiced this fear at the first meeting.

M.P.: *Reprisals against their sons or against them?*

MR. X: Against them. One woman called us before the first meeting and said, "Why should I give you my name, how do I know you're not the F.B.I. or the C.I.A.?" I think a great many of them were afraid of that. There was one meeting at which we had a mysterious visitor who just sat and listened and wouldn't give his name. At the end he gave us a speech about how proud our sons must be of us. We never found out who he was. He definitely was not a parent.

MRS. X: There was a very dramatic case of a mother who came in crying. She cried practically all through the meeting. She wouldn't give us any information about her name or her son's name or where she lived or anything else. Ultimately we learned that it was a case of having lost contact with her son. He had deserted to Sweden and then to France and he wrote her a letter telling her she wouldn't be able to contact him again. He just disappeared and she was just so heartbroken that she could hardly speak.

MR. X: One of the couples from the original list whom I contacted by telephone was bitterly opposed to what their son had done. The son was a deserter. She and her husband, whom she described as "good Americans," felt that they were disgraced by their son. In answer to my question as to whether she would want her son to come home again, she answered only if he would "do the right thing." I assumed by that she meant going back into the Army or giving himself up. But most of the other people whom I was able to contact were sympathetic to their sons. We did hear, though, of other people who virtually severed all ties with their sons if they were draft resisters or deserters.

MRS. X: There was one woman from Connecticut who called and was very much in favor of what her son did. But her husband was terribly against his actions. She wanted to come to our meeting but her husband wouldn't allow her to. She felt that if she could leave without her husband knowing it, she would show up at our meetings, but she never did. She would talk to me for a half hour at a time about her son.

MR. X: The failure to organize a parents' group for amnesty hasn't particularly made me bitter because I feel that it was caused by mechanical difficulties in obtaining the names of the parents. I can understand that many of them I have contacted felt that the time wasn't right or that it was a completely hopeless situation.

Mrs. X: As a mother, I feel sorry for the parents who don't see what wonderful youngsters these are who are trying to right a great wrong and are doing it in a very brave way. Bravery has to be measured in individual ways. I know that as far as our son is concerned, leaving home and his country took a great deal of courage.

Mr. X: It also took courage because he was so sure in his own mind that had he stayed in this country and allowed himself to be drafted, he would not have been in combat, and as a matter of fact might not have been accepted. So in our view he has done something that has required as much courage, if not more, than staying home and going into the Army. As parents, of course, we have the same feeling as any parent whose son can't come home —a feeling of sadness, of frustration, of depression that he's away from home and can't possibly ever come back. Of course, we do have the consolation that we can go to see him.

M.P.: *What does it mean to your son? He knows you are organizing and you are upset. Has he ever expressed his feelings?*

Mrs. X: He's often said to me that the only thing he is really sorry for is that he has caused us anxiety and sorrow. As far as amnesty is concerned, he has told us many times that he would never come back. He likes Canada. He is going to become a citizen and stay there but he feels it's a wonderful thing for us to try to do something for others.

Mr. X: I think it has given him a tremendous moral boost to know that we are so much behind him and that we are trying to organize the group. I know he is very interested in it. He has asked me about it several times and I know he would be very happy if he knew he could just visit in this country. Moreover, I'm not so sure that as he gets older he might not change his mind and come back here—if he could.

M.P.: *How can you compare the sacrifice that you are*

making, and that your son is making, with, perhaps, the sacrifice of someone whose son is compelled to serve and who has to wait out the year in Vietnam?

Mr. X: Ours is a life sentence, unless there is amnesty. The others have an ordeal that will probably be over in two years or whatever the length of service and the waiting time is before they get into the service. For most people, in the long run, their sons will probably return from service. Ours is the greater sacrifice, if that's the way you want to put it. Because ours is really for life. Of course, there is no comparison with the parents whose sons are killed. I wouldn't compare our situation with theirs, or those whose sons came back maimed. But my feeling in that matter is also that their sons had the same opportunity that ours did and if they all had said "no," the war would be over.

M.P.: *How do you perceive the possibilities of amnesty?*

Mr. X: The history of amnesty in this country is not good; there has never been a general amnesty after wars, only partial amnesties. The one encouraging factor is that this is not a declared war. If the Supreme Court ever declares the war or the draft unconstitutional, that would be a tremendous boost. But I don't really think that will ever come about. I would hope that with a change in the government to more sympathetic people, and with the end of the war, we might have amnesty. But I'm not really filled with any great hope.